Best wishes,
Millard K. Bushing

GENERAL TURNER ASHBY

and

STONEWALL'S
VALLEY CAMPAIGN

Brigadier General Turner Ashby, C.S.A.

GENERAL TURNER ASHBY

and

STONEWALL'S

VALLEY CAMPAIGN

by

Millard K. Bushong

Maps

by

Timothy T. Pohmer

McClure Printing Company, Inc.
Verona, Virginia
1980

Printed in the United States of America

Dedicated To Sergeant Edward Mark Bushong, my paternal grandfather, whose military service as a scout in Company E, Twelfth Virginia Cavalry, Laurel Brigade, exemplified those qualities of bravery, initiative, endurance, loyalty, and horsemanship that were typical of Ashby and his Cavalry.

Other Books by Author
Historic Jefferson County
Old Jube: a Biography of General Jubal A. Early

PREFACE

I first became interested in the romantic career of General Turner Ashby when as a young boy I listened to accounts of his daring exploits from the lips of my Confederate grandfather. As I grew older, I desired more details about the "Knight of the Valley" but books concerning his life and activities were hard to find. It seemed incredible that a Civil War hero who had so many admirers should have left posterity so little information about his short life.

In undertaking to write an account of Turner Ashby's brief but exciting career and the Shenandoah Valley Campaign of 1862, I was fully cognizant of the difficulties involved. The main handicap in such a study of the brilliant cavalryman is the almost complete lack of manuscript material. This necessitates more reliance upon supplementary sources, especially secondary accounts, some of which contain conflicting versions of what actually happened. Apparently Ashby was kept so busy scouting, patrolling, and fighting that he did not have the time, even if he had the desire, for writing. Had he lived a number of years after the war was over, he might have left us memoirs or correspondence that would have proved invaluable. Even then, his modesty would probably have prevented his giving himself proper credit.

The writing of a book such as this requires the cooperation of many persons. I have been very fortunate in the response which I have received to my appeal for information relating to Turner Ashby, and I want to thank those who helped me in any way at all.

Three Virginians have read the entire manuscript for historical criticism and have given me many suggestions reflecting their expertise on Turner Ashby and the Shenandoah Valley Campaign of 1862. They are John K. Gott of Arlington, Dr. Garland R. Quarles of Winchester, and Dr. James I. Robertson, Jr., of Blacksburg.

Others who have helped me in one way or another are the following: Nelson Alexander, Harrisonburg, Va.; Wayne Angleberger, Bridgewater, Va.; Willard M. Ansel, Charleston, West Va.; Mrs. Frank Ashby, Bluemont, Va.; Mr. and Mrs. Wilton C. Ashby, Canvas, West Va.; Mrs. Alvin V. Baird, Jr., Delaplane, Va.; Aquilla D. Bowers, Mount Jackson, Va.; Ray O. Bowman, Follansbee, W. Va.; George R. Clatterbuck, Harrisonburg, Va.; Mrs. Ralph Dorsey, Berryville, Va.; Leighton Evans, Mount Crawford, Va.; Edwin Fitzpatrick, Charles Town, W. Va.; Mrs. E. Norman Fowler, Lovettsville, Va.; Colonel William G. Gavin, Charles Town, W. Va.; James

E. Gay, Front Royal, Va.; Miss Laura Virginia Hale, Front Royal, Va.; Mrs. Rosa B. Hankey, Charles Town, W. Va.; Curtis Heisey, Bridgewater, Va.; George Langford, Harrisonburg, Va.; R.H. Legard, Jr., Narrows, Va.; Christopher McManus, Rockville, Md.; Mrs. Earl Manuel, Sr., Charles Town, W. Va.; Robert B. Miller, Inwood, W. Va.; Raymond P. Parks, Charles Town, W. Va.; Wallace W. Phillips, Middleburg,Va.; Timothy T. Pohmer, Butler, Pa.; Mrs. Emily G. Ramey, Rectortown, Va.; Samuel E. Ritchie, Dayton, Va.; Ben Ritter, Winchester, Va.; James H. Roadcap, Jr., Harrisonburg, Va.; Carlton Staples, Winchester, Va.; Ms. F.B. Trenary, Front Royal, Va.; Dr. Charles W. Turner, Lexington, Va.; and Dr. James Whitney, Augusta, Ga.

My thanks are due the staffs of a number of libraries who facilitated my research by helping me locate materials, xerox letters and manuscripts, obtain copies of photos, and provide the direction to enable me to utilize their facilities to the utmost. They are on the staffs of Duke University, George C. Marshall Library, University of North Carolina, Valentine Museum, Virginia Historical Society, Virginia Military Institute, Virginia State Library, and Washington and Lee University.

Last but not least, I want to extend special thanks to my wife, Dean McKoin Bushong, who has been constantly at my side, helping me in every aspect of work involved in the production of this book. She helped me collect the available material, offered many valuable suggestions, typed the entire manuscript, and aided in ways too numerous to mention. In addition, she has patiently borne the lot of a wife whose husband has been subjected to the many frustrations involved in pursuing a study of this type.

I, alone, am responsible for any shortcomings or errors that may exist.

Millard K. Bushong

Arcadia, Route 2
Berryville, Va., 22611
November 1, 1980

CONTENTS

ILLUSTRATIONS

GENERAL TURNER ASHBY
and
STONEWALL'S
VALLEY CAMPAIGN

CHAPTER I

BACKGROUND

The remarkable fact about Brigadier General Turner Ashby was not that he was killed early in the war but that he was not killed sooner. When a man constantly places himself in front of his troops, exhorts them to "Follow me," and proceeds to lead them toward the enemy, he is courting disaster. This is especially true when he is riding a white horse and thus offers a tempting target to Federal sharpshooters. He could not expect all enemy commanding officers to duplicate the magnanimous attitude of Lieutenant Colonel Thomas Kane of the Pennsylvania Bucktail Rifles. This Northern officer once remarked:

> I have today saved the life of one of the most gallant officers in either army, Gen. Ashby; for I admire him as much as you can possibly do. His figure is familiar to me, inasmuch as I have seen it often on the skirmish line. He was today within fifty yards of my skirmishers, sitting on his horse as if unconscious of his danger. I saw three of them raise their rifles to fire, but I succeeded in stopping two of them and struck up the gun of the third as it went off. Ashby is too brave to die in that way.[1]

Ironically, unknown to Colonel Kane, a bullet from one of the Bucktail marksmen, who did not know his commander's wish, had just pierced Ashby's heart, killing him instantly.

Turner Ashby's ancestors were of English nationality and traced their origin to Richard de Ashby, who in 1296 was lord of the manors of Quenby and South Croxton in Leicestershire. In the succeeding centuries members of the family distinguished themselves in English politics, literature, and military and naval service. The word Ashby is a combination of the Saxon "Ash" and the Danish "Bye," meaning "town," which, when translated into modern English, becomes either Ashby or Ashtown.[2]

When members of the Ashby family came to America, some settled in Virginia as early as 1635, in Maryland in 1650, and in Massachusetts in 1640. Confederate General Turner Ashby was directly descended from a line of military men. Four generations of his ancestors held commissions in the colonial wars, the Revolution, and the War of 1812. His great great grandfather, Captain Thomas Ashby, who located near Paris, Fauquier County, Virginia, between 1700 and 1710, was engaged in the Colonial service of Virginia and was active in defending the frontier against the Indians. When peace was declared, he accumulated property until he became one of the most prominent landowners in the area. It was he for whom Ashby's Gap in the Blue Ridge Mountains was named, although some writers credit his son, John Ashby, with the honor.[3]

The oldest son of Thomas Ashby, who was named John, was born in 1707 in Fauquier County and grew to manhood on his father's farm. According to tradition, he was the first white man to drive a wagon through Ashby's Gap. As told by a member of the family, John Ashby failed to take proper precautions when his wagon was going down the mountain. In those days, since the wagon chain was not then in general use, the approved way of holding a wagon in check was to cut down a tree and attach it to the vehicle. When Ashby failed to do this, the wagon in its descent ran over the horses and spilled the load on the ground. When he was asked why he had not locked the wheels, he replied, "Damn a pair of horses that can't outrun a wagon."[4]

John Ashby was one of the early settlers who crossed the mountains and located his home on the west bank of the Shenandoah River. For the convenience of the travelers who used this road linking the Virginia Piedmont with the Shenandoah Valley, he established a ferry. This became known in later years as Berry's Ferry. One of the places where George Washington actually slept was at John Ashby's home in the Valley. Washington, who was on his way to help survey Lord Fairfax's extensive holdings, was so impressed by the beauty, fertility, and accessibility of the Shenandoah Valley that he later purchased acreage along the Bullskin Run, in present Jefferson County, West Virginia. So many other members of his family, including brothers Samuel and Charles, followed his example that Zion Episcopal churchyard in Charles Town can boast that it has more Washington graves than any other place in the United States.[5]

When the French and Indian War between Great Britain and France began, settlers along the frontier became greatly concerned. They organized companies of rangers to protect their homes from the attacks of the redskins. One of these companies, known as the Second Virginia Rangers, was led by John Ashby, who was selected by his neighbors to be its captain. From 1752 to 1754 this company was located at Fort Ashby, in present Mineral County, West Virginia. The Virginians stationed here became such experienced Indian fighters that they were made the advance guard of General Sir Edward Braddock's expedition against Fort Duquesne in 1755. When the British officer refused to heed the advice of George Washington and his fellow-Virginians on the proper way to fight in America, he suffered a humiliating defeat at the hands of the French and their Indian allies.

Quenby Hall, The Ashby Castle in England

Courtesy of Mrs. Lee Fleming Reese

During this campaign Captain Ashby became acquainted with a young teamster named Daniel Morgan, who was later to become a famous general in the Revolutionary War. Morgan had incurred the displeasure of a British officer who was instrumental in having the young teamster sentenced to receive five hundred lashes. Ashby did not learn of this severe punishment until the young Morgan had been given four hundred and ninety-nine. When he remonstrated with the Britisher, he succeeded in saving Morgan from the last blow. The future American general later boasted that during the Revolution he had evened the score with the redcoats by his military service.[6]

George Washington selected Captain Ashby to carry news of the Braddock disaster to the colonial governor of Virginia, Robert Dinwiddie, at Williamsburg. Ashby made the long and difficult journey in such record-breaking time that the British commander at Fort Loudoun in Winchester did not realize that he had gone and had returned to his troops. When the Britisher upbraided the American for unnecessary delay in getting started on his journey, Ashby surprised him by producing Governor Dinwiddie's reply.[7]

Because the Colony of Virginia had granted Captain John Ashby land in present Kentucky for service in the Indian wars, he determined to travel westward in order to locate his holdings. Accompanied by three companions, the bold adventurer set out in 1774 to explore. Forming the acquaintance of Daniel Boone, he accompanied that famous frontiersman on some of his expeditions. He found his grant of 2,000 acres in the bluegrass region and along the Ohio River — some of the best land in Kentucky. Ashby also received a large tract in the Green River section, which land descended to succeeding generations of Ashbys for a long time.

The object of his western trek having been accomplished, Captain John Ashby set out for home by the way of the Ohio and Mississippi Rivers. With two companions he floated down the rivers in dugouts. They went as far as New Orleans and had numerous experiences — some quite dangerous — en route. One of the companions died on the journey down the Mississippi, the other died in Savannah, and Ashby alone was left to return home after an absence of over two years. He died in 1797 at the age of ninety.

According to a member of the Ashby family, Turner Ashby more closely resembled Captain John Ashby in his physical and mental make-up than did any other member. Turner was influenced tremendously by his ancestor's exploits and subsequently developed the same characteristics of energy, daring, love of adventure, and military spirit.[8] The future Confederate general's great grandfather was John's brother, Robert.

Turner's grandfather, John Ashby II, was a captain in the Third Virginia Regiment which was commanded by Colonel Thomas Marshall, the father of the future Chief Justice John Marshall. John II served with distinction in the American Revolution. His wife was Mary Turner, and they named one of their sons Turner, who likewise was a military man, serving as a colonel during the War of 1812. The first Turner Ashby married Dorothea F. Green of Rappahannock County, who brought to the Ashbys her dark hair and dark complexion, which became distinguishing physical characteristics of the future Confederate general. They became the parents of the following children: Elizabeth, born July 4, 1825; James Green, born June 15, 1826; Turner, born October 23, 1828; Mary Green, born January 29, 1830; Richard, born October 2, 1831; and Dorothea F., born November 10, 1835. As was quite common in the early 19th Century, several other children died at an early age.[9]

Colonel Turner Ashby, after serving in the War of 1812, moved to Alexandria where he engaged in the mercantile business. Because of deteriorating health, he spent some time abroad. Upon his return to the United States, he decided to go back to his native county of Fauquier, where he resided on an estate named *Springfield.* When an uncle of his wife died, he came into possession of *Rose Bank,* an estate adjoining that of *Springfield.* Unfortunately, he died prematurely, leaving his widow the responsibility of managing the family estate and serving both as mother and father to six young children, the eldest being not twelve years old and the youngest, an infant.

Dorothea Green Ashby was not unequal to this Herculean task. In spite of her grief at the premature loss of her husband, she tried to rear her six children in a home that was replete with the refinements and comforts of a Virginia country home owned by aristocrats. *Rose Bank* was situated on a hill which looked out over the surrounding mountains, as well as Goose Creek flowing in front of the yard. She added to the natural beauty of her home by cultivating many flowers and pieces of shrubbery. She employed the best tutors she could find and instructed her children in refined and moral disciplines. She imparted to her boys qualities that were later to make them outstanding. She taught them to ride, to shoot, to speak the truth, and to be considerate of others. All three gave up their lives to their native state. James, her oldest son, captained a company raised in Stafford County before the war began and died in February, 1861, from pulmonary disease. Turner, her second son and the subject of this biography, was killed leading his men at Harrisonburg, Virginia, on June 6, 1862, while Richard, the youngest, had paid the supreme sacrifice at the hands of the enemy near Romney, West Virginia, on July 3, 1861. Likewise the three daughters, while not distinguishing themselves as soldiers, remained true to their mother's teachings and lived happy, useful lives.[10]

Young Turner, as noted above, was born October 23, 1828, at *Rose Bank*. He was inclined to be somewhat small in size; however, his outdoor activities more than compensated for his small stature, for he developed into a man of great strength. He had the dark hair and complexion of his mother's family. After profiting from tutors in his own home, he furthered his scholastic training by attending a school taught by a neighbor named Major Ambler. Although he was not a brilliant student, he mastered the intricacies of reading, writing, spelling, and arithmetic. Since not many of his contemporaries of that section of Virginia received a collegiate education, his became the school of practical experience. What he lacked in formal education, he made up in common sense, sound judgment, and intelligent ideas.

Turner Ashby's love for the neighboring mountains, streams, and valleys was unequalled. He rarely wanted to leave the area and, until he entered the Confederate army, he spent his entire life in the locality where he was born. The farms were large, the fields were fertile, and the neighbors were congenial. Among the Ashbys' friends and neighbors in upper Fauquier County were the Marshalls, Striblings, Amblers, Paynes, Hatchers, and Dulanys. They were the descendants of colonial families of Tidewater Virginia who had emigrated westward in search of more fertile land, beautiful scenery, and an embracing and healthful climate. Their farms produced wheat, corn, oats, and rye, besides providing pasture for sheep, cattle, and horses.[11]

One of Ashby's schoolmates described the future Confederate leader as follows:

> Gen. Ashby, as a boy, was remarkable for his contempt of danger, and his freedom from the vices common among boys; he was never known to swear, or to use profane language. His contempt of danger was exhibited nearly every day; whenever the creek was swollen by heavy rains, he might be seen in it, breasting the torrent above the waterfalls, where a failure would dash him to pieces on the rocks below; whenever a colt was found too wild and vicious to be ridden by any one else in the neighborhood, it was his pleasure to mount and tame him. In combats with his school fellows, whilst he was always brave and stubborn in the fight, after it was over, he was always ready to forgive and forget.[12]

Turner's constant companion was his younger brother, Richard. The two were inseparable and developed a feeling of mutual respect and admiration that was almost incomparable. Turner, as the elder, took an extraordinary interest in watching over Richard, in siding with him in his boyish fights, and in serving as his chief protector. Although Richard felt fully capable of looking after his own interests, the older brother could not be deterred from assuming this responsibility for the younger brother.

While Turner was enjoying the advantages offered by a home like *Rose Bank*, he acquired possession of a wolf, which he called "Lupus." However, when he realized that this unusual pet was causing terror among some of the neighborhood children, he got rid of him. This consideration for others was to be one of his most desirable characteristics.

The one thing that Turner Ashby enjoyed perhaps more than anything else was horseback riding. This is still a popular pastime in Northern Virginia and many of the farms are devoted to the raising of thoroughbred horses. At an early age he became an expert horseman and was not only skilled as a rider but also as a trainer. It mattered not whether the competition was at the tournament, the hurdle-race, or the fox-chase, it was usually customary for Turner Ashby to emerge as the winner.

Of all these forms of amusement on horseback, perhaps none was as demanding of the rider as the ring tournament. This was one of the most popular forms of social diversion in Northern Virginia in the mid-19th Century. The best definition of such an event is given by Thomas Nelson Page's Negro boy in *P'laski's Tunament* who described a ring tournament as, "whar you gits 'pon a hoss wid a pole an' rides as hard as you ken, an' pokes de pole at a ring an' de one what pokes de moes, he crowns de queen."[13] The heyday of these events was about the middle of the century, and by 1885 they were rapidly disappearing; however, it is interesting to note that this custom has been preserved to this day, for every summer a ring tournament is conducted at Hume in Fauquier County and at Natural Chimneys, near Mt. Solon in Augusta County, Virginia. One is also held in the South Branch Valley of West Virginia and in parts of Maryland.

The events at the tournaments were not limited to riding. There were also picnics, pig roasting, and musical festivals. At night there were balls and torchlight processions. To climax the affairs, there were usually speeches and orations, sometimes by prominent persons from outside the county. Thus the ring tournament became a gala social occasion for Northern Virginians. The tournament kept alive the spirit of chivalry that had come down to these Virginians from their forefathers in England.

Courtesy of Mrs. Lee Fleming Reese

The Ashby Coat-of-Arms

For a number of years Turner Ashby rode in the tournaments held at Fauquier White Sulphur Springs near Warrenton, at Capon Springs, and many others. While some of the other riders bore the names of Roderick Dhu, Piedmont, Ivanhoe, etc., Turner took as a title the name of Knight of the Black Prince, or Knight of Hiawatha. When he assumed the latter title, he dressed as an Indian warrior and frequently rode a horse without bridle or saddle. His dark complexion and dark hair complemented his assumed name. It was seldom that he failed to give the best exhibition of riding skill, piercing the rings with his lance, and crowning some fair lady Queen of Love and Beauty.

In 1853 tragedy struck the Ashby home, for Mrs. Ashby was forced to sell *Rose Bank* in order to pay the family debts. Virginia did not share the prosperity of the cotton states in the Deep South and many a Virginia slave was sold "down the river" in order to keep the plantation from passing out of the hands of the family. James Madison could not obtain a loan from the United States Bank, the Jefferson heirs lost *Monticello,* and John Randolph of Roanoke threatened to run away from his slaves. Southern hospitality may have seemed glorious to writers (and to visitors!), but it was uneconomical and financially disastrous to many plantation owners. Turner's mother struggled courageously to keep her home intact and to maintain the standard of living to which her large family was accustomed, but the task proved too great for her womanly efforts. She succumbed to the inevitable and sold *Rose Bank* to Edward C. Marshall, a son of the Chief Justice. It is heartrending at any time to be forced to give up one's home, but it was especially hard on the Ashby family. They had formed a deep attachment for the large colonial house situated on the hill which enabled its occupants to view the beautiful mountains and streams. It took the family a long time to recover from this interruption to their happy existence. One can imagine their grief when they learned that the fine old house had been destroyed by fire in 1863.[14]

The new owner changed the name of *Rose Bank* to *Markham,* which was the name of the nearby station on the recently-constructed Manassas Gap Railroad. This artery, which is now part of the Southern system, ran from Manassas Junction to the Shenandoah Valley and was frequently utilized during the Civil War. Its president was the new owner of *Rose Bank.* As is frequently the case, the construction of the railroad brought a number of undesirables to the neighborhood. When some of these newcomers disturbed the serenity of the Markham area by making nuisances of themselves, young Turner Ashby organized a small cavalry company of his neighbors in order to keep the unwanted workers under control. This group, which became known as the Mountain Rangers, was kept organized after the railroad was completed and was increased by new enlistments. With Turner Ashby as its leader, it was mustered into the Virginia Militia at the time of the John Brown Raid at Harpers Ferry. At the outbreak of the Civil War, The Mountain Rangers became Company A of the newly-organized Seventh Regiment, Virginia Cavalry, and later became the nucleus of The Laurel Brigade.[15]

With the loss of the family homestead, Mrs. Ashby moved to Stafford County to make her future home with her daugher, Mary, the wife of George Moncure. Another daughter, Dora, had married George's brother, Powhatan, also a resident of Stafford County. Richard likewise followed his family to the new abode and even bought a farm there, but Turner did otherwise. The flat countryside in Stafford was a sharp contrast to the mountains and valleys of Fauquier. Like many natives from the mountain region, he was eventually to succumb to the "pull of the mountains" and return to the scenes of his happy boyhood. When opportunity presented itself, he bought a farm within rifle range and full view of his old homeplace. He named his new home *Wolf's Crag*, although the spelling of this house seems to be changed by almost everyone who writes about it. Later, Richard felt the urge to return to the vicinity of his youth, and the two bachelor brothers lived at *Wolf's Crag* until the outbreak of the Civil War.[16] Turner's new home was very appropriately named for the ruins of a castle on the steep shores of eastern Scotland. Like other persons of that era the Ashbys were probably influenced by Sir Walter Scott's novels.

When Turner Ashby returned to the area where he had spent his youth, he seems to have led a busy life. His business pursuits were divided between the operation of his Wolf Crag Farm and the conduct of a mercantile business at Markham. Because he was unhampered by family responsibilities, he was free to engage in much social life with his friends and neighbors. Although he was retiring, gentle, and unassuming in his manners, his skillful horsemanship, love of the outdoors, generous nature, and chivalric spirit caused him to be a popular figure. He was a natural leader whose men would follow him anywhere. Perhaps foreseeing that the nation was dividing along sectional lines and wishing to be prepared for any emergencies, he increased the membership and discipline of his Mountain Rangers. His associates were mostly from the same background as he was, owned their horses, loved the chase and the tournament, and were full of military ardor. They would ride long distances in order to attend the exercises and drills, as theirs was a rural area and the farms were far apart. The training which they received from these activities proved invaluable when they answered the call to arms in 1861.

Politically, Turner Ashby showed a keen interest in local, state, and national affairs. As was the case in the affiliation of many Virginia aristocrats, he belonged to the Whig Party even though this party was struggling to surmount the vexations of the slavery problem and was eventually to disappear as a major organization. Although he believed in the general principles of democracy, he was distrustful of the radical masses. While he could be courteous and respectful to all classes of society, he was opposed to the extension of suffrage to everybody. He owned some slaves whom he treated as respected individuals, and they reciprocated by being loyal, faithful, and happy.[17] In Ashby's dealings with Negro slaves, one is reminded of the conversation which the Negro sexton in the Old Chapel Graveyard in Clarke County had with the stranger seeking the whereabouts of a certain grave. "Ole Mis' Annie? Why, ob co'se I know whar my ole mistress is. She yo' gran'ma? Just to think if you hadn't spoke, we never would'er knowed we wuz related!"[18]

Turner Ashby was scrupulously honest. One of his biographers, who had served as his chaplain during the war, recalled that a merchant in Winchester frequently extended credit to the general, who would send his servant, George, to obtain articles needed in camp. When the faithful Negro assured the merchant that "Mass" Turner would be in on a particular day to settle the bill, Ashby was extended the necessary credit. The bill was paid promptly by the debtor in person, even though the general was engaged in active campaigning against the enemy. In commenting further on Ashby's character, his chaplain wrote:

As to other features of his moral character, the writer, though daily and intimately associated with him, never heard him use a blasphemous expression; he never indulged in the lesser vices of smoking or chewing tobacco; and whether at the mess-table, around the camp-fires, or at the head of the column on the march, the writer fails to remember a single instance in which a joke was told or an incident related which would have been looked upon as indelicate or improper in the presence of ladies. He was innately modest and refined in language and conversation. Previously to the war there was an opinion entertained by some that he was not at all times strictly temperate. It is apprehended that the exposure of the Bath campaign of '61 and '62 would have called out any lurking fondness which a man may have had for drink. The General then, as ever, exercised the most perfect temperance and moderation, never touching a drop when the intensity of the cold

and exposure would have justified any sane man in using what he
was never known to abuse. He was in the fullest sense of the word
a temperate man. In mild weather, and always when on light duty, he would pass weeks together without touching anything in-
toxicating, and this averment every member of his military family
will fully sustain. As a moral man, then, we may say he was
remarkable, and his morality withstood the manifold temptations
of active, wearisome, perplexing, and arduous campaigning
which showed what a man was in every particular.[19]

In connection with Turner Ashby's character as a young man,
there is an incident which enables one to appraise him more closely. His reaction to an insult perpetrated by a fellow-Virginian
against a guest from the North is perhaps typical.

When tensions in both North and South had been exacerbated
after the John Brown Raid but before the outbreak of hostilities, a
Northerner was a guest in the home of one of the oldest and most
prominent families in Northern Virginia. Not only was the man a
Yankee, but he was also a member of the Republican Party. That
particular group, which was anathema to the South, was a new
organization dedicated to oppose the extension of slavery into
federal territories. The purpose of the stranger's visit was to seek
the hand of his host's daughter. Because he was a guest,
regardless of his political views, he was frequently invited to many
of the social events in the neighborhood. Although his section of
the country and his political convictions were well-known to the
Virginians, they were not discussed and perhaps not thought of at
all.[20]

When Turner Ashby gave a reception on the occasion of a tournament, he invited his friends and neighbors, as well as their
guests. The Northerner went with his Virginia friends, mixed freely with the others present, and was treated as one of them. Unfortunately, a young man of the neighborhood who had been a rejected suitor of the Northerner's intended fiancee, said to the lady,
"Isn't it a sublime piece of impudence for a Yankee and Black
Republican to come down here now and accept the hospitality of a
Virginia gentleman after all that has happened?"

The young woman came to the defense of her guest with the
rebuking statement, "Mr. B., you should be the last person to
criticize the catholicity of my father's hospitality. You have pro-
fited by his indisposition to draw social lines too sharply. You have
been received by him as a guest on several occasions."

Realizing that his presence was embarrassing to those present,
the Northerner decided to leave; and, accordingly went to the

cloak room to get his hat and coat. While he was there, he was accosted by his late adversary with the greeting, "What I have just said had reference to you and was meant to be insulting."

The Northern guest had not been exposed to encounters of this kind, but he had enough manliness to resent it by striking his antagonist in the face with a glove. In order to prevent a brutal fight with fists, other guests intervened. As gentlemen still settled an affair of this kind by resorting to a duel, it was not long before it was decided to fight immediately in a grove near the house by the light of torches. Just then Turner Ashby, having heard what had happened, burst into the room in a towering rage. Confronting the Virginia challenger, he asked, "What is the time fixed for our meeting, Mr. B.?"

"I am to fight Mr. C.D. immediately," answered the Virginian.

"I beg your pardon," replied Ashby, "but Mr. C.D. has nothing to do with this affair. He came to my house tonight as my guest. When I invited him to come, the invitation was Turner Ashby's word of honor that he should be treated as a gentleman; it was my voucher for his character to my other guests to meet him. I am sorry to have to explain these points of good breeding to you, Mr. B., but you have shown your ignorance of them by insulting my guest. The insult is mine, not his, to resent. He is here under my protection. If you are not prepared to make a proper and satisfacttory apology at once, both to my guest and to me, you must fight Turner Ashby, and the time and place agreed upon will answer as well as any other. What do you say, sir?"

This confrontation gave an entirely new tone to the picture. To fight a duel with one unused to firearms was one thing, but to fight a duel with an opponent with Ashby's reputation as a marksman was quite different. Realizing that discretion was better than valor, the would-be challenger blamed his conduct on heavy drinking and signed the apologies which Turner wrote. The Northern visitor left Virginia with the greatest admiration for Turner Ashby.[21]

Although not actively associated with any particular religious denomination, Turner Ashby was a firm believer in the Almighty. According to his sister, when even a youth, he would usually read some portion of the Scripture before retiring; and, in her opinion, he continued this practice until the day of his death. When he entered the Confederate military service, he encouraged his chaplain to hold frequent religious services, which he usually attended. When he was mourning the death of his brother, Richard, who was killed in July, 1861, Turner commented upon the joys of

Heaven and the inadequacies of life here on earth. His chaplain felt that his failure to make an open profession of his faith in Christ was attributable to his busy military activities, which kept him occupied constantly up to the time of his death.[22] The same reason can perhaps by used to explain his failure to organize his soldiers properly and to instill discipline in them. He was too busy fighting to attend to such details.

We are indebted to Ashby's chaplain for our best picture of what physical qualities the general possessed. While he was so impressive on horseback that animal and man seemed to be one, when he was dismounted, he was not particularly striking in appearance. Of medium stature, about five feet eight inches in height and weighing about one hundred thirty-five pounds, Turner Ashby was not burdened with excess flesh but was remarkably strong for one so small. He had dark-brown eyes, which were deepset, full of expression and tenderness. While his mouth was hard to see because of his full-flowing beard, it was indicative of great firmness and decision. His smile revealed a gentleness that seemed more like that of a woman than of a man. His black beard was so long that when he was mounted, it almost seemed to mingle with the mane of his steed.[23]

CHAPTER II

JOHN BROWN

The peace and quiet of the Lower Shenandoah Valley were suddenly disturbed on October 16, 1859, when a small group of outsiders burst into Harpers Ferry, Virginia, and inaugurated a campaign of terror and murder that left an indelible mark on the area. Harpers Ferry was never the same after the John Brown incident although its name became familiar to millions of Americans who might otherwise have never heard of it. Today over a million registered visitors are attracted to the little town in Jefferson County in order to enjoy its natural beauty, its different way of life, and its history.

The leader in the unfolding drama in 1859 was John Brown, a fanatical abolitionist who was supported by Gerrit Smith, Frederick Douglass, and others in the North who wanted to eradicate slavery. Brown was born in Connecticut, moved to Ohio, and later played an active role in the attempt to make Kansas a free state. His deeds of violence, murder, and robbery in that border region caused him to become *persona non grata*; and both the President of the United States and the Governor of Missouri had offered rewards for his capture. In order to escape the heat, he had fled to Canada, there to continue his efforts to free the Negro but in a different setting. In the little town of Chatham on the other side of the border, he and a few associates met in May, 1858, in the First Baptist Church to formulate their plans. They adopted an instrument known as the Chatham Constitution which provided for an amendment or repeal of the preamble and principal articles of the United States Constitution. The new government was to have a President, Vice-President, House of Representatives, and Supreme Court, but no Senate.[1]

The locality which Brown selected for his new effort to free the slaves was the unsuspecting little Virginia town of Harpers Ferry. Strategically located at the northern approach to the Shenandoah Valley, the area offered the schemer many advantages. It boasted the United States Armory and Arsenal, which President George Washington had fathered in order to take advantage of the abun-

dant water power supplied by both the Shenandoah and Potomac
rivers which met there. Thousands of firearms were available for
the taking since the Federal defenders were few. In case the freed
Negroes would not be able to use the guns thus captured, Brown
was prepared to arm them with "pikes." These villainous-looking
weapons had a long wooden handle with a sharp metal blade attached. Even the most inexperienced slave could plunge a pike into the heart of his master in order to obtain his freedom. Brown
had over 1,000 of these simple but effective weapons sent down
from the North so that he could march at the head of a slave army
down through the heart of the Southland.[2]

Other factors which influenced the selection of Harpers Ferry
were the ruggedness and isolation of the countryside. Friendly
mountains would hide the adventurers until they were ready to
strike. Since Maryland is very narrow at this point, it would be
relatively easy to escape across Mason and Dixon's line into friendly Pennsylvania if the plans miscarried. For some time Brown had
become convinced that the Allegheny Mountains would be a
desirable area to conduct slave raids and operate the Underground
Railroad. He believed that a small force could hold a chain of forts
and stations in the mountains. With this in mind, he planned the
advance on Harpers Ferry.[3] Although the Shenandoah Valley did
not have the large numbers of Negro slaves that Eastern Virginia
boasted, there were some; and Jefferson and neighboring Clarke
County had a larger percentage of blacks, in proportion to the
number of whites, than many of the Valley counties farther south.

John Brown laid his plans well. Over a year before he was ready
to strike, he had sent his advance agent, John Edwin Cook, to get
vital information. Cook was a good choice. Intelligent, attractive,
educated, and well-born, he was able to allay the suspicions of the
curious natives by posing as a book agent, historian, teacher, and
prospector. He furnished his superior with maps of the countryside, figures of the number of slaves in the area, and names of
prominent residents who might later be seized as hostages. Of the
latter, perhaps the most important was Colonel Lewis W.
Washington whose plantation *Beall Air* was located about four
miles from Harpers Ferry on the road to Charles Town, the county
seat. This Virginia aristocrat, who was a great-grand-nephew of
the illustrious George, possessed some inherited relics which John
Brown had heard about and which he hoped to acquire. One was a
pair of pistols which Lafayette had given the general, and the
other was a sword which Frederick the Great had presented to the
Father of Our Country. The latter bore the inscription, "From the

oldest General in the world to the Greatest." For some strange reason, which perhaps as much as anything else reflected his deranged state of mind, Brown wanted these trophies to use in another struggle for liberty. In obedience to orders, Cook met Colonel Washington, visited *Beall Air*, partook of his host's hospitality, and made careful notes regarding the relics and slaves on the premises.[4]

Contrary to Cook's plans, he fell in love with a Harpers Ferry resident, Mary Virginia Kennedy, who was the daughter of his landlady. Virginia, too, was attracted to the young Northerner; and on April 27, 1859, they were married. Cook kept his great secret from his bride; and, though she realized something was troubling him, she did not press him for enlightenment.[5]

On July 3, 1859, four other strangers came to the vicinity. The oldest one introduced himself as Isaac Smith and his three companions as his sons. In reality, they were John Brown, two of his sons, Oliver and Owen, and Jeremiah G. Anderson. In reply to questions about themselves, they stated that they were prospecting for minerals in the nearby mountains and wished to rent a farmhouse which they could make their headquarters. They succeeded in finding one in Maryland, about five miles east of Harpers Ferry, near Sample's Manor, which was known as the Kennedy Farm. As it had an isolated location, it was ideally suited for Brown's purposes. The new tenants moved in and, to all appearances, were engaged in prospecting throughout the countryside. They opened an office in Chambersburg, Pennsylvania, so as to have a convenient place to which supplies could be sent.[6]

Finally the time for action arrived. Events had been planned to the last detail. About eight o'clock on Sunday night, October 16, 1859, Brown and eighteen of his men left the farmhouse for Harpers Ferry. Three others remained behind to guard the headquarters. All of the men were heavily armed and ready for any emergency. The trip to their destination took but a short while; and they soon made themselves master of the Government factories, the bridges across the two rivers, and the telegraph wires which they cut.

When the Baltimore and Ohio express train from Wheeling arrived about midnight, it was stopped and not allowed to proceed until after an interval of five hours had elapsed. When it was released, Brown made his first fatal mistake, for its conductor gave the alarm a few miles down the track. Before long things began to hum. Ironically, the first person killed in this grandiose scheme to liberate the slaves was a free Negro, Hayward Shepherd, who

Wolf's Crag, Turner Ashby's home near Markham

Courtesy of Ben Ritter

worked as a porter at the depot. When he was accosted by one of the raiders, he became frightened and ran. The resulting shot entered his body and caused his death the following day. This was but the prelude to the killing of innocent persons, for four others, including the town's mayor, were subsequently shot and killed.

Meanwhile, Brown had sent a detachment into the countryside to capture prominent persons as hostages. One of these, Colonel Lewis Washington, was taken, along with several of his slaves. The raiders also obtained the famous sword and pistols which Brown desired for moral effect. About three o'clock in the morning, they went to the home of John Allstadt and made him prisoner along with his eighteen-year-old son and the Allstadt slaves.[7]

On Monday when news of the attack spread throughout the countryside, companies of militia converged on Harpers Ferry. While Virginia contributed most of them, Maryland was represented by citizen-soldiers from Frederick. One of the independent Virginia companies, the Mountain Rangers led by Captain Turner Ashby, was mustered into the Virginia militia. Although it made the march across the Blue Ridge in less than a day, it arrived too late to participate in the fighting and was assigned to picket duty.[8]

The main fight on Monday took place around the armory, where Brown commanded in person. Before long he was surrounded and forced to take refuge, with his prisoners and their slaves, in a small brick building in the armory enclosure. It was the fire engine house and subsequently became known as the "John Brown Fort." Firing back and forth resulted in casualties on both sides, and each passing hour saw the situation in the engine house become more serious. Brown tried to arrange a truce which would allow him to retire unmolested across the Potomac. When his two negotiators were wounded in reply to his proposal, he remained in his improvised fort to await rescue efforts. He could not understand why a band of slaves did not arrive to rescue him from his predicament. In this connection it should be pointed out that not a single slave voluntarily rose in revolt against his master. Like many other Northerners, John Brown did not understand the peculiar bond that caused the Negro slave to remain loyal to his master when he had the opportunity to get rid of his shackles.

In the meantime, Cook had been carrying out his part of the raid. He had taken leave of his Virginia wife Sunday morning in order to participate in the march on Harpers Ferry that evening. Then he had been sent back to the farmhouse headquarters with

the wagons, horses, and treasures stolen from the home of Colonel
Washington. Later when he ascended Maryland Heights in order to
obtain a good view of what was transpiring in the town below, he
saw the hopeless position of the surrounded raiders. Accordingly,
he escaped temporarily to Pennsylvania where he was captured a
few days later and brought to Charles Town for his subsequent
trial and execution.[9]

When authorities in Washington heard about the unusual oc-
currences in Harpers Ferry, they prepared to take action. They
learned there was a force of ninety Marines who were available for
immediate duty. They sent this force by train to Frederick Junction, where their leader, Lieutenant Israel Green, received a
dispatch to go to Sandy Hook and there await higher authority. In
this case Green's superior officer proved to be Robert E. Lee, a
regular army colonel who was on leave at his home *Arlington*,
across the Potomac from the capital city. A special train brought
Lee and his volunteer aide, a young cavalry lieutenant named
J.E.B. Stuart, to Sandy Hook. The force marched to the Ferry and
at 11:00 o'clock in the evening replaced the volunteers and militia
who had been keeping watch over the raiders.

Early Tuesday morning Colonel Lee ordered Lieutenant Green
to select a detail of twelve Marines for a storming party. Before
they attacked the engine house, Lieutenant Stuart tried to convince Brown of the wisdom of surrendering without further bloodshed. The officer was authorized to promise the insurgents protection from the infuriated civilians while President James Buchanan
was consulted. Brown's reply was that he would not surrender,
and he demanded that he be given an opportunty to lead his men
out of the engine house, across the Potomac into Maryland, and
that he be allowed the length of the bridge before pursuit would
begin. Lee's reply was to order the Marines to make an immediate
assault on the doors of the improvised fort.[10]

Some difficulty was experienced in battering down the stout
doors of the engine house, but eventually the Marines made a big
hole in the door with a ladder used as a battering ram. When
Green leaped through the opening and ran to the side of the fire
engine, he saw Colonel Washington, who pointed out Brown.
Quick as a flash, the Marine dealt him a heavy blow with his saber.
As Brown had just moved, he did not receive the blow on his head,
as Green had intended, but on the back of his neck. The raider was
stunned by the force of the saber and fell senseless to the floor. As
he was falling, Green gave him a saber thrust in the left breast.
When the blade struck something hard in Brown's clothing, it did

not penetrate but merely bent double. The obstruction is believed to have been the buckle of the belt supporting the Frederick the Great sword stolen from Washington.

Green was unharmed as he came through the door, but a Marine private named Luke Quinn who followed him, was struck by a bullet and mortally wounded. A second attacker, who received a flesh wound, also had several teeth knocked out. By the time more Marines had poured through the door, the fight, which had lasted only three minutes, was over.

Washington and the other hostages with their slaves were released. The bodies of one of Brown's sons and several of the other defenders were inside the fort. Brown, himself, was carried outside where he soon regained consciousness. His wounds were dressed; and, as they were only superficial, he recovered rapidly. The next day, Wednesday, October 19, he was taken to Charles Town, the county seat, and turned over to the civil authorities.[11]

While the Marines had sustained light casualties, the insurgents did not fare so well. Of the twenty-two who comprised the original group, ten had been killed in the fighting, seven were captured, and five escaped. Most of the latter had remained behind at the farmhouse headquarters.

With the removal of John Brown and his men to Charles Town, the scene of activity shifted to the county seat. Although much of the fighting had occurred on property belonging to the United States Government, the question of federal or state jurisdiction does not seem to have occurred. When Governor Henry A. Wise arrived on the scene and insisted that the prisoners be tried according to the laws of Virginia, President Buchanan did not object. On October 25 the Jefferson County Magistrates' Court assembled for a preliminary hearing. Sheriff James W. Campbell conducted the prisoners, including Brown, across the street from the county jail to the courthouse.

With Judge Richard Parker of Winchester on the bench, the circuit Court met the same afternoon. The court appointed two able attorneys, Charles James Faulkner and Lawson Botts, to defend the insurgent leader. The grand jury received a report of the preliminary examination and on October 26 reported true bills against each prisoner. Because of the importance of the case, Andrew Hunter was appointed special prosecutor to assist Charles B. Harding, the county's commonwealth attorney, in presenting the state's side. Four counts were listed against the prisoners. The first was treason against the Commonwealth of Virginia; the second was advising and conspiring with slaves and others to rebel, etc.; the third was the first degree murder of all five of the victims together; and the fourth was the murder of the three citizens separately.[12]

When John Brown requested that he be allowed to have outside counsel and the foreign lawyers had not arrived, he agreed to retain Lawson Botts and get Thomas C. Green to assist him. Apparently, Faulkner, who was from Martinsburg, was dismissed. Incidentally, Thomas C. Green later served on the West Virginia Supreme Court of Appeals. The accused requested a delay in the trial because he claimed a severe injury to one of his kidneys made him unable to proceed with it. He was subsequently examined by Dr. Gerard F. Mason, a reputable Charles Town physician, who pronounced him perfectly able to stand trial. For moral effect upon the public at large, Brown asked permission to recline on a couch during the trial. The request was granted.

The selection of a jury, most of whom were non-slaveholders, enabled the trial of John Brown to get under way. It began on October 26 and ended on October 31. Halfway through the proceedings, when some of Brown's witnesses failed to appear, he claimed he had no confidence in his lawyers, Botts and Green. When they requested to be allowed to withdraw from the case, they were permitted to do so. Their places were taken by George H. Hoyt, a young attorney from Boston; Hiram Griswold of Cleveland; and Samuel Chilton of Washington, D.C.

When all the opposing counsel had concluded their speeches, the jury retired and later returned with a guilty verdict of treason and murder.[13] Judge Parker then asked the accused if he had anything to say why sentence should not be pronounced against him. Brown rose from his cot and made a long speech in which he denied most of the charges of which he had been convicted. The following quotation from his remarks to the court is of more than passing interest, "...I feel entirely satisfied with the treatment I have received on my trial. Considering all the circumstances, it has been more generous than I expected, but I feel no consciousness of guilt..."[14]

The court sentenced him to be hanged on Friday, December 2.

The trials of the other prisoners proceeded in about the same manner as that of their leader, except that they did not take as much time. As two of them were Negroes, the charge of treason was dropped although they were both found guilty of murder and inciting slaves to rebellion. The Virginia statute provided for "any free person"who committed treason, and since it was not definitely established that they were free, there was doubt concerning the application of the statute to them.

Cook had escaped into Pennsylvania but was captured and taken to the jail in Charles Town. Indicted on November 7, he was tried the next day. He was defended by Daniel W. Voorhees, at that time Attorney General of Indiana and later a United States Senator from that state. Voorhees was a friend of the Governor of Indiana, Ashbel P. Willard, who had married Cook's sister. He was a very able lawyer, as well as a gifted orator. He did not base his appeal on the letter of the law but took broader, higher grounds. He pictured the young man before him as an adventurous prodigal, who had been enchanted by the fanatical Brown. In his plea for mercy, he mentioned the brokenhearted Virginia wife and the grief that would be caused the prisoner's distinguished relatives. The attorney's arguments were very impressive; but nevertheless, the jury found the prisoner guilty on all counts except treason. On November 10, Cook was sentenced to be hanged on December 16.[15]

When the Virginia Supreme Court of Appeals at Richmond had rejected Brown's petition for a writ of error, his hopes, as well as those of the other prisoners, were dashed to the ground.[16]

In the interval between the sentencing and execution of John Brown, Charles Town and Jefferson County teemed with activity. When a series of fires broke out in the county seat area, friends of the prisoners were blamed, especially when some of the victims were recent jurors. Arson became so widespread that Governor Henry A. Wise was requested to send additional troops to help the local authorities maintain order. One of the out-of-town companies, the Richmond Grays, had in its ranks John Wilkes Booth, the later assassin of President Abraham Lincoln. Rumors of would-be attempts to rescue the prisoners caused Governor Wise to dispatch more troops until over 1,000 men were on hand. Naturally, the town's limited facilities were taxed to the utmost to accommodate such an influx. Residents invited many of the officers to be guests in their homes and some of the more appreciative strangers showed their gratitude by sending gifts to their hosts when the executions were over.[17]

On December 2, 1859, John Brown left the Jefferson County jail in an open wagon to proceed to the location of the gallows. The site of the execution was a field on the Rebecca Hunter farm on the southeast edge of Charles Town. Brown was closely guarded by the soldiers in case there might develop any rescue attempt or effort to molest him. On his way to the scaffold, he remarked to the undertaker, "This is a beautiful country—I never had the pleasure of seeing it before."[18]

According to a reporter for a New York newspaper, Brown stooped and kissed a Negro child as he was leaving the jail, and the poet John Greenleaf Whittier wrote about the incident. As a matter of fact, no such occurrence could possibly have happened. Because the prisoner was so closely guarded, it was practically impossible for an outsider to get near him, least of all Negroes, who were said to have been scarce on the day of execution. Moreover Brown's arms were tied, which would make the display all the more difficult. As final proof, the jailor, John Avis, has left a sworn statement denying that the alleged incident occurred.

After thanking the sheriff and jailor for their kindnesses toward him, Brown prepared to meet his fate. A cap was placed over his face, the rope was placed around his neck, and the trap was sprung. As life departed from his body, the only visible signs were a slight grasping of the hands and twitching of the muscles. The pulse did not cease beating until thirty-five minutes had elapsed, and then the body was cut down, placed in its coffin, and conveyed to Harpers Ferry. At the scene of his attempted raid, it was met by his sorrowful wife and then sent to North Elba, New York, for burial.[19]

Two weeks later four more conspirators, including Cook, swung into eternity. On March 16, 1860, the remaining two who were still in custody paid the supreme sacrifice for their part in the ill-advised attempt to conduct a slave insurrection in Virginia.[20]

One of the witnesses to the execution of John Brown was Captain Turner Ashby. Mounted on a snow-white horse, he was deeply impressed with what he saw and was fearful of the future for his state and nation.[21] Although, as has been pointed out, he led his Mountain Rangers to Harpers Ferry as soon as he heard about the aborted invasion, he was too late to particpate in the fighting on October 17. In the weeks following the unsuccessful raid, he was occupied with picket and patrol duty. Since rumors were widespread that attempts would be made to rescue the prisoners in the Charles Town jail, there was a regular chain of pickets along the Potomac. Ashby had the responsibility for this precaution; and in carrying out his duties, he became familiar with the physical features of the area where he was destined to launch his military career. When he had discharged his duties creditably and he was no longer needed, he returned to *Wolf's Crag* to resume his peaceful pursuits. Much to his surprise, his company showed its

JOHN BROWN ASCENDING THE SCAFFOLD PREPARATORY TO BEING HANGED.—FROM A SKETCH BY OUR SPECIAL ARTIST.

Courtesy of the Library of Congress

The Execution of John Brown at Charles Town

appreciation for his leadership by presenting him with a handsome dress-sword and beautiful silver service.[22]

There are many versions concerning the origin of the famous "Rebel Yell" shouted by Confederate soldiers during the Civil War. One explanation attributes its origin to Turner Ashby and his Mountain Rangers. Just before the John Brown Raid they were having a tournament on a meadow on *Green Garden Farm* near Upperville. As Turner Ashby, dressed as the "Black Knight," came on the field, he and his competitors made a roaring noise. When he received information about the John Brown Raid, he ordered his men to meet him at Harpers Ferry. At the scene of the raid and at Charles Town, the other units heard the rangers repeat their yell. Some of the militia members remembered this experience and tried to imitate the yell when they went into action at the First Battle of Bull Run.[23]

Although Turner Ashby played only a minor role in the events that occurred after the John Brown Raid had taken place, he was greatly disturbed at what the future might hold for his native state and country. He could not help but be aware that the increasing sectionalism which had been all too evident before would continue to fester perhaps at an accelerated pace. Whe he returned to *Wolf's Crag* after it was all over, he lost many of his gay, carefree characteristics and acquired a much more serious mien and bearing. He participated in fewer and fewer fox-hunts and indulged in serious forebodings of the future.[24] The Harpers Ferry experience had enabled him to become acquainted with Robert E. Lee, Stonewall Jackson, Jeb Stuart, and others whom he was destined to know more intimately in the forthcoming conflict. Finally his patrol activities in the Lower Valley gave him knowledge of the area that was to prove invaluable in subsequent years.

CHAPTER III

HOSTILITIES BEGIN

In January, 1860, when Turner Ashby returned to *Wolf's Crag* to resume his normal pursuits after the John Brown affair, he could not help reflecting upon the serious situation which the ill-fated raid had caused. While most people in the North, including Abraham Lincoln, condemned Brown's violent methods, there is no doubt that his trial and manly bearing at his execution had won thousands of converts to the abolitionist cause. In spite of the fact that there had been a record of insanity in his family, he had refused at his trial to use this malady as an excuse to escape the hangman's noose. He realized, correctly, that he could accomplish more by forfeiting his life on the gallows and becoming a martyr to some followers than by being incarcerated in an institution and then perhaps released within a few years. Ashby was so disturbed by the reaction to the execution that he worried constantly about the future.

One of Turner Ashby's friends and former neighbor was Major Lewis A. Armistead of the United States Army. This Virginian had been a cadet at the United States Military Academy at West Point but did not graduate. He had been dismissed from the institution because he violated military decorum when he struck cadet Jubal A. Early's head with a plate in the mess hall.[1] Early, who remained at the academy, later won fame as the Confederate commander of the Second Corps in its bold Shenandoah Valley Campaign of 1864. Armistead later joined the army, won two brevets in the Mexican War, and remained in the regular army until he resigned May 26, 1861 to enter Confederate service. He advanced in rank and won immortal fame as a brigadier general who on foot led his brigade in Pickett's Charge at the Battle of Gettysburg. Like many of his men, he was killed there near the famous little clump of trees.[2]

In 1860 while Major Armistead was home on leave, he paid a visit to Turner Ashby at *Wolf's Crag*. When the conversation included a discussion of the general situation in the country, Turner mentioned his concern over the possibility of a disruption of the Union and consequent war. The army officer exclaimed to his friend, "Turner, do not talk so; I know but one country and one

flag. Let me sing you a song and drive away your gloom." Ashby
joined him in singing "The Star-Spangled Banner."[3]

As the year 1860 progressed, it became increasingly evident
that the United States was in deep trouble. The problem of sectionalism had not disappeared but intensified. Since the Com-
promise of 1850, far-reaching events had transpired that caused
the people from one section to regard those from another with
suspicion, hostility, and even hatred. In rapid succession the
Kansas-Nebraska struggle, the Dred Scott decision by the United
States Supreme Court, and the John Brown Raid had been
dividing the nation. This sectional feeling had been partially
mitigated by the fact that the major political parties had been able
to claim a national constituency. By 1860 this was no longer true.
The Whig Party, which had never been a closely-knit organization, had foundered on the question of slavery. The Democratic
Party had managed to weather the storm and remain a national
organization by nominating for the Presidency doughfaces—Northern men with Southern leanings. It was hoped that such a
choice would carry the nominee's home state, along with several
other Northern ones, and obtain enough Southern votes to win.
This strategy had proved successful in 1852 with the election of
Franklin Pierce and in 1856 with the election of James Buchanan.
Unfortunately the party split wide open in 1860.

Meanwhile, a new political organization had appeared on the
scene. The modern Republican Party, which was formed in 1854
to oppose the extension of slavery into the federal territories, had
offered the American voters its first Presidential nominee two
years later. Although the man chosen for this honor, John C. Frémont, was not a particularly strong candidate and lost the election
to Buchanan, he made a relatively good showing. Unless the
Republican challenge could be met successfully in 1860, the
Union was in danger.

There were four Presidential nominees in 1860. The split in the
Democratic Party had become so deep that the Northern
Democrats nominated Stephen A. Douglas, while the Southern
Democrats nominated John C. Breckinridge. The Republicans offered Abraham Lincoln as their candidate. A new political
organization, the Constitutional Union Party, came into the field
for this one and only time. It was supposed to favor a moderate or
conservative course and offered the country its support of "the
Constitution, the Union, and the Laws." Its Presidential nominee
was John Bell.

Turner Ashby, greatly disturbed at the tide of events, felt that the election of John Bell to the Presidency was indispensable to the preservation of the Union, since the other candidates were sectional ones. Accordingly, he worked and voted for the Constitutional Union nominee. He knew that not many Southern Democrats would support Stephen A. Douglas and not many Northerners would vote for John C. Breckinridge. Likewise, Lincoln's candidacy would appeal to only a handful of Southerners. Although Bell managed to carry Virginia, he did not receive much support elsewhere, and Ashby's hopes descended into gloom. Typically, upon hearing of Lincoln's election, he remarked, "If war ensue, we will have the consolation of knowing that we have done all in our power to avert it."[4]

When Abraham Lincoln was elected President in November, 1860, action followed quickly. South Carolina seceded in December and it was followed in the next few months by six other Southern states. In February, 1861, the secessionists formed the Confederate States of America with the capital at Montgomery, Alabama, and made an effort to persuade the other Southern states to join the new organization.

Virginia's course of action during these momentous times was to pursue a policy of delay. Most Virginians did not regard the mere election of Lincoln as sufficient provocation for leaving the Union, but they believed in secession as a last resort. When the General Assembly called for the election of delegates to a convention in Richmond to determine ths state's course, the returns showed an overwhelming victory for the Unionists. When the convention met in February, its members elected John Janney, a Unionist, as chairman. They were able to defeat all secessionist attempts to take the state out of the union until April 17. With the Confederate attack on Fort Sumter on April 12 and Lincoln's call for 75,000 volunteers to enforce the laws of the United States, the die was cast. If Virginia remained in the Union, she was called upon to furnish 2,340 soldiers to fight against the Southern Confederacy. There was no remaining neutral. Faced with the choice of fighting against her fellow-Southerners or on their side against the North, it is not surprising that on April 17, by a vote of 88 for, to 55 against, the Virginia Convention voted to join the Confederate States of America.[5]

Events had been rapidly reaching a climax. Prominent Virginians had made plans to seize Harpers Ferry for the state even before the passage of the Secession Ordinance. Those persons involved met on the night of April 16, 1861, and included the following: former Governor Henry A. Wise, John D. Imboden, Turner Ashby, Richard Ashby, Oliver Funsten, John A. Harman, and Superintendent Alfred M. Barbour of the Harpers Ferry Armory and Arsenal.[6]

When Barbour returned to Harpers Ferry from Richmond, where he had served as a Unionist delegate to the Virginia Convention, he called a meeting of the employees of the Government arms plant. Realizing the need for skilled industrial labor in the agricultural South, he told them that the place would be in possession of Virginia and they would be paid high wages if they remained to work for the state. However, sentiment was divided, for some of the expert machinists later worked for the Union at Springfield, Bridesburg, and Washington, while others made guns for the Confederacy at Richmond and Fayetteville, North Carolina.

Unfortunately for the South, Barbour's plea backfired, for it warned the Federal garrison at Harpers Ferry. No sooner had Virginia passed her Secession Ordinance on April 17 than her militia converged on the important industrial establishment. Since the Federal garrison at this time consisted of Lieutenant Roger Jones and only forty-two regular soldiers of the Forty-Second Infantry, it was apparent that Harpers Ferry would have to be evacuated. The army officer informed his superiors of his predicament and urged them to send reinforcements. He received orders to destroy the rifle works and withdraw from the town in case its capture became imminent.[7]

When Jones learned what Barbour had said, he ordered thousands of rifles and other arms to be gathered in piles in a building and trains of gunpowder to be laid through and around them. In order to create a draft and speed destruction, he had windows opened. Everything was ready to fire the whole plant and evacuate at a moment's notice. About ten o'clock on the night of April 18, a panting messenger informed Lieutenant Jones that the Virginia militia was only a mile away. Simultaneously a group of loyal volunteers on Bolivar Heights opened fire on the vanguard of the attackers.

When the order was given to fire the buildings, the torch was applied and soon the armory and arsenal buildings were engulfed in flames. Four of the garrison who lingered too long were captured, but the remainder escaped across the Potomac River into Maryland. As the first of the 2,500 Virginians came upon the scene, they witnessed the destruction of a large number of arms. Evidence of the intensity of the flames can still be seen in Harpers Ferry where excavations by the National Park Service reveal some rusty weapons fused together. Not all the arms were lost to the South, however, for the early intervention of townspeople and workmen saved about 5,000 completed muskets and 3,000 unfinished small arms. Although most of the armory and arsenal buildings were completely destroyed, the large workshops with their valuable arms-producing machinery were saved. Dismantled and shipped to Fayetteville, North Carolina, this machinery renewed its valuable role.[8]

The soldier who was in command of the Virginia troops at Harpers Ferry was Major General Kenton Harper of the militia. He was replaced by a colonel of the militia, Thomas J. Jackson, later known as "Stonewall," who was a West Point graduate at that time teaching at the Virginia Military Institute. Jackson realized that Maryland Heights, across the Potomac from the town, was the highest eminence in the area and hence was of more military value that the others. From its top one could dominate both Loudoun Heights and Bolivar Heights, as well as the town. He, therefore, seized that strategic location. His appreciation of the importance of Maryland Heights in connection with the defense of Harpers Ferry was borne out by subsequent events.

The authorities at Richmond decided the important command at Harpers Ferry should be entrusted to an older and more experienced officer than the ex-professor from the Virginia Military Institute. They, therefore, appointed Major General Joseph E. Johnston, one of the highest-ranking officers, to take over. He arrived on May 23. Since Jackson had not been notified by the Virginia officials of the change, he was not willing to relinquish his command to another without further instructions from Governor John Letcher or General Robert E. Lee. When the latter communicated with Jackson, the change of commanders was effected immediately.[9]

When the Virginia troops at Harpers Ferry were organized into the First Brigade, Colonel Jackson was appointed its commander. It was composed of young men representing the best blood of the Confederacy. The Second Regiment in this brigade, which later achieved immortal fame as the Stonewall Brigade, received most of its members from the counties of Jefferson, Berkeley, Frederick, and Clarke.

General Johnston, realizing the impossibility of protecting Harpers Ferry, decided to withdraw to Winchester, which could be defended more easily. After burning the Baltimore and Ohio Railroad bridge across the Potomac, as well as some public buildings, the Confederates moved to the better position.

Captain Turner Ashby and his Mountain Rangers arrived in Harpers Ferry too late to prevent the destruction of the armory and arsenal, but they soon became busily engaged. They were assigned to picket duty along the bank of the Potomac between Harpers Ferry and Point of Rocks, a small railroad station on the north bank of the river twelve miles east of the Ferry. As other soldiers were joining his command, Ashby found his followers increased by the addition of several companies of infantry and a battery of six guns commanded by Captain John D. Imboden. He performed his assigned duties in such a manner as to win the praise of his superiors. Not only did he interrupt the passage of railroad trains and Chesapeake and Ohio Canal boats, but he also assisted many men from Maryland to cross the river and join the Confederates. His scouting activities caused him to be constantly in the field.[10]

While Ashby was occupied with these activities in the Harpers Ferry area, a new organization was being formed that was eventually to include his command. An elderly graduate of West Point who had seen previous military experience, Colonel Angus W. McDonald of Winchester, had applied for and obtained from the Confederate War Department permission to raise a mounted force to be specially employed in the defense of the upper Potomac border. When he obtained the necessary orders, McDonald organized his command in his home town. In selecting officers to assist him in his endeavor, he was attracted to Turner Ashby, the energetic cavalryman who had displayed an aptitude for scouting at Harpers Ferry. When McDonald offered the young cavalier an opportunity to serve in this capacity, he was delighted to receive an affirmative reply. This was the beginning of the Seventh Virginia Cavalry Regiment.

Before the transfer to Colonel McDonald's command could be carried out, Ashby received a rude shock. While Jackson was still in charge at Harpers Ferry, J.E.B. Stuart had been commissioned lieutenant colonel and ordered to report to the river town for assignment to duty. When Jackson ordered all of the cavalry companies to be consolidated into a battalion to be commanded by Stuart, Ashby was greatly offended. Even though Stuart was a West Pointer and a regular army officer, Ashby was older and thought he was entitled to the first promotion. This view was shared by his men for their leader had already become their idol. Turner informed Imboden of his disappointment and announced his determination to resign from the army. Imboden, who felt the cavalry leader was justified in his resentment, urged him to see

Jackson in person. Accordingly, Ashby rode his black Arabian mount to his senior's headquarters, where he received satisfaction. Jackon agreed to divide the companies between Stuart and Ashby and to ask for the latter's immediate promotion. Thus there would be two regiments of cavalry, one of which would be led by Colonel McDonald with Ashby as second in command. When the senior officer's infirmities forced him to retire in a few months, Ashby was promoted to take his place.

One exploit which made Jackson more reluctant to lose the services of the brave trooper was the successful completion of a spying expedition to Chambersburg, Pennsylvania. Ashby had borrowed a farmer's homespun suit, hired a plow-horse, and impersonated a horse-doctor. He had filled his saddle-bags with a remedy for spavin or ringbone, had visited the encampment of Union General Robert Patterson, and had returned in the night with a vast amount of information.[11] Such daring and initiative were bound to cause Jackson's admiration.

Ashby's performance also attracted the attention of General Joseph E. Johnston, who, consequently, was very anxious for the young horseman to serve in the First Regiment under Colonel J.E.B. Stuart, then Johnston's cavalry commander at Harpers Ferry. Ashby informed Johnston that he preferred to remain with McDonald and that he had already been ordered to help organize the Seventh Virginia and that the Governor of Virginia had expressly provided that the Virginia troops, when mustered into Confederate service, would preserve their regimental organization. Correspondence between Ashby and Johnson produced the following letter from the general:

> Harpers Ferry, June 16th, 1861
> Captain: Your party has just reported to me. Let me offer you my cordial thanks for your services—especially the last. I assure you that the knowledge that you were between us and the enemy made me sleep very soundly last night and that your presence among the troops, under my command, would always have such an effect.
> Whenever I may be serving under circumstances agreeable to you, be assured that it would be a matter both of professional and personal gratification to me, to be associated with you.
> With the hope of meeting you often hereafter,
> I remain, respectfully and truly,
>
> J.E. Johnston.[12]

On July 23, Ashby received another letter from Johnston informing him that he had been promoted lieutenant colonel in the Virginia Cavalry, with orders to report to the general; however a following paragraph in the same epistle gave Ashby the option of remaining with McDonald or reporting to Johnston.[13] It is perhaps needless to add that the newly-appointed lieutenant colonel made the choice of remaining with the Seventh Virginia.

The Seventh Virginia Cavalry Regiment, which had been organized on June 17, 1861, consisted of the following officers and companies:

Colonel	Angus W. McDonald, Winchester, Va.
Lieutenant Colonel	Turner Ashby, Fauquier County, Va.
Major	Oliver M. Funsten, Warren County, Va.
Adjutant	A.W. McDonald, Jr., Hampshire County, Va.
Surgeon	Dr. A.P. Burns
Assistant-Surgeon	Dr. Thomas L. Settle, Fauquier County, Va.
Chaplain	Rev. J.B. Avirett, Frederick County, Va.
Asst.-Quartermaster	Capt. T.P. Pendleton
A.C.S.	Capt. John D. Richardson, Clarke County, Va.

Company A, Capt. Richard Ashby, Fauquier County, Va.
Company B, Capt. John Q. Winfield, Rockingham
            County, Va.
Company C, Capt. S.D. Myers, Shenandoah County, Va.
Company D, Capt. Macon Jordan, Page County, Va.
Company E, Capt. Walter Bowen, Warren County, Va.
Company F, Capt. George F. Sheetz, Hampshire County,
            Va.
Company G, Capt. Frank Mason, Maryland
Company H, Capt. A. Harper, Shenandoah County, Va.
Company I, Capt. E.H. Shands, Rockingham County, Va.
Company K, Capt. William Miller, Shenandoah County,
            Va.[14]

In the organization of this command, it will be noted that Turner Ashby was second in command directly under Colonel McDonald. His brother, Richard, succeeded him in charge of Company A, formerly the Mountain Rangers. According to one admirer, Richard was the handsomest and most soldierly figure in the entire regiment and was more robust-looking and more commanding in appearance than his elder brother.[15] While the regiment was being formed in Winchester, the McDonald home became headquarters. The enlisted men pitched their tents under the trees in the yard and, although the Ashby brothers were offered an opportunity to sleep in the house, they declined and preferred to share the discomfort of their men. The regiment marched away on June 17 or 18 along the Northwestern Turnpike toward Romney. Its first mission was to destroy the bridges of the Baltimore and Ohio Railroad over the Cheat River, thus interrupting Federal use of that important artery. The Cheat River bridge consisted of two through iron spans supported on two stone masonry abutments and one pier. The structure was twenty-seven feet above the bed of the stream and was three hundred twenty feet long. It was seventy-six miles west of Cumberland, Maryland, near Rowlesburg in Preston County, now West Virginia. Most of the Confederate troopers' route was through a mountainous and hostile country.[16]

The second day after leaving Winchester, the Confederates reached Romney, where they remained to complete the work of organization and to await the arrival of equipment which had been sent from Richmond. Scouts rode ahead of the main body in order to ascertain the whereabouts of Union Major General George B. McClellan, who had been conducting successful operations in what is now West Virginia. Because of the necessity for obtaining provisions for the soldiers and forage for their horses, it was decided to divide the regiment. Turner Ashby established his camp about six miles from Romney on *Ridge Dale*, the estate of Colonel George W. Washington.

An important addition to the Seventh Virginia Cavalry Regiment was the infantry company from Rockingham County under the captaincy of John Q. Winfield known as the Brock's Gap Rifles. When McDonald realized he needed additional men to complete his organization, he and Ashby appealed to the footsoldiers to "jine the cavalry." Captain Winfield in a letter to his wife expressed his disappointment upon joining the Tenth Virginia Infantry Regiment and stated he was "tired of delay and inaction." Not wanting to remain in the interior of the state and participate in dress parades while "the insolent foe behind us were polluting the soil of my native state," he weighed the differences between the two arms of service. He was influenced when he heard that McDonald and Ashby would have discretionary powers of command and were resolved to drive the enemy back into Maryland, Pennsylvania, or wherever they could be found. However, he decided to leave the choice of arms to his men and was greatly elated when they preferred to be cavalrymen.[17]

Ashby kept a busy schedule while he was encamped on the Washington estate. He established a picket post across the nearby Potomac River, from which he sent out daily scouting parties almost to Cumberland, Maryland. This town was occupied then by a Federal force commanded by Colonel Lew Wallace, later famous as the author of *Ben Hur*. Although Hampshire County and its environs were generally favorable to the Confederate cause, like many of the border counties, it contained some Unionists. Some of them prowled around the Confederate camp, obtained what information they could, and relayed it to the nearest Federal authorities. There was one suspect whose activities caused his arrest to be eagerly sought by the Confederates. When McDonald communicated with Ashby about this individual, the latter sent out a scouting party of eleven men on June 26 and put his brother, Richard Ashby, in charge of the expedition.

Unfortunately, on this particular day the younger Ashby did not ride his regular mount. His favorite horse had been pushed so hard by carrying his master on so many patrols that Richard decided to give him a rest. The replacement, while a serviceable animal, was not as accustomed to the rider's guidance. When Richard was unable to find his quarry, he decided to push closer to the Federal lines and followed the bed of the Baltimore and Ohio Railroad toward Cumberland. In doing so, he ran into an enemy ambush. Seeing that he was greatly outnumbered, the Confederate officer withdrew to a more defensible position. He elected to bring up the rear. When he was withdrawing, his horse fell while attempting to negotiate a cattle-guard along the railroad. Athough unhurt by the fall off his horse, Ashby soon found himself unhorsed, alone, and being charged by enemy cavalrymen. He determined to sell his life as dearly as possible and fought his opponents until he was overwhelmed in a vicious hand-to-hand fight. Weakened by a number of wounds, the young captain was finally knocked prostrate. As he was lying helpless on the ground, he received a serious wound in the abdomen from a bayonet thrust. It is said that this wound resulted from his replying in the affirmative when he was asked if he were a secessionist. After rifling his pockets and taking his spurs, the blue-clad troopers left the scene.[18]

When Turner Ashby was informed by a friendly mountain girl that heavy firing had been heard in the direction taken by his brother, he set out to ascertain what had happened. He arrived at the scene of the encounter and saw evidence of a struggle; but he was unable to find anyone who could give him an account of the fight. Accompanied by ten of his troopers, he followed what he thought was the enemy's line of retreat. Before long, he overtook the Federals who had taken possession of Kelly's Island, a long, narrow island in the Potomac River. Without hesitation the intrepid officer led his men to the attack; and after suffering several casualties, the little group reached the island. He urged his followers to reserve their fire and use their bowie knives. Such was the ferocity of the Confederate attack that they routed their opponents. Ashby emptied eleven out of twelve cylinders of his revolvers, killed three of the enemy, and received a slight wound in his leg. His dark bay mount was also wounded by the same ball. Among the articles captured on the island were Richard's horse and spurs. Not finding his brother, Ashby returned to the Virginia shore and retraced his steps to the site where the first engagement had taken place. Careful searching of the area revealed the object of his quest, who, though almost dead, had managed to drag himself to some nearby bushes in order to seek shelter from the sun's burning rays. Richard was so weakened from his wounds that he had scarcely enough strength left to ask for a drink of water. After giving the dying man a stimulant, the men made a stretcher from a blanket and two poles. They then carried him to their camp where he occupied a room at *Ridge Dale*, the mansion owned by Colonel George W. Washington. The Confederate surgeons thought at first he might recover from his eight wounds because of his great vitality, but after suffering severe pain for seven days, he died on July 3, 1861.[19]

Turner Ashby's grief at the loss of his brother was almost unbearable. The two had been inseparable since early childhood and enjoyed a mutual affection rarely seen even in brothers. According to some accounts, he was so overcome by the tragedy that he broke Richard's sword into several pieces which he threw into the grave and then got on his knees and swore revenge; however, Ashby's chaplain refutes this story and asserts that the elder brother's grief was so great that he remained silent and made no outward expression of his loss. He did, however, take the time to write the following letter to his sister, Dorothea, who, it will be recalled, had married Powhatan Moncure of Stafford County:

Camp Washington, July 7th, 1861
Dear Dora:
  I received your letter a few days ago and take this evening to write you a few lines, urging and entreating, that you may all look upon our affliction as patriots, not selfishly mourning over our untimely loss, but regarding it as a sacrifice made upon the altar of our country, which we ought to congratulate ourselves that we could furnish. Poor Dick went into the war like myself, not to regard

himself or our friends, but to serve our country in this the time of
peril. I know your Ma and Mary will all be too good soldiers to grudge
giving your country the dearest sacrifice that you could provide.
Yours is the good fortune to be called upon to provide so great an offering. His country has lost the services of a brave man with a strong
arm, which he proved upon her enemies in losing his life. As he has
ever won praises from them for the greatest bravery they ever saw,
you all (and I mean this for you all) do not know what a weight it
would take from me to know you bore our loss like soldiers. I had
rather it had been myself. He was younger and had one more tie to
break than I. But seeing him through the time of his prostration from
his wounds, I know that he felt that he was but losing his life in the
cause of duty, and seemed entirely resigned, not desponding at the
doubts which he knew there existed in his life. We all believed a part
of the time that he would recover; at one time, he thought so too.
But the exposure without attention for several hours upon the
battle-field so prostrated him as to make it hard for reaction to take
place, which kept him from having any appetite. He lived until the
eighth day suffering very little for one so cut to pieces.
    He was buried with all the honors of war, and never was greater
respect paid to the memory of one man; it was indeed a triumph of
his bravery. I had him buried in a beautiful cemetery in Romney; and
should I live through the war, I will have him moved to Fauquier.
Mine has been the heaviest loss. I lose the strength of his arm in the
fight as well as the companion of my social hours. I mean to bear it
as a soldier, and not as one who in this time for sacrifices regards
only his own loss. You must all try to bear it in the same way. Let it
be your boast that you have given a brother for the safety of your
country and the preservation of your homes, and Ma that she has
given a son for such a cause as ours. When men die as he has died,
(and as he prepared to die), for liberty, it shows our enemies that we
cannot be conquered. It saves the lives of many.
    George is well and sends his love to his wife. Our movements
from here are not yet determined. I may not write often, but should
there be anything the matter will do so at once.

Yours truly.
Turner Ashby.[20]

Captain Richard Ashby was buried with all the honors of war in
the Indian Mound Cemetery near Romney. Later his remains were
disinterred and removed to the Stonewall Cemetery in Winchester in
the grave of his illustrious brother Turner who was killed less than a
year later.

The attempt to destroy the Cheat River Railroad bridge was abandoned when Confederate scouts reported that the Baltimore and
Ohio in that area was well-protected by Federal infantry. To pursue
the goal with cavalry alone seemed to be courting disaster, especially when it was known that Colonel Lew Wallace was in Cumberland
with an Indiana regiment. On July 17, Confederate authorities

ordered Colonel McDonald to return to Winchester and the next day his command began the ride.[21] Federal Major General Robert Patterson had crossed the Potomac at Harpers Ferry and was expected to march on Winchester. A battle appeared imminent at Manassas or Bull Run, where General P.G.T. Beauregard awaited an attack by Brigadier General Irvin McDowell from Washington.

Members of the Seventh Virginia Cavalry had been greatly impressed with the bravery and leadership qualities exhibited by the Ashby brothers in the fighting around Romney. Richard's tragic death had left its imprint, and Turner's revenge on the enemy made him the idol of the regiment. He was thus enabled to draw around him a large personal group of supporters so devoted that they would follow him anywhere.[22]

Although neither army was prepared for battle at Manassas, both Federals and Confederates were forced to engage in combat because of public opinion. United States Congressmen, newspaper reporters, influential citizens, and the Northern public in general were practically unanimous in demanding that their ill-prepared army attack the equally ill-prepared Confederates. It mattered not that the Union had not had sufficient time to prepare its troops for battle. The cry of "On to Richmond" was so vociferous that the professionals were powerless to resist. It was widely believed in the North that once the southward movement began, Richmond would fall like a ripe apple ready for the picking.

Their opponents at Manassas were equally as confident. Many Southerners believed that one of their soldiers could whip twenty Yankees. Their commanding general in the area was P.G.T. Beauregard, a West Point graduate and a regular army officer who enjoyed the reputation of the "hero of Fort Sumter." Even Beauregard himself declared:

> No people ever warred for independence with more relative advantages than the Confederates; and if, as a military question, they must have failed, then no country must aim at freedom by means of war... The South, with its great material resources, its defensive means of mountains, rivers, railroads, and telegraph, with the immense advantage of the interior lines of war, would be open to discredit as a people if its failure could not be explained otherwise than by mere material contrast.[23]

Ashby's Cavalry missed the first battle of Bull Run, which was fought by the Confederates commanded by General P.G.T. Beauregard and the Federals led by Brigadier General Irvin McDowell, as has been noted above. The highest-ranking Union officer was Lieutenant General Winfield Scott; but since he had served in the War of 1812, he was hardly fit for field duty in 1861. In fact, he was so incapacitated that he had difficulty in mounting his horse. He had recommended that an officer who had served under him in the Mexican War, Robert E. Lee, be offered command of the armies of the Union; but Lee, in an agonizing decision, though opposed to slavery and secession, felt that his first obligation was to his native Virginia. Consequently, the thankless command of the Federals fell upon the shoulders of McDowell, another West Pointer, who was a capable officer but wholly unequal to the impossible task of leading the Union army into battle before it was ready. Fortunately for him, his opponents were equally unprepared.

The Union commander at Harpers Ferry, Major General Robert Patterson, like General Scott, had served in the War of 1812 and the Mexican War. He had been placed in charge of the military departments of Pennsylvania, Delaware, Maryland, and the District of Columbia, when he was ordered in mid-July to prevent Johnston from reinforcing Beauregard at Bull Run while McDowell was advancing against the Confederates. Although numerically superior to Johnston in the Valley, he failed to engage him in battle. His reason for this inactivity was that he had not received orders to attack. When Johnston gave him the slip, Patterson received considerable criticism and was mustered out of service July 27, 1861. The key to the Confederate victory at First Bull Run was Johnston's joining Beauregard and Patterson's failure to join McDowell. Had Patterson kept Johnston in the Valley or had he joined McDowell, in all probability First Bull Run would have resulted in a victory for the Federals.

When Ashby's cavalrymen reached Winchester on the evening of July 19, they found that Johnston's Valley Army, including the Stonewall Brigade, had already left for Manassas. The route was across the Blue Ridge Mountains through Ashby's Gap to Piedmont Station now Delaplane, where the men took passage on the cars of the Manassas Gap Railroad. Ashby's men were expected to cover the movement in Johnston's reinforcing Beauregard. When the cavalry leader participated in a bold scout behind enemy lines on July 20, he was gratified to ascertain that the Unionists were entirely ignorant that Confederates had left the Valley for Manassas Junction and were ready to participate in the First Battle of Bull Run on July 21.

Having completed his assignment regarding Patterson, Ashby led his troopers eastward. He marched, in turn, across the Shenandoah at Berry's Ferry, through the Blue Ridge at Ashby's Gap, and occupied Upperville, where he spent the night. Although he heard artillery firing on the march, he did not realize that a great battle was taking place until he reached Haymarket. Having no marching orders, Ashby and a few companions rode over the nearby battlefield. Although he rejoiced in the Southern victory in the first great contest of the war, he was disappointed at not having been a participant. He believed, as did others in his command, that if they had not been delayed by the necessity of transporting the infirm Colonel McDonald in a wagon, they would have made it to Manassas in time to join the fight. The Seventh Regiment spent the evening at Bristoe Station, on the Orange and Alexandria Railroad, about six miles from Manassas Junction.[24]

The meaning of the word Manassas has intrigued many persons. According to one account, it owes its origin to a conversation between two Negro slaves who lived on neighboring plantations, a few miles east of Fairfax Station. A faithful old slave belonging to a Mrs. Taylor met his neighbor and addressed him as follows: "Uncle Willis, kin yer tell me how dey got dis name Manassas fur this place down dar what dey has all dem big guns?"

"I dunno, Brer Ephraim, cep'ting 'tis we is de man, and dem Yankees whar cum down here is de asses; dats how we gets de name Manassas, I speck."[25]

When Confederate authorities feared an attack on Staunton from the west, they ordered McDonald's cavalrymen back to the Valley. Their route led through Fauquier and Rappahannock Counties over the Blue Ridge through Thornton's Gap, into Luray (Page) Valley, and finally to the Main Valley through New Market Gap. Since their march through Fauquier took them within riding distance of Markham, Turner was undoubtedly tempted to ask for a short leave of absence to visit his old home, *Wolf's Crag*. Realizing his obligations as a soldier, however, he resisted the temptation. In fact, his devotion to duty was so great that not once in his military career was he furloughed or absent from his post.[26]

From New Market the Confederates proceeded southward to Staunton, where they learned of a change in orders. Instead of going westward to meet an expected attack from Brigadier General William S. Rosecrans which never materialized, they were sent northward to the Lower Shenandoah Valley to protect the border counties from enemy attempts to destroy the crops. Because of the fertility of its soil, the Shenandoah Valley has frequently been called "The Granary of the Confederacy." At Winchester the command was divided. McDonald took six companies to Romney, while Ashby took the four remaining organizations to Kearneysville, on the Baltimore and Ohio Railroad between Martinsburg and Harpers Ferry. His responsibility was to protect the men employed in taking up the materials of the railroad. This important transportation facility had never been repaired after Johnston had put it out of commission by destroying bridges during his previous occupancy of the area. In fact, earlier the Confederates had "borrowed" B&O rolling stock at Harpers Ferry, sent it to Winchester over the Winchester and Potomac line, conveyed it over country roads to Strasburg, put it on the Manassas Gap rails, and used it to transport Johnston's army to Manassas in time to turn the tide of the battle.[27]

Besides destruction of the railroad, Ashby was also ordered to render the Chesapeake and Ohio Canal useless. This waterway on the Maryland side of the Potomac followed the meanderings of that stream all the way from the nation's capital to Cumberland, Maryland, a distance of 184 miles. While the canal lost in its race with the railroad and, in fact, never reached the Ohio, its slow-moving boats pulled by horses or mules hauled vast quantities of coal and other materials to the eastern seaboard. As much of this western coal was used by Federal warships in their merciless blockade of the Confederacy's ports, any interruption to this traffic would yield great benefits to the munitions-deficient South. Since the canal needed dams to divert water from the Potomac and locks to overcome the differences in elevation in this long journey, it was vulnerable in many places.

To accomplish these objectives, Ashby established his camp near Shepherdstown, along the Potomac, and extended his picket lines for some distance from the river. Since raiding parties from Maryland were frequently crossing the river in order to annoy the Virginians and interrupt the dismantling of the railroad, the Confederate troopers were kept quite busy. While in the Shepherdstown vicinity, Ashby availed himself of the opportunity to renew the acquaintance of Colonel Alexander R. Boteler at *Fountain Rock*. The latter was a prominent politician who had represented his district in the United States House of Representatives and later in the Confederate Congress. As a result of Ashby's visits to *Fountain Rock*, he and the politician became close friends. Unfortunately, because of its owner's prominence. *Fountain Rock* was burned to the ground in July, 1864 on orders of Union Major General David Hunter. Besides the loss and inconvenience to the Boteler family, the unnecessary act of destruction deprived future historians of the opportunity to utilize Boteler's extensive collection of manuscripts.[28]

On one occasion when Colonel Ashby and several of his fellow Confederates stopped at *Fountain Rock* to enjoy a late supper, they found that they had been preceded by a number of their men. In spite of the demands on the Boteler household for food, Mrs. Boteler was equal to the occasion and fed them all. When one trooper who had enjoyed a hearty meal, especially Mrs. Boteler's cakes, offered to pay, asking how much he owed for his food, the reply was, " Nothing at all. If I had it in my heart to charge a Confederate soldier for a meal, my husband would sue for a divorce immediately." Although the soldier remonstrated with his host and stated that he had been "used to pay for what he got all his life," she remained obdurate and refused to take a cent. When the incident was reported to Ashby, he laughed and told Mrs. Boteler that she made "a most excellent wife for a member of Congress."[29] Ashby's friendship with Boteler undoubtedly facilitated his promotion to a full colonelcy later.[30]

Having accomplished his mission in the Shepherdstown-Kearneysville area, Ashby moved his camp to *Wheatlands,* the home of George W. Turner, who as an innocent civilian at Harpers Ferry was one of the non-combatants killed by the John Brown raiders. Although a graduate of West Point, he had forsaken a military career to be a member of the landed aristocracy and had become prominent in Jefferson County affairs. As *Wheatlands* was located south of Charles Town between the county seat and the little village of Rippon, it was a better place to watch the Federal force that was assembling at Harpers Ferry. However when the enemy became more active, Ashby moved his camp closer, east of Charles Town in the direction of Harpers Ferry.

Turner Ashby's first large engagement in which he had the sole responsibility of command occurred on October 16, 1861, when he skirmished with a Federal force commanded by Colonel John W. Geary. The latter was an army officer who had served in the Mexican War and had been Governor of Kansas during the civil war in that territory. The encounter took place on Bolivar Heights just west of Harpers Ferry. Federal forces had crossed the Potomac from Maryland on October 8 in order to remove wheat from the large flour mill of Abraham Herr on the Island of Virginius in the Shenandoah River at Harpers Ferry. The wheat was being ferried across the Shenandoah when Geary learned that Confederates were approaching from the direction of Halltown. Geary had about 600 troops, while Ashby had 480. The Confederate advance drove in the enemy's pickets to Bolivar, where it was stopped by companies from the Third Wisconsin and Twenty-eighth Pennsylvania Regiments. Ashby's force consisted of 300 militia armed with flintlock muskets, 180 of McDonald's cavalry, and a small artillery force which employed one rifled four-pounder gun and one badly mounted twenty-four pounder. Since the latter gun was a makeshift piece which was mounted on common wagon-wheels, it is not surprising that it broke down and had to be spiked. This loss was a serious one because Ashby had no replacement for it and was opposed by an enemy who had superior guns. He realized the importance of having adequate artillery so much that he was determined in the future to improve that arm of service. The resulting organization of Chew's Battery which supported him in his later battles justified his evaluation of his weakness on Bolivar Heights. Although some Confederate cannon and sharpshooters had taken position on Loudoun Heights, across the Shenandoah, they were silenced by Union batteries posted on Maryland Heights, a higher eminence across the Potomac.

When Geary was reinforced by the acquisition of more infantry and artillery, Ashby's men fell back to the position occupied by the enemy's pickets at the beginning of hostilities. Ashby reformed his line on a neighboring elevation known as School-House Hill and awaited Geary's approach.The Federals withdrew across the Potomac during the night, whereupon the Southerners regained possession of Harpers Ferry.[31] Both sides claimed victory in the Bolivar Heights affair, but since both commanders retreated after slight losses, the skirmish can more accurately be termed a draw.

Casualties in this affair were relatively light. The Federals lost four killed, seven wounded, and two captured, while their opponents suffered one killed and thirteen wounded. One of the latter was John Yates Beall of *Walnut Grove*, Jefferson County, who was then a private in the Second Virginia Infantry, Stonewall Brigade. Being at home on furlough, he volunteered for the fight. He later became active in a scheme to liberate Confederate officers imprisoned on Johnson's Island in Lake Erie, but the plan miscarried because of a betrayal by a woman jilted by one of the conspirators. Beall was subsequently captured in civilian clothes at Niagara, taken to Governor's Island, tried before a military commission, found guilty of being a guerrilla and spy, and sentenced to be hanged. In spite of strenuous efforts made by his friends to enable him to escape the hangman's noose, he was executed on February 24, 1865. His remains were brought to Charles Town and buried in Zion Episcopal Churchyard. The tombstone marking the grave bears the inscription, "Died in the service and defense of his country."[32]

The Bolivar Heights skirmish and the advent of winter concluded Ashby's military activities for several months. In summary, the campaigns in the Lower Shenandoah Valley since the beginning of hostilities had benefited the Confederacy in a number of ways. For one thing, the capture of the armory and arsenal at Harpers Ferry, with its valuable arms-producing machinery, was an important addition to the South's meager industrial capabilities. The few days at Harpers Ferry when the militia had held full sway proved beyond doubt that not much dependence could be placed in that state organization. These same men, when incorporated into the Confederate army and properly trained by competent officers, proved to be excellent soldiers. Although Stonewall Jackson had been in command at Harpers Ferry for only twenty-five days, he had enough time to organize and bring under control a large number of volunteers. He became so familiar with that area that he knew how to capture Harpers Ferry and its Federal garrison when ordered to do so in September, 1862. When Jackson's successor, Joseph E. Johnston, held the river town until June 15, he kept Washington authorities in a state of alarm over the safety of the nation's capital and deprived the Union of the uninterrupted use of its best commmunication with the West—the Baltimore and Ohio Railroad. Johnston's evacuation of Harpers Ferry and taking a position at Winchester instead demonstrated his appreciation of the indefensibility of the town bordered by the two rivers. The skill with which he gave Patterson the slip and marched to reinforce Beauregard at Manassas contributed greatly to the Confederate victory at Bull Run. Finally, the qualities of leadership displayed by Johnston, Jackson, Stuart, Ashby, and others in the 1861 Lower Shenandoah Valley campaigns inspired among their followers in the ranks a respect and devotion that proved valuable in the future.[33]

Colonel Angus W. McDonald, First Commander of the Seventh Virginia
Cavalry Regiment

CHAPTER IV

REORGANIZATION

"If you wanna have fun,
Jine the cavalry."

While many Civil War books and articles have been written about the exploits of the infantry and artillery, the arm of service that has been generally overlooked is the cavalry. The mounted men were the envy of the foot-soldiers and were generally considered to have an easy life riding back and forth, doing little fighting, escaping harsh discipline, and performing like knights of old.

The horse-soldiers were the recipients of many jokes made at their expense by other soldiers. "Whoever saw a dead cavalryman or a dead mule?""A fight is about to begin; there go the cavalry heading for the rear!" Perhaps the contempt which others had for the mounted men is best illustrated by the following anecdote, which Major General Fitzhugh Lee, the commanding officer's nephew and a famous Confederate cavalryman, told on himself. As he was riding away from Appomattox after the surrender, he met an old infantryman who, he later learned, had been visiting his home in North Carolina. The Confederate cavalry officer reported the following conversation as having taken place:

"Ho, there," cried General Lee,"where are you going?"

"I've been off on a furlough and am now going back to join General Bob Lee," replied the foot-soldier.

"You needn't go back but can throw your gun away and return home, for Lee's surrendered."

"Lee's surrendered?"

"That's what I said," replied Fitz.

"It must have been that damned Fitz Lee, then. Rob Lee would never surrender." Whereupon the old soldier shouldered his musket and, with a look of contempt, resumed his journey to rejoin his regiment.[1]

On another occasion, a field officer of a certain cavalry brigade invited some of his fellow-officers to dine with him. Among the items on the bill of fare was apple brandy, which was imbibed very freely. While the officers were indulging themselves, an old colonel arose, with great gravity, and said, "Gentlemen, my regiment met the enemy yesterday and overcame him. We killed 50, wounded 100, and captured 250 prisoners." When his colleagues had congratulated him on his success, the group consumed more apple jack. After a few more rounds the colonel bragged again, "I omitted to inform you of a terrible conflict my regiment had with the enemy yesterday. We killed 500, wounded 1,000, and captured 1,500 prisoners." Again he was congratulated on his victory, again the brandy flowed freely, and again the old colonel rose to the occasion. This time he staggered to his feet and said, "Gentlemen, I neglected to tell you of the most terrific battle of the war. On yesterday my command encountered the enemy, and killed 10,000 of them, wounded 20,000, and captured 25,000 prisoners of war."

The host, who had also drunk too much, sprang to his feet, seized the jug, and exclaimed, "Here, Colonel, for God's sake, take another drink and kill the whole Yankee army."[2]

The cavalry was very different from the infantry and artillery. The latter two arms performed the "heavy work" in the great battles and were depended upon to give a commander the victory he so ardently desired. If a soldier were killed or badly wounded, that was, of course, the end of his military career; but if he survived, he could usually look forward to several months of inactivity while the antagonists prepared for another confrontation. In winter the infantrymen or artillerists got even more relief from arduous campaigning. Then the wheels of the guns sank in the slushy soil and wagons could not be moved to bring rations to the hungry soldiers if they were on the march. Consequently, they settled down in their relatively comfortable camps, built various kinds of shelter, and entertained themselves as best they could until spring arrived and dried the wet terrain. Then they prepared to resume the conflict.

Cavalry life was different. The horse-soldiers did not suffer the enormous casualties experienced by their comrades-in-arms in battle, but they continued their work long after the infantryman or artillerist had settled down into his life of repose. They fought throughout the year in winter as in summer. Since they were the "eyes and ears" of the army, they could not rest. They must be in the saddle constantly and watch by night as well as by day. They must guard against surprises at all times and must remain in the saddle, often without regular rations and sleep while the infantrymen have been resting in camp and enjoying a life of relative leisure.[3] This conclusion is not meant to minimize the work of the infantry and artillery but merely to emphasize the contrast offered by cavalry service.

The Confederate cavalrymen were quite different from their Northern counterparts. One Northern writer has described the Southern horseman as follows:

> ...The young bloods of the South, sons of planters, lawyers about towns, good billiard players, and sportsmen—men who never did work and never will—war suits them, and the rascals are brave. They are fine riders and bold to rashness and dangerous subjects in every sense. They care not a sou for niggers, land, or anything. They hate Yankees and don't bother their brains about the past, present, or future. As long as they have good horses, plenty of forage, and an open country, they are happy. They are splendid riders, shots, and utterly reckless. Stuart, John Morgan, Forrest, and Jackson are the types and leaders of this class. They must all be killed or employed by us before we can hope for peace. They are the best cavalry in the world, but it will tax Mr. Chase's [Salmon P. Chase] genius of finance to supply them with horses. At present horses cost them nothing, for they take where they find and don't bother their brains who is to pay for them.[4]

While this general characterization undoubtedly has its inaccuracies, it does contain some truths and helps explain the role of the Confederate horsemen. They labored under many difficulties. The Government was not able to supply horses for all the men who volunteered for this arm of service. It entered into a contract with the soldier to take his horse at a fair valuation, furnish food and keep him shod, and pay a per diem of forty cents for his use. If the horse should be killed, its owner was paid the muster valuation; but if it should be captured or worn out in the service, the owner absorbed the loss. In this case, he was compelled to furnish another mount or to be transferred to some other arm of the service. At first, the adoption of this policy did not prove to be much of a hardship, for Virginia and other Southern states were full of fine horses. However, as the war took its toll, the lack of good horses became a serious problem. At times half of the command were absent at one time and many cavalrymen were reported "absent without leave" because of their inability to obtain a steed and return to their commands within the allotted time. Since it would be unjust to punish them, discipline was relaxed and the cavalry became too much a volunteer association. This breach of army regulations caused considerable annoyance to strict disciplinarians like Stonewall Jackson and others who sometimes became very critical of their cavalrymen.[5]

The lack of discipline in the Confederate cavalry may be partially explained by the fact that many of the men were well-to-do farmers and planters who were more used to giving than obeying orders. Consequently, they chafed under military rules and regulations. This was particularly true during the first two years of the war. They felt free to criticize every officer from the general down to the lieutenant. When the army was reorganized and elections were held in front of Major General George B. McClellan's lines at Yorktown in 1862, many capable officers whose ideas of military discipline were more in line with regular army life were not retained by their commands. Their places were taken by "more sociable and better fellows." In some instances this was beneficial; in most cases, it was harmful to the improvement of the effectiveness of the army. In this connection, it is interesting to note that three of the Confederacy's greatest cavalry generals, Nathan B. Forrest, Wade Hampton, and John Hunt Morgan, entered the service without previous military experience. The name of Turner Ashby might justifiably be included in this group. Had not his brilliant career been ended by a Yankee bullet on that fateful day in June, 1862, near Harrisonburg, there is no telling how far he would have advanced in the Confederate service. All of these cavalry generals were natural leaders, popular with their followers, and extremely valuable to the cause which they served.

In order to improve the discipline of his cavalry by preventing straggling, General Braxton Bragg of the Confederate Army of Tennessee ordered that cavalrymen absent from their command without proper written authority would be deprived of their horses and immediately assigned to the nearest regiment of infantry from their respective state.[6]

In the reorganization of the Confederate army, great gaps were made in the cavalry. Many doctors were promoted to surgeons in other arms, some influential persons obtained other positions, elderly men were released to return to the less demanding task of going home to raise supplies for the army, and some left because of ill health—never to return to the bugle call of "boots and saddles" or "to horse." Their places were filled by recruits, often boys from sixteen to twenty years of age, who needed but a few months' experience to become excellent soldiers. Other vacancies were filled by transfers from the infantry, who were sometimes influenced by the desire for what was considered an easier service and the comforts of horseback. Their disappointment may well be imagined when they discovered that they sometimes had to fight as infantry all day and then provide food for their horses at night. Early the next morning they had to find food for their horses, as well as themselves, and repeat the activities of the previous day. Many of the newly-recruited cavalrymen were poor, some of them very poor, and it was somewhat of a mystery how they kept mounted. When their horses had been captured or incapacitated for service—for these they would get no pay—they impoverished themselves or denied their families so that they could remain with their commands and not be transferred to other arms of the service. However, the process of attrition gradually reduced the number of cavalrymen until toward the end of the war their units were nowhere near what their full strength should have been.

Besides the task of providing forage for their horses, the Confederate horse-soldiers labored under other difficulties. They wer e handicapped by the lack of proper arms and equipment. At the beginning of the war the troopers had to furnish their own saddles and bridles. The English Roundtree saddle, which had been used extensively at home, proved ill-suited to military use, for the constant activity soon made soreback horses. Later the Government provided a saddle that was more satisfactory. The supply of arms was sadly deficient. At first many riders were supplied with shotguns, although some counties had armed their volunteer companies with good pistols. Some regiments from North Carolina were furnished with Enfield rifles. Because the cavalrymen found Confederate carbines and sabers unsatisfactory, they discarded these and used trophies taken from the Federals. In this way they were able to obtain saddles, bridles, arms, ammunition, and even horses which enabled them to fight on more even terms.[7]

In the fall of 1861, the stage was being set for events of far-reaching significance in the Lower Shenandoah Valley. On October 13 Stonewall Jackson was promoted to major general, and on November 4 he was ordered to take command of the Valley District, with headquarters at Winchester. The Confederacy had established the Department of Northern Virginia, which consisted of the Valley, Potomac, and Aquia districts. As soon as Jackson arrived in Winchester, he sought to increase the little force he found on hand. He had learned that Federals across the Potomac were building up their strength, and he was determined not only to defend the headquarters city but also to repel any attempt of the enemy to invade his district.[8] He obtained much of the information about enemy dispositions from Turner Ashby.

When Lieutenant Colonel Ashby went to confer with Jackson, he renewed the friendship that he had formed during their previous associations. He came away more favorably impressed than ever by the hero of Bull Run. In order to clarify his status under the new command system, he wrote Adjutant General Samuel Cooper in Richmond. In his letter he stated that he had previously been receiving orders only from the Confederate War Department, and he wanted to know if this should continue to be the case or should he report to Jackson.[9] Ashby was quite happy to learn that he would be associated with the commander of the Valley District.

Ashby's operations had been so handicapped by the lack of artillery that he determined to seek authority to organize a battery to be attached to his command. In his engagement with Geary at Bolivar Heights, he had failed to obtain cooperation of the artillery on Loudoun Heights, and he did not want a repetition of this occurrence. By having a battery directly under his command, he could exercise full responsibility.

The result was the organization of Chew's Battery, which was destined to become one of the most famous artillery units in the entire Confederate army. It was established on November 11, 1861 under special authority of the Secretary of War. Unlike regular artillerymen, who walked behind the guns on foot, each member of Chew's Battery rode his own horse. Wherever the cavalry went, the horse artillery accompanied it. Its commander and first captain was Roger Preston Chew of Jefferson County, who was then only eighteen years of age. A graduate of the Virginia Military Institute, where he ranked eighth in a total class of seventy-five members, he joined with several other schoolmates in forming his famous organization.[10] The original officers, besides Captain Chew, were Milton Rouss, first lieutenant; and J.W. McCarty and James Thomson, second lieutenants. A fourth officer, James H. Williams who was also a lieutenant, had not been trained at the Lexington military school but had been a practicing attorney in Dubuque, Iowa, and had served as a member of the state legislature. Originally, the battery included thirty-three men, in addition to its officers. The company had three pieces of artillery—one a rifled gun called the "Blakeley," one howitzer, and one six-inch rifled gun. When Ashby suggested that all the men be mounted, Chew's Battery became the first mounted battery of flying artillery organized in the Confederate army. It accompanied

Ashby's Cavalry throughout Jackson's Valley Campaign of 1862 and did yeoman service with the cavalry advances, as well as checking the enemy on the retreats. It has been said that what Jackson was to Lee, Ashby was to Jackson, and Chew was to Ashby.

After the deaths of Ashby and Jackson, the company served with the battalion of Stuart's Horse Artillery. Its membership increased during the war to a total of 197 men and Chew became a lieutenant colonel. When Lieutenants Rouss and McCarty resigned and joined the cavalry in 1862, Thomson was promoted to first lieutenant, with Williams and J.W. Carter serving as second lieutenants. In 1864 Captain Chew was promoted to the command of Stuart's Horse Artillery, while Thomson succeeded him as captain of the battery and E.L. Yancey became a second lieutenant.[11]

Even General Robert E. Lee's surrender at Appomattox did not daunt Chew's Battery. When news of the impending disaster became known, the organization, along with the cavalry brigade of General Thomas T. Munford, cut its way through the Federal lines with its eleven guns in an attempt to join the army of General Joseph E. Johnston in North Carolina. However, when the artillerymen received news of Johnston's surrender to General William T. Sherman, they disbanded as a group. In order to prevent their pieces from falling into the hands of the enemy, Chew's men buried them along the banks of the Staunton River. To mislead the enemy even more, they took the carriages and caissons to a remote spot and burned them. In 1903 an attempt was made with Colonel Chew's help to locate the guns, but it was unsuccessful.[12]

Since the idea of horse artillery was unique, it might be worthwhile to explain its composition and operation. Most persons are familiar with the word artillery, which means big guns and cannon, mostly on wheels. Leaving out of consideration the big guns, such as siege pieces or such big guns as are in forts or permanent works, not on wheels or movable, field artillery, light batteries, or horse artillery are left. Ordinary artillery operated with infantry in the field and when there were changes of position, the cannoneers rode on the limber chest. The horse artillery was attached to the cavalry in the proportion of about a battery to a division of cavalry. Ideally, there should have been a battery to a brigade of cavalry, but the scarcity of horses in the Confederacy, especially as the war was extended, deprived the South of this luxury, except in the western theater of operations. In that area the redoubtable Lieutenant General Nathan Bedford Forrest seemed to be more successful in taking horses from the enemy.[13]

In the Army of Northern Virginia, there were seven or eight batteries of horse artillery, which were organized into a battalion commanded by a lieutenant colonel. As has been stated above, the last commander was Colonel Chew. Usually a horse battery was equipped with four twelve-pound guns, sometimes Napoleons, sometimes three-inch rifled ordnance. Six horses pulled each gun and each left-hand horse carried a driver. Six horses were also used to pull a caisson which belonged to each gun. This carried the ammunition. The horse battery differed from the other artillery units in that all the cannoneers were mounted and there were two extra men to hold the horses when the battery went into action. A horse battery maneuvered into action at a gallop and changed position as frequently as practicable to save the men and horses when the enemy got their range too accurately.

The following is a very accurate description of a Confederate horse battery in action:

Down the crowded highway galloped a battery, withdrawn from some other position to save ours. The field fence is scattered while you could count thirty, and the guns rush for the hills behind us, six horses to a piece, three riders to each gun, over dry ditches where a farmer would not drive a wagon, through clumps of bushes, over logs a foot thick, every horse on the gallop, every rider lashing his team and yelling. The sight behind us makes us forget the foe in front. The guns jump two feet high as the heavy wheels strike rock or log, but not a horse slackens his pace, the cannoneer leaning forward in his saddle. Six guns, six caissons, six horses each, eighty men race for the brow of the hill, as if he who reached it first was to be knighted. A moment ago the battery was a confused mob; we look again, and the six guns are in position, the detached horses hurrying away, the ammunition chest open, and along our lines the command, "Give them one more volley and fall back and support the guns."

We have scarcely obeyed when "Boom, boom!" opens the battery, and jets of fire jump down and scorch the green trees under which we fought and despaired. What grim cool fellows those cannoneers are! Every man is a perfect machine. Bullets splash dust in their faces, but they do not wince; bullets sing over and around them, but they do not dodge. There goes one to the earth, shot through the head as he sponged the gun. The machinery loses just one beat, misses just one cog in the wheel, and then works away again as before. Every gun is using short-fuse shells. The ground shakes and trembles. The roar shuts out all sounds from a battle line three miles long, and the shells go shrieking into the swamp to cut trees off short, to mow great gaps in the bushes, to hunt out and shatter and mangle men until their corpses cannot be recognized as human.

GENL. TURNER ASHBY

Brigadier General Turner Ashby, "Knight of the Valley"

> Now the shells are changed to canister, and the guns are served
> so fast that all reports blend into one mighty roar. The shriek of a
> shell is the wickedest sound in war, but nothing makes the flesh
> crawl like the demoniac, singing, purring, whistling grapeshot
> and the serpent like hiss of canister. Men's legs and arms are not
> shot through, but torn off; heads are torn from bodies and bodies
> cut in two. Grape and canister mow a swath and pile the dead on
> one another.[14]

One Confederate general said there might be a question as to
who fired the first shot in the war and who fired the last shot, but
there could be no question as to who fired the most shots and the
most rapid shots. It was the horse artillery of Stuart's Corps, Army
of Northern Virginia.

According to Lewis Brady, a private in Chew's Battery, a group
of his fellow-artillerymen made military history when they charged an enemy battery with theirs, captured it, and turned the guns
on the retreating Federals. Lieutenant J.W. Carter had managed
to assemble fifteen fellow-artillerymen to accompany Brigadier
General Thomas L. Rosser on his famous New Creek raid in
November, 1864. Carter had been unable to get more of the men
because of the scarcity of good horses. According to Brady, this
was the only time during the Civil War that a battery charged and
captured a battery.[15]

Early in December, 1861, Lieutenant William Thomas Poague
with two Parrott rifles captured from the enemy at First Bull Run
was ordered to report to Colonel Ashby in Charles Town. When he
reached the Jefferson County seat of government in the evening,
he learned that the cavalry officer was staying at the hotel. Upon
receiving a request to come to his superior's room, Poague found
him sitting up in his bed with nothing on but a red flannel shirt.
Ashby received him kindly, expressed his regret at Poague's having to make a night march from Winchester, and told him to
report for duty the next day.

On the appointed day Poague accompanied Ashby and a few of
his troopers to the neighborhood of the Potomac above Harpers
Ferry. Turner had learned that a group of Federals across the river
had boasted that they were going to bag him as he made his
scouting sorties along the river. Mounted on his black stallion and
taking a handful of followers with him, Ashby made his way to a
house on the Virginia side. Within a short time he returned with
some prisoners. As a parting gesture to the enemy, Lieutenant
Poague sent a few shells across the river which demoralized the
bluecoats. A further search for Federals on the Virginia side proved unsuccessful.[16]

Meanwhile Ashby's activities had not gone unnoticed. Confederate authorities in Richmond had decided to enlarge his command. On October 7, 1861, Colonel Robert H. Chilton, assistant adjutant-general, wrote him a letter containing a special order increasing his command to four companies of Colonel McDonald's cavalry regiment and four companies of infantry composed of Virginia militia. In addition, he was to enlist enough men to organize a company of artillery. In the same letter the bold cavalry leader was authorized to do as much destruction as possible to the Chesapeake and Ohio Canal. Ashby had been keeping a close watch on the amount of traffic in canal boats and noted that it had been increasing. Many of the boats carried tons of coal, as well as other supplies, for the Union; and the Confederate authorities determined to interrupt traffic on the waterway.[17]

Meanwhile Ashby's good friend, Alexander R. Boteler of the Confederate Congress, had been using his influence to have him promoted to a full colonelcy. In a letter dated October 24 to Confederate Secretary of State, R.M.T. Hunter, the congressman emphasized his reasons for advocating the promotion. He pointed out the desire to enlist an additional force of several hundred men who would not volunteer to serve unless they were assured that Ashby would be their commanding officer. They were not willing to serve under Colonel McDonald and, unless a promotion were forthcoming, Ashby would continue to be second in command. Such was the reputation that Turner was establishing that no one else could take his place among his followers. Boteler's confidence in the cavalry leader was so great that he was willing to promise if Ashby were made a colonel and given the strength of a regiment, the military situation would be greatly improved. An embarrassing military relationship was that some of the militia officers were full colonels who ranked Ashby and handicapped his efforts to command. Boteler also indicated that he had written the Secretary of War.[18]

The intercessions of Colonel Boteler, as well as those of others, brought results later. Ashby received letters from Secretary of War Judah P. Benjamin authorizing him to raise cavalry, infantry, and artillery troops. In a letter dated February 22, 1862, the cabinet officer further instructed him to organize ten companies of cavalry. He could accomplish this objective either by re-enlisting, recruiting existing companies, or recruiting new companies. When the ten companies had been raised and mustered into Confederate service, Ashby could organize them into a regiment.

The Secretary of War followed this action with the promotion to colonel. The commission, which was dated March 12, 1862, was forwarded to Ashby two days later by General Jackson, who concurred that the full colonelcy was well-earned.[19] Their confidence in the cavalry leader was justified when he reported on March 17 that he had enlisted in Confederate service eighteen companies, one of artillery and the rest cavalry. Although some of the companies had previously been under his command, others were entirely new. The optimistic colonel indicated that he expected to organize four or five additional cavalry companies, as well as several of infantry. He also requested Benjamin to provide him with guns and equipment. He illustrated his need for the latter by stating that in a charge made a few days earlier some of the troopers rode bare-back armed with clubs.[20]

Although military encounters had been minimal in the Lower Valley after the Bolivar Heights affair in October, 1861, Turner Ashby had been very , active. His scouting and patrol duties covered a wide area and kept him constantly in the saddle. In order for him to have a more centrally-located headquarters, Jackson ordered him to move his camp from *Flowing Spring* to Martinsburg, the county seat of Berkeley County. Because cold weather had arrived, he wanted to obtain the use of some vacant houses for his men. Ashby never allowed his men to take possession of occupied houses. He, himself, declined better quarters on numerous occasions, for he felt that he should share the hardships of his men. This constant consideration for his enlisted men explains, in part, their respect and admiration, which, in turn, explains much of his success as a military commander. For instance, after the affair at Bolivar Heights with Geary when Ashby had returned to camp, even though it was nine o'clock at night, he rode to the courthouse in Charles Town to visit his wounded. He stopped to converse with each of his men in the temporary hospital, asked about the wounds, and offered to help in any way he could.

From his command post in Martinsburg, Ashby covered long distances in order to keep Jackson informed about the enemy dispositions and activities. On several occasions during the winter of 1861-1862 he would ride from Martinsburg to Winchester, returning by way of Bloomery and adjacent picket-posts—a distance of nearly seventy miles in fourteen hours. Quite often he would perform these duties by himself or accompanied by just a few of his followers. He never thought of delegating unpleasant patrols to subordinates if he could carry them out himself.[21]

Stonewall Jackson, who subscribed to Napoleon Bonaparte's thesis that "an active winter's campaign is less liable to produce disease than a sedentary life by camp-fires in winter's quarters," decided to put his thoughts into action. Specifically, he intended to destroy Dam No. 5 in the Potomac River, since this man-made structure was one of several that diverted river water to the Chesapeake and Ohio Canal. It will be recalled that this waterway stretched on the Maryland side of the Potomac from Washington to Cumberland, Maryland, and was a major carrier of coal to the nation's capital. For several months Confederate authorities in Richmond had been cognizant of the desirability of putting the canal out of commission. If the dam could be damaged to such an extent that it would no longer be able to divert water to the canal, the transportation facility would not be able to operate. If the dam were destroyed in the winter, in all probability canal boats would not be employed until spring. Usually, they were not used extensively in the winter because of freezing conditions, but a break in the dam would prolong the period of inactivity.

When previous attempts to destroy the dams had failed, Jackson determined to try again, even though it was December and the Confederates would have to plunge into icy waters to accomplish their objective. Accordingly, on December 16 the Stonewall Brigade left their camp near Winchester and marched to Martinsburg on their way to the Potomac Dam No. 5. The infantrymen were accompanied by the Rockbridge Artillery, as well as Chew's Battery and, naturally, Ashby's Cavalry.

The Confederates arrived at the river and soon learned that they had undertaken a formidable task. Not only was the dam stoutly-built but they were also exposed to a galling infantry and artillery fire from the enemy across the river. This forced them to do their work at night. Although the task of destruction was begun on the night of December 17, it was not until the 21st that Jackson was satisfied with the accomplishment of his objective and a big breach was opened in the dam.[22]

Lieutenant Poague of the Rockbridge Artillery had one of his guns to engage the Federals and also one from Chew's Battery. He had an opportunity to see Ashby in action for the first time and was so impressed that he had this to say:

> We soon found ourselves under fire, for the enemy seemed to be searching the whole region with his fire. Jackson was afoot and right in front and now and then would duck his head as shells came near. As we neared the top of the ridge we found every man and officer behind a big tree and all dodging first to one side and then to the other,

Captain McLaughlin and Colonel J.T.L. Preston being as nimble as
any of the lot. Jackson did not take to a tree, but occasionally bowed to
those infernal shells.

Did I dodge? Yes: just as low as my saddle pommel would allow. But
who was that man out there walking slowly back and forth near the
deserted guns in the open field with arms folded apparently enjoying
a quiet promenade, totally indifferent to the hellish fire raining all
about him? That was Turner Ashby—a man of the coolest courage
and finest nerve I ever knew or saw in the Army...[23]

The final step in the reorganization of the cavalry in the Lower
Valley had been the retirement of Colonel McDonald and his replacement by Colonel Ashby. For some time it had been obvious that a
change in leadership was imperative. McDonald was a brave and
loyal commander, but he was simply unable to command a regiment
of cavalry on active duty in the field. What is perhaps more important,
he had lost the confidence of his men. He had suffered some reverses
in his fights with a greatly superior enemy near Romney and these did
not enhance his popularity with his subordinates. In this connection
one of his officers, Captain John Winfield, had the following to say:

...Previously to the defeat at Romney, there were many circumstances which conspired to make Colonel McDonald unpopular
with his command. He had reached the period of his life when the infirmities of age incapacitated him from commanding a regiment of
cavalry. He could rarely ride on horseback and dared not expose
himself to inclement weather, or to the ordinary inconveniences of a
camp life. Every attempt to defy the dangers of exposure resulted in a
painful attack of rheumatism; so that in a few months after he took
command of his regiment he was more or less an invalid, with little
hope of ever being otherwise. To secure discipline and efficiency in a
regiment, especially one of raw troops, the constant presence and personal superintendence of the commanding officer is indispensable.
Hence it was but a short time before the regiment were discontented
with him, desiring, as was natural, a more active and vigorous commander. Their eyes, too were turned upon Ashby, the next officer in
rank.[24]

When McDonald returned to Winchester in a fruitless effort to
reorganize his command after a disastrous defeat at Romney, he
found so much dissatisfaction among the officers and men that he
sought an interview with Jackson. Stonewall concurred and relieved
him from command of the Seventh Cavalry Regiment. He was given
the less arduous duty of overseeing the artillery defenses of Winchester. As might be expected, his replacement was Lieutenant Colonel Turner Ashby.[25]

While he was stationed in the Martinsburg area, Turner Ashby took
time out from his military duties to join the Masonic Order. Entering
as an apprentice, he rose in rank to become a Master Mason in Equali-
ty Lodge No. 136, Martinsburg. Always interested in the welfare of his

fellow-man, Turner thus had an additional incentive to develop his character along those lines.[26]

General Jackson made several other trips to Dam No. 5 as he hoped to complete the work of destruction begun earlier. Because of the cold December weather, he was not able to accomplish much. As he was returning to Winchester on one of these occasions, he noticed a persimmon tree containing some of the fruit he like to eat. He dismounted, climbed the tree, and helped himself to the sour persimmons. After he had eaten his fill and started to descend, he was greatly embarrassed by getting so entangled in the branches that he could go neither up nor down. His predicament was such that he had to call for help. To his great relief, his staff obtained some rails from a nearby fence, made a pair of skids, and watched him slide to the ground.[27]

CHAPTER V

BATH AND ROMNEY

Confederate occupation of the Winchester area during the winter of 1861-1862 was not without its problems, especially after Stonewall Jackson assumed command of the Valley Army. The new leader was a product of the mountains of Western Virginia whose loss of both parents when he was very young had left its mark upon him. He was inclined to be serious and rarely laughed. Aspiring to a military career, he entered the United States Military Academy at West Point in 1842, having received a recommendation for appointment from Congressman Samuel L. Hays. Because of inadequate preparation and the rigorous demands of the military academy, his cadet days required the utmost effort for him to graduate; however, his perseverance and dedication to hard work paid off, and he was graduated in 1846, ranking seventeenth in a class of fifty-nine. His fellow-cadets paid him the compliment of saying that if the course had been a year longer, he would have come out first.[1]

Jackson served with distinction in the war with Mexico and won two brevets. In 1851 he resigned to teach at the Virginia Military Institute, remaining there until the outbreak of hostilities in 1861. Although the cadets made him the butt of many jokes, they gradually grew to respect him. He had many strange habits, some of which inclined his critics to think he was insane. One of his biographers stated that when at study he sat bolt upright and never touched the back of his chair. He was obsessed with the idea that if he bent over his work, the compression of his internal organs might increase their tendency to disease.[2] He was very religious, uncommunicative, demanding, modest, and, above all, he was a strict disciplinarian. He expected unquestioned obedience to orders.

In contrast with their commander, many of the soldiers in his army were volunteers whose concept of military service was the enjoyment of life. They were young, independent, impatient, resentful of authority, and inclined to view military service as more of a lark than the serious business it was. While Jackson had achieved some degree of success in transforming people like these into effective soldiers, as in the case of the Stonewall Brigade, he had a constant struggle to impose his ideas on his soldiers.

Since Jackson wished to isolate his command from the distractions of Winchester's social life, he established his camp four miles north of the town. Winchester was declared off limits to the regular soldiers, who were denied admission by a circle of militiamen picketed around the town. They had strict orders not to allow the regulars to pass unless those desiring to enter had the proper military authorization. Since Jackson was not disposed to humor the unnecessary whims of his men, it was very difficult to obtain official permission. Consequently, it became necessary to resort to subterfuge. Sometimes the regulars flanked the posts, sometimes they forged passes from General Jackson, and sometimes they used more subtle methods to get past the militia. On one occasion they marched in a body to the picket post, where one of their men informed the officer in charge that Jackson had ordered them to enter the city and arrest all members of the brigade found there without official leave. The ruse worked. After the Confederates had passed the militia outpost, they broke ranks and visited friends in the city.

On another occasion some members of the Stonewall Brigade obtained permission to visit Winchester on a Sabbath day so as to attend church services. They used the opportunity to remain a week. When they finally returned to camp, they expected to be disciplined for having been gone so long when they had been authorized only to attend church. Their leader explained the long absence to the fact that the pranksters had discovered that the church meeting was a "protracted" one which lasted a week. As their company commander had a sense of humor, he did not press the matter; and the men escaped punishment. Another ploy which succeeded was to pretend that one of their number had gone insane and was being taken to jail in the city. Any doubts about his insanity were dispelled when he made such violent attacks and demonstrations on the pickets that they were glad to be relieved of him by allowing the whole delegation to pass through the lines.[3]

As has been illustrated by the earlier attempts to destroy some of the dams supplying water to the Chesapeake and Ohio Canal, General Jackson was not averse to a winter campaign. He thought that his troops would be better off if kept occupied than if they were permitted to spend the winter months in idleness. Consequently, when he was reinforced in late December by the arrival of Brigadier General William W. Loring with his division of 6,000 men, Jackson was ready for action. Loring had been guarding the road from Staunton to Parkersburg. When he received orders to join Jackson at Winchester, he left a small force west of Staunton to guard the Allegheny Mountains. The addition of Loring's force, with Ashby's Cavalry, raised the strength of Jackson's Valley Army to about 10,350, consisting of 7,500 volunteers, 2,200 militia, and 650 cavalry. This force was about equal to that of the enemy at Romney. Jackson wanted more troops; but, realizing the impossibility of obtaining them, he determined to do the best he could with what he had.[4]

Unfortunately, the arrival of Loring and his command was not as promising as it seemed at first glance. Loring, himself, was an experienced officer who had participated in the Seminole War in Florida in the 1830's, had lost an arm at the Battle of Chapultepec in the Mexican War, and had fought Indians on the frontier. When he was sent to western Virginia in 1861, he had resented being under the command of General Robert E. Lee.[5] While he undoubtedly possessed a great amount of personal courage, he lacked the ability to handle a high command in the army. He was especially remiss in instilling the necessary discipline and morale in his troops.

Loring's army, which was known as the Army of the Northwest, retained its separate identity even when merged with Jackson's Valley Army. Although Loring's division consisted of three brigades, the units were not up to full strength. One, commanded by Colonel William B. Taliaferro, included the first Georgia, Third Arkansas, and Twenty-third and Thirty-seventh Virginia Regiments and was the first to reach Winchester. Taliaferro, scion of a line of Tidewater Virginia aristocrats, had served in the Mexican War and had been a member of the Virginia General Assembly. He had enough political influence to get himself promoted to the command of the Virginia militia in 1859, when he was in charge of the state troops at the John Brown execution. His unnecessary regulations handed down to the troops which he commanded for the Confederacy alienated his men to the point where they would have been most happy to see him removed from office.[6]

The remainder of Loring's men consisted of the brigade of Brigadier General S.R. Anderson whose troops—the First, Seventh, and Fourteenth Regiments—were all from the state of Tennessee. The Third Brigade, which included the Twenty-first, Forty-second, and Forty-eighth Virginia Regiments and the First Regular Battalion, was commanded by Colonel William Gilham. The latter had been a colleague of Jackson's at the Virginia Military Institute, where Gilham had served as a professor of infantry tactics. Two batteries of artillery, commanded by Captain L.M. Shumaker and L.S. Marye, completed the reinforcing group.

The most serious deficiency of this motley addition to Jackson's Valley Army was its lack of discipline and respect for those in authority. This shortcoming boded ill for the future and almost caused the Confederacy to lose the services of the irreplaceable Jackson when it came into conflict with his ideas of military deportment. On the

march from Huntersville to Winchester, Loring's men had been subjected to the first severe storm of the winter and had abandoned many
of their tents, blankets, wagons, horses, and even weapons. The lax
control which their officers had over them was taxed even more when
the men broke ranks to partake of good food offered by the Valley
women along the route. As it was the holiday season, homesickness
took its toll, and Loring's force was not completely assembled at Winchester until the day after Christmas.[7]

Although the weather continued to be bitterly cold, Jackson planned his moves as soon as conditions were more favorable. He formulated the idea of keeping his men busy by launching an attack
against the Federal garrisons at Bath [Berkeley Springs] and Romney.
He hoped to capture the forces located there, augment his commissary with supplies taken from the enemy, interrupt communications along the Baltimore and Ohio Railroad, keep the scattered
Federal forces from uniting, and cement western Virginia, his own
native area, more strongly to the eastern part of the Old Dominion.
Although this was an ambitious undertaking against an opponent
greatly superior in numbers and equipment and was full of risk even
in good weather, it seemed the height of folly to undertake it in the
dead of winter. Jackson, however, was not deterred by uncertain
climatic conditions but merely bided his time until things took a turn
for the better.

Jackson had not long to wait. The unseasonably cold weather after
Christmas gave way to a mildness that seemed more in keeping with
spring in the Valley. Three days of good weather began on December
29, and Jackson had his men draw enough rations for five days. He
planned to leave for Bath early in the morning on New Year's Day,
1862. The day was so deceptively mild that many of the soldiers
relieved themselves of blankets, overcoats, and other camp gear
which they relegated to the company wagons. The force consisted of
three brigades of infantry, five batteries of artillery, and Ashby's
Cavalry.[8] Although Jackson had hoped that his army would begin its
march at 5:00 A.M., which some units did, he was disappointed to
learn that Taliaferro's Brigade did not get under way until noon and
some of the militiamen did not leave until 4:00 P.M.

Suddenly disaster struck the Valley Army. The wind shifted to the
northwest, the temperature dropped to zero, and snow and sleet added to the discomfort of the marching columns. By dusk the vanguard
had covered only eight miles northwest of Winchester to Pughtown
and the wagons were bringing up the rear—too far behind to relieve
the discomfort of the men. Besides suffering from the cold, the men
had nothing to eat. They made the best of a bad situation, however,

by building huge campfires and sleeping together in what was known as "hog-fashion." This was simply the expedient of several soldiers combining what blankets remained and wrapping themselves up as close together as possible.[9]

General Jackson himself was not spared the discomforts caused by the unusually cold weather, although his condition was somewhat mitigated by some whiskey given him by a gentleman of Winchester. Believing it to be wine and not noticing the taste, he imbibed too freely. When he had satisfied his thirst, he gave the bottle to his staff, who soon emptied its contents. Before long he complained of being very warm in spite of the frigidity of the weather and unbuttoned his overcoat. Becoming unually loquacious, he discussed a number of interesting topics and elaborated on the sudden changes of temperature which frequently plagued the Valley. In the words of Henry Kyd Douglas, his youngest staff member, "General Jackson was incipiently tight."[9]

The snow continued throughout the night, and the wind sent chilly shivers up the spines of the ill-prepared soldiers. They tried to combat the elements as best they could by building large campfires and wrapping themselves in the few blankets available. One of the infantrymen had the misfortune to see his blanket catch on fire, which disaster caused him to exclaim, "I wish the Yankees were in Hell!" He was answered by another unfortunate with the remark, "I don't. Old Jack would follow them there, with our brigade in front!"[10] When Jackson was later told of some of these amusing incidents, he indulged in hearty laughter, something very unusual for him. He usually confined his less serious moments to a smile.

In spite of the hazardous condition of the roads, the wagons caught up with the main army on January 3. However, Jackson, realizing the necessity for speed, ordered his men to content themselves with a few mouthfuls and to resume the march. Since many of the men had not eaten for thirty hours and hence could not withstand the cold as well as if they had full stomachs, Brigadier General Richard B. Garnett, the commander of the Stonewall Brigade, allowed his troops to fall out and prepare a more satisfying meal. When Jackson demanded to know by whose authority these men had left ranks, Garnett replied that he was responsible. Jackson, in his zeal to make up for time lost on the march from Winchester, informed his subordinate that time did not allow for a cooked meal. When Garnett remonstrated that it was impossible for the men to press on without their rations, the unsympathetic Stonewall reminded him that, "I never found anything impossible with this brigade!" The brigadier resumed the march at once.[11]

As was usually his custom, Jackson did not reveal his destination to his men; however, when the troops reached Unger's Store and headed northward, it was obvious that the next objective was Bath [Berkeley Springs] in Morgan County, an ancient watering-place that had attracted even George Washington in days gone by. The bad weather which covered the roads with sleet and ice continued to slow the marching columns so that they did not reach Bath until about noon on January 4.

Meanwhile, Ashby's Cavalry had been sent on a detour instead of accompanying the main body. Accompanied by Chew's Battery, as well as several companies of the Stonewall Brigade, Ashby proceeded to Dam No. 5 on the Potomac. Like the troops under Jackson, this force retained only a small amount of camp equipage. Leaving the river, they headed westward toward Bath and on the way passed through Hedgesville. At a road intersection farther along they established a camp. They suffered the same discomforts experienced by their comrades under Jackson, for the snowstorm and the bitterly cold weather did not differentiate between the two groups. They built numerous campfires and utilized what few blankets that remained. Ashby, himself, wrapped up in two elk-skins that his brother Richard had given him. When his chaplain saw the cavalry commander hidden by the elk-skins with nothing but his dark eyes and beard exposed, he remarked on the similarity to an Indian warrior.[12]

When the Confederates converged on Bath on January 4, Jackson ordered General Loring's three brigades to move directly into town along the graded road from Winchester. Ashby's Cavalry with Chew's Battery was to approach across a mountain from the east, while the militia was expected to attack from the west. When Loring's men proved unequal to the assigned task, Jackson sent Ashby to capture the town, which he did with his usual celerity. Most of the Federal defenders escaped and headed for Hancock, Maryland, across the Potomac and about eight miles from Bath. Some stores and other supplies were captured and put to good use by the Confederates. The Federals had retreated into two directions—toward Hancock and toward Sir John's Run. Ashby sent a group headed by Captain John Q. Winfield to march to the latter objective, while he followed the enemy to Hancock. Although Ashby overtook the Federal rear guard near Hancock, he was able to engage it in combat for only a short while, after which the enemy retreated across the Potomac.

The next day Jackson tried to persuade the Federal commander across the river to surrender. With this in mind, he ordered Ashby to arm himself with a flag of truce and with a single companion to cross the river and try to convince the enemy commander to avoid further bloodshed by giving up the town. The negotiators met a Federal group on the Maryland bank who, obeying orders of their own commander, blindfolded the Confederate cavalry officer and conducted him to headquarters. His name was so well-known to the bluecoats that they crowded around him in order to get a glimpse of "the great rebel Ashby." The Federal commander, however, refused the surrender offer and the two Confederates got into their boat and recrossed to the Virginia shore. Jackson then ordered some of his batteries to fire into the town in retaliation for previous Federal shelling of Shepherdstown even when there were no Confederate soldiers present. The advent of darkness ended the firing on Hancock.[13]

January 5 brought more snow. The weather became too cold for the troops to cut firewood. Jackson reluctantly allowed them to burn fence rails in order to survive. Altogether about six inches of snow were on the ground. Since men on picket duty were not permitted the luxury of a campfire, one can easily imagine their discomfort. According to one of these who was assigned to this duty, "If I should use the army parlance and say [I] stood picket...I should have missed it. I *ran* picket for hours around and around a big tree; I had to do it to keep from freezing."[14]

Jackson planned to construct a pontoon bridge two miles upstream from Hancock so he could move in force against the Maryland town and augment his supplies with booty taken from the enemy. He was forced to abandon this plan because of the time required to complete the river crossing. A more convincing argument against the enterprise, besides the inclement weather, was the arrival of 1,500 reinforcements for the Federal garrison in Hancock. He sent his troops to wreak destruction upon the Baltimore and Ohio Railroad, particularly by destroying trestles and cutting the telegraph lines. Thus he was able to cut communication between enemy garrisons east and west of Hancock. Realizing that he had accomplished about all that he could under such adverse conditions, he moved his army southward on January 7 against the next objective, Romney, the seat of government for Hampshire County.[15] The van reached Unger's Store at dark.

The slippery roads continued to tax the ingenuity of officers and men. Since they were described as "one glare of ice," it was extremely difficult to keep the supply wagons and artillery in line. One expedient resorted to was to detail four men to go with each wagon in order to keep it in what passed for a road. When traversing a curve, the soldiers tied ropes to the top of the wagon-bed in the rear and all swung to the upper side of the road. Since the horses were smooth shod, it was practically impossible for them to retain their footing.

Courtesy of The Jefferson County Civic Center Museum

Lieutenant Colonel Roger Preston Chew, Organizer of Chew's Battery and Later Commander of Stuart's Horse Artillery

One animal would slip and fall and when he got on his feet, another would take his place on the ice. Sometimes all four horses would be down at the same time. Even Jackson himself was observed dismounting and putting his shoulder to the wheel of a wagon to keep it from sliding back.[16]

The condition of men and horses made a halt imperative. Near Unger's Store Jackson took time out to rest his command and to have his horses shod. While there, he received the unwelcome news that the Federals had attacked and routed a small force he had left at Hanging Rock, between Winchester and Romney. Believing the enemy force at the latter place to be much larger than it actually was, he feared that he might be caught between two Federal commands. He dispatched several hundred infantrymen to Hanging Rock. When the bluecoats withdrew to Romney, these Confederates followed. Jackson learned later that the attack at Hanging Rock had been made to curtail his offensive operations.[17]

While the Confederates were still in camp, Ashby brought the welcome news that the Federals had evacuated Romney, leaving behind huge quantities of tents, medical supplies, food, and munitions. They had mistaken two companies of Ashby's Cavalry for the main Confederate army. Jackson was not long getting his men in motion. On the way to Romney while he, Loring, and Ashby were riding along, they came to the banks of a small stream whose waters had been turned into ice. Fearing that the ice was not thick enough to sustain the weight of both horse and rider, Stonewall rode upstream to where the crossing was not as wide. He was followed by all the others, except Ashby, who remarked, "General, I will cross here." He withdrew from the bank, gave his mount the spur, and cleared the stream beautifully. One of his companions noted that "so perfect was Ashby's seat, and so exactly did his movements coincide with those of his horse, that the only motion visible in the rider was the settling of the folds of his cape as he landed on the opposite bank." When it was observed what a fine example of horsemanship this was, the viewer remarked, "And yet, the man was so modest with it all, merely remarking that he had had to take many a bolder leap in a foxhunt."[18]

The remainder of the Valley Army finally arrived in the deserted town of Romney and hoped it would be given an opportunity to recover from the arduous campaigning of the previous weeks. In this reverie it was doomed to disappointment for the aggressive Jackson had already formulated plans to move against Cumberland, twenty-five miles north-west of Romney. This Maryland town was an important railroad depot, contained numerous Federal stores, and was in an area of strategic bridges of the Baltimore and Ohio Railroad. He planned to employ Garnett's Stonewall Brigade and Taliaferro's Brigade of Loring's division in this new venture. However, the depleted condition of both commands, plus a state of near mutiny on the part of many of the men, caused him to abandon any more offensives.[19]

Instead, the Confederate Army of the Shenandoah went into winter quarters. Two militia brigades were sent to Bath and Moorefield, while a third one took up position just outside of Romney. Loring's undependable divison was expected to occupy the town itself, while the Stonewall Brigade was ordered back to the Winchester neighborhood so as to be within supporting distance of the other units. Ashby's Cavalry would resume its earlier role of scouting the Potomac area so it could keep track of enemy movements.[20]

Unfortunately, the commanding general's dispositions met considerable opposition from many of his subordinates, both officers and men. Loring's division in particular was incensed by what seemed preferential treatment for "Jackson's pet lambs," as the Stonewall Brigade was called. Not accustomed to the hard marching and strict discipline which they had been subjected to during the preceding weeks and becoming increasingly disenchanted with conditions in the Hampshire County seat, the Army of the Northwest resented its lot. Many had already deserted, and most of the remainder were so discontented as to be unreliable. Their commander, who should have known better because of his military background, encouraged this rebellious spirit and was quite outspoken for a subordinate officer. Jackson's decision to leave Loring at the lonely outpost of Romney while the remainder of the army wintered in the hospitable arms of Winchester was the straw that broke the camel's back.[21]

As the Confederates scoured the countryside in the Romney area, they could hardly believe their eyes. The Federal retreat had left its mark. This was especially true after the Hanging Rock raid. One description of the devastation inflicted upon the Southerners by the retreating enemy is as follows:

> The blackened chimneys stand like milestones to mark the desolating tracks of the enemy, and the entire absence of fences and other marks of cultivation show where have been the abiding places of the former owners...About 7 miles from Romney was the little village of Frenchburg, where now not a vestige of civilization remains but the bare chimneys of the houses and the large banks of torn bricks and tile, still smoking & smoldering...Really this country has seen fire and sword, there is not a vestige of fence or house in sound condition within five miles of Frenchburg. This was a flourishing town of about 1,200 inhabitants; it had more fine buildings than any little place I ever saw of the same size. But now

it is sad to see it. The occupation of a friendly army is desolating enough, where effort is made to restrain the men, but an enemy's camp indeed around a town is the presence of destruction itself.[22]

The spirit of insubordination in Loring's division in Romney grew and festered. Rather than attempting to combat this cancer that was destroying the efficiency of the Army of the Northwest, Loring and some of his officers encouraged it. When eleven brigades and regimental officers condemned the occupation of Romney in a petition which they signed and presented to him, Loring endorsed it and sent it to Confederate Secretary of War Judah P. Benjamin in Richmond. Realizing that it had to be sent through military channels, Loring forwarded the petition to Jackson. Although Stonewall disagreed vigorously with its contents, he, nevertheless, forwarded it to higher echelons.

Rumors that Federal forces under Major General Nathaniel P. Banks at Frederick were preparing to cross the Potomac and advance on Harpers Ferry or Winchester caused authorities in Richmond to intervene. Instead of relying on the military judgment of Jackson, who was kept apprised of enemy movements by the ever-vigilant Ashby and leaving the matter for him to decide, President Jefferson Davis instructed his Secretary of War to send the following telegram to Jackson: "Our news indicates that a movement is being made to cut off General Loring's command. Order him back to Winchester immediately."[23]

Politics had taken precedence over military judgment. The commander of Loring's Thirty-Seventh Virginia Regiment, Colonel Samuel Fulkerson, had written a friend in the Confederate Congress his opinion that Romney was of no military importance and should be evacuated. Colonel William B. Taliaferro was even more critical of Jackson, for he wrote: "The best army I ever saw of its strength has been destroyed by bad marches and bad management...Not one [man] will re-enlist, not one of the whole army. It will be suicidal for the Government to keep the command here."[24] In order to assure political support for the withdrawal from Romney, Taliaferro even went to Richmond in person and used his persuasive powers to good effect.

Jackson was justifiably furious. Good soldier that he was, he obeyed orders and recalled Loring to Winchester. Then he promptly wrote a letter of resignation, which he forwarded to his immediate superior, Major General Joseph E. Johnston, at Manassas. The letter reads as follows:

Headquarters Valley District
Winchester, Va.
January 31, 1862

Hon. J.P. Benjamin, Secretary of War
     Sir—Your order requiring me to direct General Loring to return
with his command to Winchester immediately has been received
and promptly complied with.
     With such interference in my command I cannot expect to be of
much service in the field, and accordingly respectfully request to
be ordered to report for duty to the Superintendent of the Virginia
Military Institute at Lexington, as has been done in the case of
other professors. Should this application not be granted, I respectfully request that the President will accept my resignation from the
army.
     I am, sir, very respectfully, your obedient servant.

T.J. Jackson
Major General, P.A.C.S.[25]

     The effect in Richmond of the receipt of this resignation can well
be surmised. The very thought that the Confederacy was about to
lose the services of one of its few generals who had distinguished
himself at First Bull Run was enough to stir up a vigorous reaction.
General Johnston had not been aware of what was happening in
the Valley until he received Jackson's letter of resignation. As he
had experienced the same type of interference from Richmond
with his own command and as he knew how ruinous such a policy,
if continued, could be to Confederate hopes, he took what steps he
could to rectify the situation. He appealed to Jackson and offered to
join with him in trying to get the Confederate authorities to recon-
sider their action. If this proposal availed nothing, Johnston was
prepared to join Stonewall in resigning. He also wrote Jefferson
Davis complaining about Benjamin's action, but he received no
comfort from the Confederate President in the latter's reply.[26] Unfortunately for the Confederate hopes of success, Davis and
Johnston disagreed a number of times and this enmity became
more pronounced as the war progressed.
     Nor was Johnston the only high-ranking Southerner to cham-
pion Jackson's cause. Virginia Governor John Letcher was so
disturbed that he wrote Jackson that he, by being Governor of the
Commonwealth, was authorized to withdraw Jackson's letter
when it reached the War Department. In order to achieve more
positive results, Letcher sent Congressman Alexander R. Boteler to
Winchester to try to persuade Jackson to change his mind. Letcher
felt that if anyone could convince the Valley commander to reverse

himself, Boteler, a close friend, could. Letters from persons in all walks of life poured into Richmond and into Jackson's Valley Headquarters. They emphasized the obligation of duty and the loss to the Confederacy if the resignation were allowed to remain. After Boteler had talked with his friend for some time, he was able to succeed in his mission.[27] Governor Letcher was greatly relieved to receive a written authorization from Jackson to withdraw the resignation. Loring was transferred to the deep South, where he was soon promoted to major general, but he failed to achieve distinction throughout the remainder of the war.

As it turned out, the fears of the Confederate authorities that Loring's command might be cut off proved without foundation. Jackson's resignation request was not due to the misconception that Secretary Benjamin or President Davis had about events in Northwestern Virginia, nor was it due to the reflection on his ability as a field commander. There was a more important principle at stake which cut the ground from under the feet of a commander in the field. If Jackson's troops were thus allowed to defy his orders by appealing to higher authority, he would be unable to maintain the discipline over them that is essential to military success. What is more important, a dangerous precedent would be inaugurated which would impair the efficiency and success of Confederate armies in all theaters of war. Nothing but disaster would result from the continuance of such a policy. Jackson's determined handling of this incident had taught the Confederate War Department a lesson in military ethics and usage it did not forget. Never again did it interfere with Stonewall Jackson in such an inexcusable manner.

All in all, the campaign against Bath and Romney which had begun under such optimistic auspices in the early part of the New Year can hardly be said to have been a success. Few Federals were killed, few prisoners were taken, and what little territory that had been wrested from the enemy was soon reoccupied by them after Loring's withdrawal. Morale was at a low ebb. The ranks were decimated by men who had become sick as a result of the harsh weather. The universal opinion was that the expedition had been a failure, in spite of Stonewall's professed belief that it had been otherwise. Lieutenant William Poague of the Rockbridge Artillery expressed himself as follows:

> In all the war I never had a similar experience—never endured such physical and mental suffering as on this trip. The expedition seemed to everybody to be a dismal failure. Our confidence in our leader was sorely tried. Loring's part of the army was in a state of

semi-mutiny, and Jackson was hissed and hooted as he passed them. This I had from a friend in the Georgia Regiment who teased me a great deal about the "crazy general from Lexington."[28]

Nor was Private John O. Casler of the Thirty-Third Virginia Regiment, Stonewall Brigade, any more complimentary. He wrote:

> We were out nearly one month, and had miserable weather all the time, and did no fighting, except some little skirmishing, but we lost more men from sickness than if we had been engaged in a big battle. We accomplished nothing, for the enemy retreated across the Potomac, only to come back again as soon as we had left. Winchester was full of soldiers sick with the pneumonia, and they died by hundreds.[29]

As for Turner Ashby, if he had any thoughts about the sanity of his commanding general, he kept them to himself. His troopers had suffered as much as the infantrymen and artillerymen. He was at all times ready to obey any order which came from above and never questioned its wisdom or necessity. Even though not a West Pointer, he had learned the lesson of unquestioned obedience by his brief experience in the army. After the retreat from Romney Ashby established his headquarters at Martinsburg and continued his surveillance of General Nathaniel P. Banks at Frederick, Maryland, who was preparing to launch the famous Shenandoah Valley Campaign of 1862.[30]

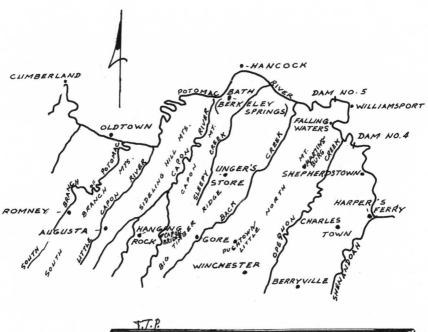

BERKELEY SPRINGS - ROMNEY CAMPAIGN
JANUARY 1862

0   10   20   MILES
SCALE

CHAPTER VI

ASHBY FAILS JACKSON BUT LATER REDEEMS HIMSELF

Stonewall Jackson's Shenandoah Valley Campaign of 1862 was one of the most remarkable accomplishments in the annals of warfare. There is probably no other campaign in history that affords a better example of strategic diversion and the intelligent use of interior lines of operation. With an army never exceeding 17,000 men of all arms, Jackson immobilized 64,000 Federals scattered among four armies. There is no doubt that his activities in the Valley saved Richmond from capture by Major General George B. McClellan. Continually demanding reinforcements to accomplish his objective of taking the Confederate capital, the Union general was denied additional troops time after time. On three different occasions McDowell's corps of 40,000 troops was ordered from Fredericksburg to Richmond and on three different occasions these orders were rescinded because of some new activity on the part of Stonewall Jackson in the Valley.

The Shenandoah Valley, or the Valley of Virginia, was important strategically for a number of reasons. Running in a northeast-southwest direction, it was a natural avenue of approach for the Confederates to threaten Washington. Protected by the Blue Ridge Mountains on the east and the Alleghenies on the west, with cavalry guarding the few passes or gaps, a Southern invading force could make its way without difficulty northward to Harpers Ferry, sixty miles from Washington. On the contrary, it would work to the disadvantage of a Union force seeking to capture Richmond, for the farther south the Northern invaders went, the greater distance would intervene between them and the Confederate capital. Should the Confederates desire to by-pass Washington and invade the North, the Valley offered a well-protected supply line. Two railroads, the Manassas Gap and the Virginia Central, pierced this region from the east, thus facilitating the movement of men and supplies. At the northern end of the Valley, the Baltimore and Ohio Railroad and the Chesapeake and Ohio Canal served the Union. Vitally important communications for the Federals, these arteries were continually exposed to hit-and-run attacks. Finally, as has been noted before, the productivity of the rich limestone soil furnished the Southerners with so many foodstuffs that the Valley became appropriately dubbed the "granary of the Confederacy."[1]

In order to understand better the military activities in the Shenandoah Valley, it is necessary to learn more about its geography. The Shenandoah River, which gives the region its name, is divided into its North and South Forks. Flowing northward and parallel for about fifty miles, these two streams unite near Front Royal, where they become known jointly as the Shenandoah. This stream unites with the Potomac at Harpers Ferry. Under the latter name the waters continue their relentless march to the sea after passing the capital city of Washington. One important geographical feature is a mountain range called Massanutten which splits the Valley for a distance of fifty miles. The western valley retains the name Shenandoah while the eastern one is usually called the Luray or Page Valley. The existence of the Massanuttens, in particular, was to enable Jackson to play hide-and-seek with his adversaries who were generally strangers to the region and, therefore, unfamiliar with its topographical features.

In the spring of 1862, the Union was ready for its big push to capture Richmond and bring the war to a successful conclusion. Major General George B. McClellan, who had achieved success in saving western Virginia for the Union, had succeeded the unfortunate Irvin McDowell in command of the Army of the Potomac. Reorganizing the Federal forces after their defeat at the First Battle of Bull Run, McClellan had whipped them into the best army that had ever been seen on the American continent. Part of his overall strategy included the advancing of Major General Nathaniel P. Banks across the Potomac to dislodge Jackson at Winchester. Banks, who had been elevated to his position by virtue of having been Governor of Massachusetts and Speaker of the United States House of Representatives, had an army of about 23,000 men, including 3,000 cavalry. He had established his headquarters at Frederick, Maryland.[2]

The Confederate defense consisted of the right at Fredericksburg, which was commanded by elderly Major General Theophilus Holmes. Its center was located at Manassas under the able command of General Joseph E. Johnston, while the left flank was protected by Stonewall Jackson and his Valley Army. Jackson's brother-in-law, Major General D.H. Hill, was at Leesburg to serve as a link between Stonewall and Johnston. Jackson asked Confederate authorities to augment his command with Hill's force, but the request was denied on the premise that it was needed to defend Richmond.[3]

The Shenandoah Valley Campaign of 1862, from beginning to end, was secondary to the Federal effort against Richmond. The invading armies of the Union occupied the perimeter of a curve which extended from the James River below Richmond, through Fredericksburg, Manassas, Harpers Ferry, and up the South Branch of the Potomac. Their numbers were vastly superior to the Confederate defenders and included McClellan's army of 100,000; McDowell's corps of 40,000, the defenders of Washington, 20,000 to 30,000, Banks's army, 15,000 to 20,000; and Major General John C. Frémont's force of 15,000. The total of such impressive numbers was over 200,000 soldiers. In addition, these Federals were superbly equipped by the factories of the North. To oppose this threat, the Confederates were unable to assemble more than 100,000 men whose equipment was markedly inferior.

If all of these Federal armies had been collected into two or three armies under a single head and given an intelligent commander, it is difficult to see how they could have failed to capture Richmond and defeat the main Confederate army. Unfortunately for Union hopes of success in 1862, their commanders were all independent of each other and reported directly to Washington. There was a unity of command, but it was vested in Secretary of War Edwin M. Stanton whose "contempt for all sound principles and usages of war appears to have been exceeded only by his ignorance of them." It should seem that it would not have required a great knowledge of the principles of strategy to unite those Union armies and crush their weak foe; but it was Mr. Stanton's lack of such military knowledge that enabled Lee and Jackson to keep the Federal armies apart; that enabled them first to defeat Frémont west of Alleghenies, then Banks, then Frémont and Shields on opposing sides of the river at Port Republic; then, finally to throw every man against McClellan astride the Chickahominy."[4]

Besides having the leadership provided by such fine general officers as Robert E. Lee, Joseph E. Johnston, Stonewall Jackson, and others, the South was vastly superior in cavalry. This was especially true early in the war, but by the time of the battle of Gettysburg in July, 1863, the Federal troopers had gained the edge, which they retained until the end of hostilities. One reason for the loss of this advantage was that it was difficult for the Confederates to provide and sustain the quality of their horses as the war continued. Another reason was the death in action of some of their famous cavalry commanders. There is no denying the fact that

Jackson's success in the Valley Campaign was, to a great extent, due to his cavalry leader, Turner Ashby, who by March, 1862, had become the idol of the Valley Army. His reckless daring had won the admiration not only of his own men but also of the enemy. A Federal officer commented, "I think even our men had a kind of admiration for him as he sat unmoved upon his horse, and let them pepper away at him as if he enjoyed it."[5] By March, 1862, Ashby's one shortcoming, his ignorance of drill and discipline, was evident. This deficiency was somewhat offset by the willingness of his men to follow him wherever he led. They were impressed not only by his personal bravery and leadership qualities but also by his prodigious energy. While on picket duty, he would often ride seventy or eighty miles in one day.

Because of Turner Ashby's personal popularity, his squadrons never lacked recruits and he eventually commanded twenty-seven companies of cavalrymen, although some writers give him a lesser number. The horse-loving Virginians preferred the cavalry to all other arms, and the size of the regiments was limited only by the difficulty of obtaining horses. Because of the lax discipline, absence of drill, and the excitement and adventure that fell to the lot of the mounted soldiers, Ashby's command acted as a magnet in attracting men from other arms. When Private George Baylor transferred from the infantry to the cavalry, he remarked, "On horseback, I felt like a new man, and contemplated the war from a much more favorable standpoint."[6] Added to their equestrian accomplishments was the fact that most of Ashby's troopers were from the Valley or adjoining counties and hence were thoroughly familiar with every country lane, every ford, every mountain, and every valley. Some of them could be found who had friends in every town in the Valley, and they knew the names of many who lived on the numerous farms. They were admirably suited to service as vedette, picket, scout, and, if necessary, fighter. Most of them were young and one who had already served four years and was only nineteen when the war ended in 1865 remarked, "We thought no more of riding through the enemy's bivouacs than of riding round our fathers' farms."[7] Since Jackson expected his cavalry not only to warn him of the Federals' advances but also to gather information about their strength, dispositions, and other movements, he could not have found men better qualified if he had searched the world over.

If the Federal artillery was superior to that of the Confederates because of the quality of guns and ammunition and the infantry was at least as good as the rebels, the Union cavalry, at least the first two years of the war, left much to be desired. Although the Northern troopers greatly outnumbered their Southern counterparts, that was their only advantage in the mounted arm. In many places of the North, horsemanship was practically. an unknown art. No special requirement was needed by either horses or men in order to gain a place in the Federal cavalry. Since many of the men were unfamiliar with the proper care of horses, the number of sick animals reached astronomical proportions. While the Confederate troopers usually carried a firearm, many of their opponents had only the saber; and in wooded country the gun or pistol gave its owner the advantage. According to one description of the Union cavalry in 1862:

> During the first two years of the war, therefore, the Federal cavalry, generally speaking, were bad riders and worse horsemasters, unable to move except upon the roads, and as inefficient on reconnaissance as in action. For an invading army, information, ample and accurate, is the first requisite. Operating in a country which, almost invariably, must be better known to the defenders, bold scouting alone will secure it from ambush and surprise. Bold scouting was impossible with such mounted troops as Banks possessed, and throughout the Valley campaign the Northern general was simply groping in the dark.[8]

No wonder one of Banks's brigadier generals felt hopelessly outclassed when he admitted that, "As cavalry Ashby's men were greatly superior to ours. In reply to some orders I had given, my cavalry commander replied, 'I can't catch them, sir; they leap fences and walls like deer; neither our men nor our horses are so trained.' "[9]

As the opposing armies began maneuvering in the spring of 1862, it seems appropriate to investigate the principal generals, for a knowledge of their characters helps one to understand their actions. As has already been related, the man chosen to lead the armies of the Union against the Confederates was Major General George B. McClellan, who had succeeded Irvin McDowell after the latter had been discredited by the Union defeat at the First Battle of Bull Run. McClellan had achieved success in everything he had undertaken and, consequently, was immensely popular with the people, with the newspaper press, and with the army. In the West Point graduating class of 1846, McClellan had ranked second, while the plodding Stonewall Jackson had been seventeenth, and George E. Pickett at the very bottom of the 59-man group. McClellan had served with distinction in the Mexican War and had been a U.S. Government observer in the Crimean War. Resigning from the army, he reentered civilian life and ultimately became vice-president of the Illinois Central Railroad. At the outbreak of the Civil War, he was made a Major General of Ohio volunteers before he was transferred to the regular army with the same rank. His military successes in what later became the state of West Virginia are usually credited with saving that part of the Old Dominion for the Union.[10]

With its commander possessing all of the foregoing favorable characteristics, the Union Army of the Potomac seemed headed for success. This was all the more likely when McClellan demonstrated undeniable ability in organizing the defeated Federals into an excellent army, second to none in training and equipment on the American continent. Unfortunately for the Union, in spite of all of his good qualities, McClellan had one short-coming that was destined to rob him and his magnificent army of the fruits of victory. He was cautious to the extreme that he never wanted to take a chance. In a military sense his nature was defensive. He was exceedingly slow in all of his operations. He was always minimizing his own strength and exaggerating that of his opponent. By relying on Pinkerton detectives to keep him inform-ed, he was usually misinformed and thus was greatly handicap-ped in all of his operations. If he were too cautious to undertake the offensive successfully, he was superb on the defensive, for the latter was his genius. However, in this evaluation of McClellan it should be pointed out that he was pitted against Lee, who was his equal in every respect, his superior in most, and who possessed in the highest degree the essential talents that McClellan lacked.[11]

McClellan's strategy in the spring of 1862 was to transfer his ar-my from the outskirts of Washington to the peninsula formed by the James and York Rivers. He then planned to push up the penin-sula so as to approach Richmond from the southeast.

Activities began on March 7 when D.H. Hill complied with Johnston's orders and evacuated Leesburg. As Johnston withdrew southward two days later toward the Rappahannock, Jackson was left isolated at Winchester. When he learned that Banks had crossed the Potomac River and was advancing on Win-chester, Stonewall withdrew southward. Banks's van entered the Valley outpost on March 12. The Federal invader commanded at least 23,000 men, including 3,000 cavalry and 80 pieces of ar-tillery. To contest his advance Jackson had only 3,600 infantry, Ashby's Cavalry of 600, and 6 batteries totaling 27 guns.[12]

Even before the bluecoated invaders entered Winchester, Ashby had fought a furious skirmish on its northern outskirts. On March 7 he had succeeded in forcing the body of Federals to retreat.

Courtesy of the Virginia State Library

Federal Charge at the Battle of Kernstown

Jackson sent his infantry to the aid of his cavalry, but it was not needed. Four days later he convened a meeting of his brigade and regimental officers for a council of war. He planned to move his army southward to Newtown [Stephens City], allow time for a rest, and then retrace its steps in order to make a night attack on Banks. When he revealed this plan to his subordinate officers, he was greatly surprised to find that they opposed it to a man. General Richard Garnett, the commander of the Stonewall Brigade, informed them that their troops were too far south of Winchester to make such a plan feasible. Because of a misinterpretation of orders previously given, the supply wagons had proceeded farther south than Stonewall intended; and since the army had joined them, an eight-mile march northward would be necessary. Realizing the sensible objections offered to the execution of the night attack, the army commander reluctantly abandoned his bold scheme and gave orders that the march southward would be resumed in the morning. As he was leaving Winchester to join his troops, Jackson remarked to Dr. Hunter McGuire, his medical director, "That is the last council of war I will ever hold."[13] It was.

While Jackson was retreating from Winchester, Turner Ashby brought up the rear, harassing the enemy at every opportunity. He seemed oblivious to personal danger. Before he left the town, he was reported by his admirer, John Esten Cooke, as having had a very unusual experience. According to the account:

> The long column defiled through the town, and Ashby remained the last, sitting [on] his horse in the middle of Loudoun street as the Federal forces poured in. The solitary horseman, gazing at them with so much nonchalance, was plainly seen by the Federal officers, and two mounted men were detached to make a circuit by the back streets, and cut off his retreat. Ashby either did not see this maneuvre, or paid no attention to it. He waited until the Federal column was nearly upon him, and had opened a hot fire— then he turned his horse, waved his hat around his head, and uttering a cheer of defiance, galloped off. All at once, as he galloped down the street, he saw before him the two cavalrymen sent to cut off and capture him. To a man like Ashby, inwardly chafing at being compelled to retreat, no sight could be more agreeable. Here was an opportunity to vent his spleen; and charging the two mounted men, he was soon upon them. One fell with a bullet through his breast; and, coming opposite the other, Ashby seized him by the throat, dragged him from his saddle, and putting spur to his horse, bore him off. This scene, which some readers may set down for romance, was witnessed by hundreds both of the Confederate and the Federal army.[14]

This account of Ashby's bravery may or may not be accurate, but it serves to illustrate how deeds of valor became associated with his name. If there were any other eyewitnesses to the event, they have never offered their testimony to its support. Another account of Ashby's departure from Winchester on this occasion is supplied by the Reverend James B. Avirett, Ashby's·chaplain and first biographer. He does not mention the encounter with the two Federal troopers but merely states that the cavalry leader took time to accept a biscuit from a Winchester lady, even though the enemy was pressing him closely.[15]

Major General Nathaniel P. Banks, the Federal commander in the Valley in March, 1862, was a politician rather than a military man. As has been pointed out, he had served as Speaker of the United States House of Representatives and Governor of Massachusetts, which gave him enough political clout to win a major generalship. He was described as "having courage but was short on talent and experience." Although he had 16,000 men at Frederick during the Romney Campaign and might at least have tried to interfere with Confederate movements, he had done nothing. Jackson could not fail to note his caution and inaction when Banks had a good opportunity to upset Confederate plans. Even when Brigadier General James Shields, another political general although he had fought in the Mexican War, joined Banks with his division of 9,000 men, Jackson was not particularly concerned. Believing that "if this Valley is lost, Virginia is lost," he determined to assume the offensive at the first good opportunity.[16]

Jackson withdrew southward to Mount Jackson, which is forty-two miles from Winchester. Banks had sent Shields's division in pursuit but the bluecoats had stopped at Strasburg, only eighteen miles from Winchester. They later pushed on to Woodstock. As Jackson had been ordered to try to prevent Federals in the Valley from joining McClellan's army, he was greatly interested when he received word from Ashby that Shields was retreating to Winchester. Ashby, who had just been promoted to a full colonelcy, had been scouting and skirmishing in the region north of Mount Jackson. When Jackson heard about Shields's northward march, he feared that the Federals were leaving the Valley and he hastily set his army in pursuit. By evening of March 22, the Confederates had reached Cedar Creek, where they established their camp.

Ashby, who had been leading the Confederate advance, reached the outskirts of Winchester on March 22 and even succeeded in capturing several wagons from the enemy. In the ensuing skirmishing, a shell fragment from Chew's Battery broke the arm of

General Shields, who had been placed in command by Banks. The latter had left to visit in Washington but was recalled to Winchester while he was at Harpers Ferry.[17]

Unfortunately for the Confederates, this skirmishing by Ashby and Chew was responsible for an incident that caused the Valley Army to lose its first battle of the campaign—the Battle of Kernstown. As the Confederates were so close to the town, it was possible for some of the Winchester ladies to get word to Ashby's scouts that the Federals were evacuating the outpost and that a large column had moved to Berryville that morning. When it was reported that only four regiments remained as rear guard and they were under orders to leave the next day, Ashby felt that the Confederates could regain possession of the town with a minimum of effort. Having no reason to doubt the accuracy of this important information, he relayed it to Jackson. The Confederate army had begun the march northward, and along the way Stonewall received additional information from what he described as a "source which had been remarkable for its reliability" which corroborated Ashby's findings.[18] According to his official report of the Battle of Kernstown, Jackson wrote, "Apprehensive that the Federals would leave this military district, I determined to follow them with all my available force."[19]

About 2 P.M., Sunday, March 23, the Stonewall Brigade reached Kernstown, four miles south of Winchester. It had marched thirty-six miles since the previous morning. Jackson's Presbyterian background made him reluctant to begin a battle on the Sabbath, but he balanced his religious feelings against reality and decided that it would be dangerous to postpone the fight until the next day. He had ascertained that the Federals had a position from which they could see his own lack of strength, and he was concerned that they might gain reinforcements during the night. Because of the rapid marching he demanded of his "foot cavalry," his little army had been so reduced by straggling that he could muster barely 3,000 infantry. His cavalry and artillery brought his total force to about 3,500. Unknown to Jackson, his information about the enemy's strength was inaccurate, for instead of meeting only Shields's rear guard of four regiments, his opponent had his whole division of 9,000. The Union general had managed to conceal the bulk of his force from the Confederates. As Shields had been hospitalized and Banks had left for Harpers Ferry, the field command of the Union army at Kernstown was assumed by Colonel Nathan Kimball, a physician by profession but who had had some previous military experience. Shields, although hospitalized five miles away, maintained contact with Kimball.

Ashby skirmished with the Federals during the morning of March 23; and when the vanguard of the Stonewall Brigade arrived, he sent it into action. It consisted of four companies led by Captain John Nadenbousch. Brisk fighting ensued and when Ashby noticed large numbers of bluecoats ahead, he broke off the engagement and brought his forces back to a position along the Valley Pike. [20] This was the situation when Jackson arrived on the scene.

No sooner had Jackson reached the battle area than he made his dispositions. Noticing that the enemy artillery on a nob called Pritchard's Hill, west of the Valley Pike, was threatening Ashby, he decided to leave the cavalry leader with part of his troopers to create a diversion while he moved his main force to the left. There he would have the advantage of higher ground. The small brigade of Colonel Jesse Burks supported Ashby and acted as a general reserve. Jackson hoped that his main force would be able to move around the Federal right and get between the enemy and Winchester. Ashby's second in command, Major Oliver R. Funsten, took about half of the troopers to screen the flanking movement to the left of the Valley Pike. Carpenter's Battery moved rapidly to its position and was soon exchanging shells with Federal gunners. Within a short time Confederate infantry had seized Pritchard's Hill. Jackson then moved the brigade of Colonel Samuel Fulkerson, supported by that of General Garnett, to the higher ground on his left. He brought up more batteries which proved able to command the Federal position. Colonel J.M. Patton's Twenty-first Virginia and Colonel John Echols's Twenty-seventh Regiment advanced as skirmishers ahead of the artillery and thus brought on a general infantry engagement. As these Confederates were advancing, they noticed a stone wall or fence ahead of them. Since some of the bluecoated enemy realized the advantage of this barrier at about the same time, a race to reach it first was in earnest. The Confederates won and poured such a hot fire into the faces of their opponents that the latter fled in great confusion.[21]

Other Federals took their place. While the fighting in this part of the battlefield continued, there occurred one of those episodes which emphasizes the human side of the American soldier. While the Sixty-second Ohio Regiment in its first battle was advancing toward the stone wall and was being subjected to a fire so devastating as to cause it to lose 25 percent of its men killed and wounded, the bluecoats witnessed an unusual act of bravery. When the attackers were only thirty yards away, the color-

sergeant of the Fifth Virginia Regiment jumped over the stone wall
with his flag and dared the enemy to come on. The Federals were
so impressed with this foolhardy act of bravery that they withheld
their fire. Someone shouted, "Don't shoot that man; he is too
brave to die," and not a shot was fired at him for several minutes.
When their patience was finally exhausted, they ordered him back
to the Confederate side of the wall. Quick to realize that he must
not tempt his luck too much, the color-bearer saluted the
bluecoats, jumped over to his side of the stone wall, and witnessed
the resumption of the battle.[22] The mortality of color-bearers in
this part of the fighting was so great that Henry Kyd Douglas of the
Second Virginia Regiment saw seven of them fall.[23]

The Confederate line consisted of Fulkerson's brigade on the
left, Garnett's in the center, and the Twenty-first Virginia and artillery on the right. Ashby with about half of his force and Chew's
Battery was on the extreme Confederate right near the Valley
Pike. The remainder of his cavalry, under Major Funsten, was on
the extreme left. General Shields, who was incapacitated because
of his arm wound, nevertheless, dispatched instructions to Colonel Kimball to shift the equivalent of six regiments from his left to
his right. He thought Jackson had 11,000 men to oppose his division, which he claimed had only 7,000.[24] The Federal reinforcements continued the attack and put relentless pressure on
the graycoats, especially the Stonewall Brigade. In order to protect
themselves from enemy artillery and rifle fire, the men took advantage of whatever cover they could find. When there was a lull
in the firing, they would advance; but when the enemy pressed
forward in ever-increasing numbers, the Confederates fell back.
Their situation was becoming serious and, when they began to
give out of ammunition, it became critical. So rapid was the firing
that even though they borrowed from their dead and wounded
comrades, there was not enough ammunition for their needs.

Jackson saw the need of reinforcing his own left. Ashby continued to engage the Federals in order to relieve pressure on the
left but was not able to make much headway. Jackson rushed
Garnett's Fifth Virginia and the remainder of Burks's Brigade to
bolster the Stonewall Brigade. Before they could reach Garnett's
hard-pressed troops, he had made an agonizing decision. The
situation in front of him was hopeless, and Federal cavalry was
threatening to outflank Funsten's small force of troopers. Not being able to contact Jackson who had departed to rally the reserves,
and faced with annihilation if he remained where he was in line of
battle, he assumed the responsibility of ordering the Stonewall

Brigade to retreat. He defended his action with the remark, "Had I not done so, we would have run imminent risk of being routed by superiority of numbers, which would have resulted probably in the loss of part of our artillery and also endangered our transportation."[25]

The result was disastrous. When the Stonewall Brigade retired, it exposed Fulkerson's men on the left and caused them to fall back also. When Jackson brought up his reserves, he noticed men with empty cartridge boxes going to the rear. As he rode to the front, he met one of these soldiers and had the following conversation with him:

"Where are you going?" Stonewall asked. When the soldier replied that he had fired all his cartridges and did not know where to get more, the general shouted, "Then go back and give them the bayonet!"[26]

As Jackson saw more of his men heading toward the rear and realized they belonged to the Stonewall Brigade, he sought Garnett and commanded him to halt the retreat. At the same time he saw a drummer boy whom he told to beat the rally. In the noise and confusion of the battle, it was difficult to hear the drum. As the general strained his eyes to see if his two reserve regiments were advancing, he was unable to locate them. When he learned that Garnett had sent word to Colonel William Harman of the Fifth Virginia Regiment to halt and take a position to support their retreating comrades, he realized the best he could do was to wait for nightfall to end the fighting.[27]

Even as the Confederates had been forced to retreat, they continued to fight at every opportunity. Although they had charged several times in order to regain positions from which they had been driven, they were unable to stop the onrushing hordes of Federals who maintained the pressure. Perhaps the best description of their valor was given by Colonel E.H.C. Cavins of the Fourteenth Indiana, who later had this to say:

> The Confederates fell back in great disorder, and we advanced in disorder just as great, over stone-walls and over fences, through blackberry-bushes and undergrowth. Over logs, through woods, over hills and fields, the brigades, regiments, and companies advanced in one promiscuous, mixed, and uncontrollable mass. Officers shouted themselves hoarse in trying to bring order out of confusion, but all their efforts were unavailing along the front line, or rather what ought to have been the front line. Yet many of the brave Virginians who had so often followed their standards to victory, lingered in the rear of their retreating comrades, loading as they slowly retired, and rallying in squads in every ravine and behind every hill—or hiding singly among the trees. They continued to make it very hot for our men in the advance.[28]

Colonel Harman, reinforced by one of Burks's regiments, had been trying to gain time for the remainder of the army. Threatened by Federal infantry in their front and on their right, as well as cavalry on their left flank, the Confederate reserves belonging to Harman and Burks suffered heavy casualties. Their efforts had not been in vain, however, for they delayed the attackers until nightfall came to the aid of the hard-pressed graycoats and ended the one-sided contest. The Battle of Kernstown was over.

Although Turner Ashby had failed to provide Jackson with accurate information about the enemy in this engagement, his actions upheld his fighting traditions. He had misled Jackson because he had been misled. However, his few troopers, aided by the ever-present Chew's Battery, faced heavy odds and put up such a stout-hearted resistance that the Federals were unable to outflank the Confederate right. Major Funsten with the remainder of the horsemen checked Federal cavalry on the Confederate left flank. When hostilities ended, Ashby protected the retreating army so well that the exhausted Confederates spent the night at Newtown, about five miles from the battlefield where their wagons had been parked. Some of Ashby's men thought that their leader had saved Jackson's army from destruction.[29] Ashby's troopers went into camp at Bartonsville, about three miles to the north and continued their screening role. Jackson, who was not known for complimentary remarks about his men, had this to say about his cavalry commander, "Colonel Ashby fully sustained his deservedly high reputation by the able manner in which he discharged the important trust confided to him."[30]

In the Battle of Kernstown, the Confederates had suffered heavy casualties. Almost one-fourth of the Stonewall Brigade, whose five regiments had boasted 1,418 men, had been listed as killed, wounded, or missing. Jackson's total loss was 700 as opposed to Shields's 590.[31] Two or three hundred prisoners were captured by the Federals.

Jackson lost one of his staff officers, Lieutenant George Junkins, because of his zeal to win. When it was dusk and confusion reigned on the battlefield, Junkins mistook a regiment of retreating Federals for Confederates and in his efforts to rally them, he found himself a prisoner of war.[32]

Jackson would not admit that he had been defeated at Kernstown. In his official report he relates his failure to recover Winchester but feels that the calling back of troops that were leaving the Valley, plus the losses inflicted on the enemy, justified the actions he had taken. On the evening of the battle while he was warming himself in front of the campfire, he was surprised to be greeted by one of Ashby's youngest troopers with the remark: "The Yankees don't seem willing to quit Winchester, General!"

To which he replied, "Winchester is a very pleasant place to stay in, sir!"

The cavalryman persisted, "It was reported that they were retreating, but I guess they're retreating after us."

The conversation ended when Jackson replied, "I think I may say I am satisfied, sir."[33]

Although tactically Kernstown was a defeat for the Confederacy, strategically it was a Southern victory. General Shields was firmly convinced that Jackson would not have dared to attack him unless he had ben expecting reinforcements. Consequently, the Federal general requested assistance from General Banks, who returned with his other division. Thus, as he had been ordered, Jackson had kept McClellan from being reinforced by Banks. But Kernstown had more far-reaching results than this. It caused President Lincoln to detach Brigadier General Louis Blenker's division of 10,000 from McClellan and send it by way of Strasburg to Major General John C. Frémont, who commanded what was known as the Mountain Department located in present West Virginia. However, if Banks decided he needed Blenker's help, he was authorized to keep this division in the Valley. Frémont, who was better known as the Pathfinder through the Rocky Mountains, had formulated an ambitious plan to march 300 miles to Knoxville, Tennessee, a strategic rail junction. However, he abandoned this plan and instead decided to operate in the Valley. Lincoln also decided to withhold McDowell's corps of 40,000 men from reinforcing McClellan.[34]

Lincoln did not stop here. He broke up McClellan's territorial command, the Department of the Potomac, and left McClellan in charge of only the Federal forces south of the Rappahannock River to threaten Richmond. He placed McDowell in command of the Department of the Rappahannock and gave him the responsibility of protecting Washington. He left Banks in charge of the Department of the Shenandoah and extended Frémont's Mountain Department to include West Virginia and part of Kentucky and Tennessee. Since these commanders were all independent of each other and reported directly to Washington, one important principle essential for military success—unity of command—was completely missing in the organization of the Union armies. What command that was exercised was undertaken by Lincoln, or more

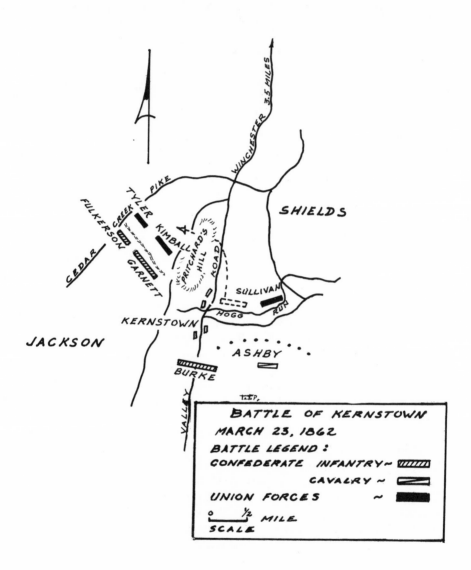

BATTLE OF KERNSTOWN
MARCH 23, 1862
BATTLE LEGEND :
CONFEDERATE INFANTRY ~
CAVALRY ~
UNION FORCES ~
0   ½   MILE
SCALE

particularly by Secretary of War Stanton, both non-military men.[35] When they were opposed by Lee, Johnston, and Jackson, the outcome of the Peninsula Campaign against Richmond and the Shenandoah Valley Campaign of 1862 should not surprise anyone.

The day after the Battle of Kernstown Jackson retreated southward to Mount Jackson, where he halted to lick his wounds and to gather reinforcements for a renewal of the struggle. Although he did not know the odds he would be facing, the enemy reorganizations would cause his feeble army of 3,000 to oppose 35,000 Unionists. Obviously he had a legitimate claim to extra troops if any could be spared from the hard-pressed Confederate forces defending Richmond.

Ashby learned that ladies of Winchester were permitted by the Federals to visit the battlefield of Kernstown, tend to the wounded, and make arrangments for the burial of the dead. Federal surgeons, in particular, were very cooperative and elicited commendations from the Southerners for their solicitude and help. One enemy officer, however, decided to jest about his exploits when he stopped at the door of a house in Winchester. According to this account of the incident, the following conversation took place between this officer and the residents of the house as he pointed to one of the vehicles near the gate:

"We've got your great Ashby here; he is badly wounded, and if his wound does not kill him, we don't guess he'll ever fight any more."

When one of the sympathetic residents replied, "Mother, let us get something for Col. Ashby to eat," the Federal officer answered her, "No, you'll do no such a thing; we intend to kill him."

The young lady then begged for his life and was greatly relieved when she was told that the officer was only jesting.[36]

In the only account of Turner Ashby's actually being captured by the enemy it is related that a Sergeant Pierson of the First Michigan Cavalry accomplished the unusual feat. Ashby had been taunting the Federals by riding to the crest of a hill in full view of his pursuers who were very anxious to capture him. Although the reckless Confederate leader would usually withdraw when necessary, on this occasion he lingered too long and he was surrounded before he was aware of his danger. The enemy had approached within fifty rods and attempted to beat him to the only avenue of escape, a cross-roads. Sergeant Pierson, who rode the only horse capable of matching Ashby's famous white charger, managed to reach the cross-roads at the same time as his quarry. Ashby fired his pistol but was unable to score a hit. A spirited hand-to-hand encounter followed which resulted in Pierson's dragging Ashby from his horse and holding him until other Federal troopers appeared. Pierson was a bigger and stronger man than his foe and used this natural advantage to the utmost.

Although his captors disarmed Ashby, they made the mistake of allowing him to ride his white horse, which had stopped when Ashby was pulled from his back. The blue coats had not proceeded very far with their prisoner when the white horse wheeled around suddenly, jumped over a high fence, and galloped away. The surprise of the Federal troopers was so great that they could not fire accurately at their rapidly-disappearing foe. Not long afterwards Ashby was discerned once again on a distant hill defiantly looking at the Federals.[37]

CHAPTER VII

ASHBY RESIGNS: JACKSON BACKS DOWN

While Jackson's army was retreating southward to Mount Jackson after the battle of Kernstown, Turner Ashby had not been inactive. His main responsibility was to command the rear guard for the Valley Army so as to give his superior time to bring off the infantry, artillery, and wagons. This required constant skirmishing with the Federals who were attempting a cautious pursuit. The day after the battle blue-clad troopers advanced about a mile south of Middletown, nearly opposite the limestone home named *Belle Grove* which had been built by Major Isaac Hite, Jr., the grandson of a valley pioneer. Chew's Battery occupied a commanding position and continued to blaze away at the enemy horsemen but was unable to check their pursuit. At a very critical time in this encounter the loud voice of Ashby was heard exhorting his men to, "Charge them, boys! Charge them!"[1] The bold cavalry leader had sensed the need for quick action and led a squadron of troopers from a nearby woods so as to gain a position between the threatened guns and the approaching riders. The maneuver was successful, for Ashby not only checked the enemy's approach, thus saving the precious guns, but he even burned the bridge over Cedar Creek in order to delay further pursuit.

In the skirmishing that followed, Ashby used those tactics in which he was particulary skilled. With the help of the dependable Chew's Battery, he would seize a strong position on a hill, open on his pursuers with artillery, and force them to form a line of battle with their overwhelming numbers. When the Federals got close enough to make it dangerous to remain where he was, Ashby would withdraw to another hilltop where the whole process would be repeated. He would vary his tactics to suit the occasion. Not being a graduate of West Point or the Virginia Military Institute, Ashby did not always follow the prescribed methods of warfare. If he thought the remedy to a particular problem was a cavalry charge, he would place himself in front of his men and exhort them to follow him with drawn sabers. The sight of Turner Ashby mounted on his white horse and followed by a group of hard-riding cavalrymen as the Confederates charged recklessly into the enemy's ranks was usually enough to create panic in the Federals. Their only recourse was to retire in hot haste.[2]

Ashby seemed oblivious to all danger and was absolutely without fear. That he exposed himself recklessly to enemy fire there can be no doubt. The same could be said about other Confederate leaders, especially during the later years of the war, for history is full of the records of brave men who threw caution to the winds and courted death in an effort to fight for a hopeless cause. On one occasion during the skirmishing near Mount Jackson when the bullets were whistling all around, Captain John Henderson rode up to the cavalry commander, who had been so busy strengthening his defenses the preceding night that he had gone without food and sleep.

"Good morning, Colonel," said Henderson. "I have brought you some breakfast, but this is rather a warm place to enjoy it."

"Never mind that," said Ashby, "your kindness is well-timed, for I am very hungry."

When Henderson handed him some hard-boiled eggs, Ashby thanked him, shared them with a fellow-officer, and after eating this frugal repast, reentered the fray.[3]

When the Valley Army went into camp near Mount Jackson, Jackson was greatly elated to learn that the Confederate Congress had adopted a resolution of thanks to his command for its "gallant and meritorious service in the successful engagement with a greatly superior force of enemy, near Kernstown."[4]

Jackson's force had been augmented by recruits called to the service when Governor John Letcher issued a proclamation calling out all the militia of the Valley and adjacent counties. When Jackson proceeded to enforce this necessary conscription in Augusta County, he had a rare stroke of luck. Among those who reported to Stonewall was Jedediah Hotchkiss, a New Yorker who had been teaching school near Churchville in Augusta County but who had cast his lot with the fortunes of his adopted state. He had served under Robert E. Lee in the ill-fated campaign of 1861 in western Virginia. His exertions undermined his health so much that he contracted typhoid fever and returned to his home to recuperate. When Governor Letcher's proclamation became effective in Augusta County and Hotchkiss had recovered sufficiently to reenter the service, he determined to seek engineering duty. He had proved to be a valuable map-maker and since the Confederacy was deficient in this type of skill, Jackson welcomed him to his staff with the following statement, "I want you to make me a map of the Valley, from Harpers Ferry to Lexington, showing all the points of offence and defence in those places. Mr. Pendleton will give you orders for what ever outfit you want. Good moring, Sir." [5] He continued to serve the demanding Jackson until the latter's death in May, 1863, after which he made maps for Generals Ewell and Early. He achieved the enviable reputation of being the "foremost map-maker of the war and his name appears more frequently than that of any other topographer in the pages of the *Official Records*, and no less than half of all the Confederate maps that eventually found their way into the *Atlas* were from his hand." [6]

One unfortunate result of the Battle of Kernstown was the relief of General Richard Garnett as commander of the Stonewall Brigade. It will be recalled that when the Confederate position on the left had become hopeless, the brigade commander had ordered a retreat without authorization from Jackson. It mattered not that Garnett was from a prominent Tidewater Virginia family, that he was a cousin of General Robert Garnett who had been killed at Carrick's Ford in 1861, and that he had been graduated from West Point the year before Jackson entered the Military Academy, that he had had previous military experience, and that he had led the Stonewall Brigade with credit. Jackson believed that Garnett's withdrawal was not necessary and on April 1 he relieved him of command, placed him under arrest, and took steps to have him courtmartialed.

The charges cited the following specifications alleging Garnett's neglect of duty: that he had not put his brigade into position properly, that he had separated himself from his command, that he had not been with his leading unit, that he had no troops within supporting distance of his front regiment, that regiments had become intermingled, that he had absented himself from his command, that he had given the order to fall back "when he should have encouraged his command to hold its position, and that he had sent an order to reserve forces to withdraw." [7] Although Garnett pressed for a resolution of these charges, nothing was done because military necessity demanded that the Confederate hierarchy devote its time to more serious matters. As for Garnett, he was a pallbearer at Jackson's funeral, served in Longstreet's corps, and died leading his brigade in Pickett's Charge at Gettysburg, within twenty-five yards of Federal cannon.

Jackson's treatment of Garnett was an unpopular move in the Valley Army, especially in the Stonewall Brigade. For several weeks his presence among the soldiers was greeted with an icy silence. According to Henry Kyd Douglas, "the officers and men of General Jackson's old brigade almost unanimously differed with him. Their regret at the loss of General Garnett was so great and their anger at his removal so intense and universal that their conduct amounted almost to insubordination."[8]

The new commander of the Stonewall Brigade was Brigadier General Charles S. Winder, a West Point graduate and a capable officer who was later killed by artillery at the Battle of Cedar Mountain, August 9, 1862. Because he succeeded the popular Garnett, he was destined to suffer ostracism by both officers and enlisted men until he partially won their respect. Like Stonewall, he was a strict disciplinarian; but, unlike Stonewall, he was not able to win their affection. One officer, however, who became his good friend, was Turner Ashby.

Ashby's constant patrol activity and his reckless exposure to danger made him have many narrow escapes from death. He once remarked that he did not fear the bullets that were aimed at himself, as he considered the Federals as poor marksmen, but he was concerned about the damage a stray bullet might do. On one occasion he attempted to burn the bridge over the North Fork of the Shenandoah, near Rude's Hill, and came very close to being captured or killed. He ordered Chew's Battery into position on Rude's Hill so it could cover the bridge, as well as the turnpike. After commanding his troopers to cross, he remained behind to fire the bridge, which had been prepared for the torch. He had placed a guard on the bridge with orders to set it on fire; but when a body of Federal cavalry approached, the Confederates fled. Ashby remained behind to kindle the fire, but four Federals headed for him, ordering him to surrender. Although their fire missed him, one ball passed through the lungs of his famous white charger, mortally wounding him and rendering him unmanageable. His men, seeing their brave leader in great danger, returned and shot the enemy who had visions of "bagging Ashby." Thus his life was saved to be forfeited another day.[9]

Much interest has been manifested in Ashby's white charger, and the writer has made a prolonged effort to learn his name but has been unsuccessful. Perhaps this animal has been overshadowed by more famous mounts, such as Lee's "Traveler" and Jackson's "Little Sorrel." This horse was apparently given to the cavalry leader by James H. Hathaway, who, seeing his son better mounted than Ashby, made his son give up the horse.[10] Wallace W. Phillips, a resident of Middleburg in Fauquier County, thinks that the name of the white horse may have been "Bald Peter," which was also the name of the white horse belonging to Captain John Ashby. It will be recalled that the latter was the one who made the quick trip to Williamsburg to apprise Lieutenant Governor Robert Dinwiddie of Braddock's defeat. Mr. Wallace recalls that Miss Betty Settle, daughter of Dr. Thomas Settle, who was Turner Ashby's personal physician, showed him the bridle Ashby's white horse was wearing when the charger received his mortal wound. He is not sure whether or not the name "Bald Peter" was mentioned when the bridle was displayed, but he believes it was possible. Turner Ashby's other horse, a black stallion, was so spirited and unmanageable that Ashby was apparently the only one who could ride him. Turner preferred to ride the white animal, however.[11]

The increase in size of the Valley Army while it was encamped near Mount Jackson affected Ashby's command. It seemed as if almost anyone who could get a horse wanted to follow the cavalry leader who had displayed such bravery, initiative, and leadership. As a result, Ashby's force was increased to a total of twenty-six companies. This was more than twice the authorized regimental size and more than Ashby could discipline, train, equip, and lead, although he never admitted that his force had exceeded the number he could control in battle. While this augmentation of his command was desirable, it exacerbated the chief weakness of the cavalry leader. He simply found it impossible to organize and administer such a large force. Had he been a graduate of one of the military academies, he would perhaps have had a better appreciation of the need for proper organization. The same comment might be made about the cavalry's need for discipline. Ashby's idea was that if he gave his men personal leadership by riding in front of them in battle, they would follow him anywhere. It is true that even though he had a large number of troopers, he usually did not have many of them under his immediate command. Many were absent on outpost and scouting duty. Although he theoretically had 600 men at Kernstown he actually mustered fewer than 300 on the battlefield. In the same battle Union troopers had succeeded in capturing many of Major Funsten's men during the confusion on the Confederate left.[12] In his official report of the engagement at Kernstown, Ashby admitted that many of his cavalrymen were absent and that he had not expected an encounter until the next day. Consequently, he gave his orders accordingly. He also mentioned the fact that his troopers and their horses had suffered from insufficient food and rest the preceding week.[13]

Nor was Ashby's inability to keep his troopers where they could be used the most efficiently the only objection Jackson had to his leadership. In spite of the Confederate prohibition on transfers, the name of Ashby continued to gather additions to his command. On April 21 almost an entire company of infantrymen from the Second Regiment of the Stonewall Brigade formed the Baylor Light Horse, Company B, Twelfth Virginia Cavalry. Most of its members were sons of farmers from Jefferson County who were commanded by their fellow-countian, Captain Robert W. Baylor.[14] The scattering of the many cavalry companies deprived them of Ashby's leadership and required those on detached duty to be directed solely by their captains, some of whom were incompetent. At Columbia Furnace near Woodstock on April 16 an entire company of sixty men had been captured along with their horses because of failure to mount a guard. On the 19th Jed Hotchkiss had discovered many men on outpost duty who had become drunk on applejack. Consequently, in a skirmish with the enemy the Confederate troopers fled precipitously and were not seen for ten days.[15]

Such conditions could not be condoned and when Jackson received a communication from General Lee inquiring about cavalry organization, he decided to take drastic action. On April 16, Lee's adjutant general, Colonel Walter H. Taylor, had written to ask whether the companies had been organized into regiments and whether the election of officers, as required by law, had been held. Lee reminded Jackson that if the requisite number of officers were to be obtained, it would be necessary that the men be well drilled and disciplined. Ashby's command at this time consisted of twenty to twenty-six companies, depending on whose version one accepts, and included about 1200 horsemen. To command this force there was but one colonel and one major above the rank of captain.[16]

In order to correct the deficiencies in the administration of his cavalry arm and improve its discipline, Jackson decided to divide his troopers so as to have a more efficient organization. One evening when Ashby rode into camp after spending the day visiting his picket-posts he received the following communication:

Headquarters, Army of the Valley

The General Commanding
    Hereby order companies A,B,C,D,E,F,G,H,I,K, of Ashby's

cavalry to report to Brigadier-General Taliaferro, and to be attached to his command; the other companies of the same command will report to Brigadier-General Winder, to be attached to his command.

Colonel Turner Ashby will command the advance-guard of the Army of the Valley, when on an advance, and the rear-guard when in retreat, applying to Generals Taliaferro and Winder for troops whenever they may be needed.

By order of
Major-Gen. T.J. Jackson.[17]

The effect of this order was to deprive Colonel Ashby of his command. He had no troops of his own but could borrow men from Taliaferro and Winder when he needed them!

Ashby quite naturally was very indignant at this treatment at the hands of Jackson. He expressed himself as feeling that his superior was over-stepping his authority, inasmuch as the Confederate War Department had authorized him [Ashby] to form his command. He even went further and stated that if he and Jackson were of equal rank, he would challenge to a duel the man whom he had served so faithfully and held in high repsect.

Believing that a great injustice had been perpetrated against him, Ashby wrote out his resignation and had it delivered to Jackson in his tent at Conrad's Store [Elkton], where the army had established itself. As the resignation had to go through military channels, it was sent to General Winder who forwarded it to Jackson. Ashby was supported in his position by his subordinate, Major Funsten, who submitted his own resignation.

Although Funsten was a brave and capable officer, he could probably be replaced. Ashby, however, was an entirely different case. His popularity among his troopers was so great that in all probability no one could take his place. His men enjoyed following a leader who would not hesitate to risk personal injury in order to inspire them. They liked the constant skirmishing and bragged that at Edinburg their leader had fought the enemy twenty-eight times during one month.[18] As a matter of fact, this constant engagement with the enemy contributed to the cavalry's lack of discipline. Jackson kept Ashby so busy scouting, patrolling, and fighting that he did not have the time to organize and discipline his troopers—if, indeed, he had the disposition. Ashby's method may have been the best that could be employed under the circumstances. He believed that war required constant contact with the enemy and making him fight for every foot of ground as he was advancing. The cavalry leader felt this was much more important than spending endless hours on dress parades and regimental maneuvers. Whether or not this opinion of the nature of warfare may be open to debate, there is no debate about how successful it was in masking Jackson's movements, keeping him informed about the Federals, beating the enemy in small, as well as large, encounters, and attracting the chivalry of Virginia and Maryland to his colors.[19]

Then the much-maligned General Winder rendered the Confederacy one of his greatest contributions. Even if he were almost as stern a disciplinarian as Jackson, he could not fail to recognize that, disciplinarian or not, Ashby's presence was indispensable to the success of the Valley Army. As has been pointed out, he and the cavalry leader had learned to understand and appreciate each other from the beginning of his Valley service. As a result, they had become very good friends. Accordingly, when Winder learned of the rift between the two great Valley Confederates, he sought out Ashby and conferred with him, after which he went to see Jackson. He was able to help convince Stonewall to confer with his aggrieved cavalryman.

Jackson penned a request to Ashby in which he asked the cavalry leader to come to his headquarters for a talk. Ashby complied and on the morning of April 25 conferred for several hours with his superior officer. Jackson asked him to withdraw his resignation and reminded Ashby that he [Jackson] had withdrawn his resignation in the Loring affair after he had been requested by General Johnston and Governor Letcher.

Ashby replied that he had resigned in earnest and that he wanted his resignation forwarded to the Secretary of War. He repeated to Jackson what he had told his officers that but for the fact "he had the highest respect for Jackson's ability as a soldier, and believed him essential to the cause of the South, he would hold him to personal account for the indignity he had put upon him."[20] Having expressed himself thus, Ashby departed. When he returned to his command, he told several of his officers about the meeting. He added that when his resignation was effective, he planned to organize an independent command and operate in the Lower Valley and Piedmont area. He was greatly elated when all of his officers present announced their intention to follow him.

Stonewall Jackson realized that he had made a mistake in depriving Ashby of his command, and he was not too proud to admit his error. He did what he could to atone for his bad judgment. Realizing that if he persisted in this course, every cavalryman in the Valley would follow Ashby wherever he led them and that disorganized cavalry was better than none at all, Jackson issued a subsequent order restoring Ashby to his command. He explained his capitulation in a letter to General Lee dated May 5, 1862, by saying, "Ashby claimed that I could not interfere with his organization, as he was acting under the instructions of the late Secretary of War, Mr. Benjamin, who had authorized Ashby to raise cavalry, infantry, and heavy artillery...such was Colonel Ashby's influence over his command that I became well satisfied that if I persisted in my attempt to increase the efficiency of the cavalry it would produce the contrary effect as Colonel Ashby's influence, who is very popular with his men, would be thrown against me."[21]

Jackson's second order "detailed" but did not "assign" the cavalry to Ashby, who remained in titular command of the advance and the advance only. However, although Jackson technically retained control of the cavalry companies, the practical effect of his subsequent order was to give Ashby unlimited control. Accordingly, Ashby and Major Funsten withdrew their resignations and the crisis was eased.[22]

As Jackson was planning to retreat southward in the event that Banks advanced, he made plans to move a huge Baltimore and Ohio Railroad locomotive from Mount Jackson to Staunton to be used in the Confederacy, which urgently needed this type of rolling stock. The problem was to haul the engine over the Valley Pike since there was a rail gap between Mount Jackson and Staunton. This was nothing new to the Confederate engineers, who had previously moved locomotives captured at Martinsburg and Harpers Ferry by Jackson. There was another railroad gap from Winchester to Strasburg.

Because of the size of the locomotive at Mount Jackson, its removal presented many problems. It was first necessary to raise it with jacks, remove whatever could be taken off, and place in position on the macadam road. Forty horses hitched four abreast furnished the motive power. When they proved inadequate to negotiate Rude's Hill, it was necessary to enlist the additional aid of hundreds of soldiers and civilians who attached ropes. The distance of forty-two miles was finally covered, only to have the locomotive break loose and overturn within sight of its destination. It was eventually righted and placed on the rails of the Virginia Central Railroad, where it served the Confederacy. This successful enterprise was repeated when more rolling-stock was hauled from Mount Jackson to Staunton.[23]

Belle Boyd, Confederate Spy

Although General McClellan had instructed General Banks to "push Jackson hard," Banks remained at Strasburg until April 1, thus denying the Federals the fruits of their victory at Kernstown. He should have launched a vigorous pursuit of Jackson's small and defeated force immediately following the battle on March 23. He did advance his cautious cavalry to Tom's Brook, five miles south of Strasburg, but there they remained and hence failed to gather important information about Jackson and Ashby. The Confederate cavalry leader, who was supported by an infantry brigade at Woodstock, kept watch on the enemy on the north side of Tom's Brook. In the absence of accurate information about Jackson's strength, Banks credited him with 15,000 men. He knew that Joseph E. Johnston, who commanded the Army of Northern Virginia before Lee, had retreated southward from Centreville and that McClellan had embarked for Fortress Monroe to begin the Peninsula Campaign. Banks believed that Major General James Longstreet had joined Jackson at New Market; but in this, as in most of his intelligence about the Southerners, he was wrong. Finally on April 2, when he had learned that Jackson had not been reinforced, he crossed Tom's Brook for the southward advance and reached Woodstock, where he went into camp.[24]

Banks's caution was due partly to the geography of the Valley. It will be recalled that Massanutten Mountain was a practically impassable obstacle except for the gap through which the New Market-Luray road passed. Banks feared that if he advanced too far southward from Strasburg, Jackson or Ashby would use this range as a screen and, advancing northward into the Luray Valley, would get in his rear at Front Royal or Strasburg and cut his communications. He, apparently, never considered the idea of moving southward to New Market, crossing into the Luray Valley, and thus forestalling the Confederates. Exclusive of the soldiers whose job was to guard his communications, Banks still had 15,000 to oppose Jackson's 6,000. [25]

On April 17 Banks left his Woodstock camp and marched southward. When McClellan began his Peninsula Campaign to approach Richmond from the southeast, Joseph E. Johnston moved to get between him and Richmond. Johnston left Major General Richard S. Ewell with his division of 8,000 muskets on the upper Rappahannock to cooperate with Jackson in the Valley. In order to keep Banks from crossing the Massanutten Mountain and get between Ewell and himself, Jackson retreated southward to Harrisonburg and then eastward to Conrad's Store [Elkton], near Swift Run Gap in the Blue Ridge. At the latter pass in the mountain Jackson was in communication with Ewell at Gordonsville and with the authorities at Richmond. Banks garrisoned Harrisonburg.

Meanwhile another Federal general, John C. Frémont, had formulated a plan to move on Staunton from the west, and, after capturing that important town, to move to Knoxville so as to protect the loyal residents of eastern Tennessee. His advance, commanded by Brigadier General Robert H. Milroy, approached Staunton by way of Monterey and McDowell. The Confederate defender of the mountain passes west of Staunton was Brigadier General Edward Johnson, who had two brigades totalling 3,000 men. Because of his long drawn out association with the mountains, he had acquired the nickname of "Allegheny."[26] When he found that his position was being threatened by enemy forces at McDowell, Harrisonburg, and Moorefield, he retreated to West View, which is only seven miles from Staunton.

It will be recalled that after Jackson's retreat up the Valley, Shields had been ordered to take his division from the Valley to Fredericksburg, where he was to unite with McDowell. The two Federal forces planned to join McClellan in his effort to take Richmond; however, General Lee, who acted as Jefferson Davis's military advisor before Joseph E. Johnston was wounded at Seven Pines, communicated with Jackson with the view of diverting McDowell to the Valley. In accordance with this strategy, it was decided to reinforce Stonewall's little army with the commands of both Ewell and Allegheny Johnson. This union of Confederate forces would increase Jackson's strength to 17,000 or 18,000.

Although the rupture between Jackson and Ashby had been settled to all outward appearances, Jackson still felt that the cavalry should be organized into regiments at the earliest practicable moment. When Congressman Boteler urged that his friend Ashby be promoted brigadier general, Jackson in a letter to Boteler dated May 6 replied as follows:

> ...
> With regard to Colonel Ashby's promotion I would gladly favor it if he were a good disciplinarian, but he has such bad discipline and attaches so little importance to drill, that I would regard it as a calamity to see him promoted. I desire so soon as he gives proper attention to these matters (which are so essential to success in operations with large masses of troops) to see him promoted. I recommended him for a colonelcy, and will always take pleasure in doing all I can for his advancement consistent with the interest of the Public Service...[27]

Nevertheless, Boteler persisted in his objective of having the cavalry commander promoted; and his persistence was rewarded when Turner Ashby was handed his commission as brigadier general on May 27, 1862, in Winchester. His service record dates his promotion May 23 but because of the impending battles its delivery was delayed. The paper informing him of this advancement was handed to him by Captain Sandie Pendleton, Jackson's staff officer, with the remarks, "I do this with great pleasure, General Ashby, hoping that as you are soon to command a brigade, the country may expect less exposure of your life."[28]

While Jackson had the choice of several alternatives in meeting the Federal thrust coming at him from different directions, he decided to protect Staunton with its storage of supplies from Milroy who headed Frémont's advance. Then he planned to confront Banks. He did not want to betray his movement westward or to expose his flank to Banks by taking the most direct route to Staunton. Instead he ordered Ashby to screen his movements. The cavalryman on April 29 and 30 drove back the enemy cavalry and demonstrated in front of Harrisonburg. Leaving Ewell at Swift Run Gap to threaten Banks's communications if the Federal officer advanced on Staunton, Jackson crossed the Blue Ridge Mountains at Brown's Gap and marched to Mechum's River Station on the Virginia Central Railroad, about six miles west of Charlottesville. Naturally most people, both Confederates and Federals, believed he was leaving the Valley in order to join in the defense of Richmond.

At the railroad station the cars were awaiting Jackson's arrival. Great was the joy of the soldiers when they realized that the trains were headed west to Staunton instead of east to Richmond. After reaching Staunton, Jackson marched westward to meet Frémont's advance headed by Milroy. Along the route he was joined by Allegheny Johnson's division.[29]

On May 7 Johnson's force encountered the Federal outposts and drove them into the village of McDowell. As it was late in the afternoon, the main engagement was fought the next day. When Milroy had asked for additional help, he was reinforced by the brigade of Brigadier General Robert H. Schenck from Franklin. Most of these men belonged to Ohio and West Virginia regiments and had the reputation of being good fighters. Some evidence of their qualifications for battle is illustrated by the fact that they had covered thirty-four miles in twenty-three hours. Johnson's division still leading Jackson's advance, gained the top of Sitlington's Hill in the Bull Pasture Mountains on the afternoon of May 8. The

Federal camp at McDowell was well located with respect to defense, for the only approach for Jackson was over the turnpike that crossed the Bull Pasture River.

Jackson sought a trail so that he could cross the stream at another place which would enable him to outflank the enemy; however, Schenck, the senior Federal officer, did not wait, but boldly assumed the offensive himself. This was a risky proceeding inasmuch as he was greatly outnumbered by the Confederates. Although he was repulsed, he did not withdraw until nine o'clock at night. The Confederates bivouacked on the battlefield and took up the pursuit the next day. They were unable to catch up with the Federals, who impeded their pursuers by setting the woods on fire on both sides of the road. Having driven the enemy back to Franklin, Jackson took the road to Harrisonburg to strike at Banks, who, meanwhile, was retreating north to Strasburg. Frémont's troops in West Virginia could join him only by a long, circuitous route.

Although the Battle of McDowell was a victory for Jackson, the Federals had the satisfaction of inflicting twice as many casualties on the Confederates as they, themselves, suffered. Among the seriously wounded was General Johnson.[30]

Meanwhile Ashby and his troopers, as usual, had been busy while Jackson had moved out of the Valley, then back into it, and then won the Battle of McDowell. He had screened Jackson's movements and then was ordered to divide his command. He sent ten companies to go with Jackson to McDowell, while he took the remainder to watch Banks. The Union commander, fearful that Confederates might get in his rear and cut his communications, retreated northward to New Market, closely followed by Ashby. On this occasion the cavalryman experienced one of his few illnesses while in the service. He was confined to camp several days by an attack of fever that was accompanied by dysentery—a common ailment in the Confederate army. He received such good nursing care in the Mount Crawford area that he fully recovered from his malady. Two of his companies, those commanded by Captains Sheetz and Winfield, attracted Jackson's favorable comment by the way they put into effect the lessons learned from Ashby, for Stonewall found them invaluable in the McDowell Campaign.

Major General Richard S. Ewell, who had remained at Swift Run Gap in the Blue Ridge, began to form some unique ideas about his superior, Stonewall Jackson. Ewell had been left to watch Banks while Jackson was engaging in the McDowell Campaign. In short, he came to the conclusion that Jackson was crazy. As usual,

Jackson had not taken his subordinates into his confidence about his intentions, and Ewell didn't know what to do. To make matters worse, he could not ask Jackson, whose whereabouts were unknown. When he heard that Banks was marching upon him from Harrisonburg, he exploded as follows to Colonel James A. Walker, who commanded the Thirteenth Virginia Regiment in his division, "Colonel Walker, did it ever occur to you that General Jackson is crazy?"

Walker had been a cadet at the Virginia Military Institute when Jackson was a teacher there and was reluctant to express himself so frankly about the commanding general of the Valley Army. Consequently, he replied to Ewell's question with the observation, "I don't know, General. We used to call him 'Fool Tom' Jackson at the Virginia Military Institute, but I do not suppose that he is really crazy." This was remarkable restraint for Walker, inasmuch as while a cadet under Jackson at V.M.I. he had had a serious confrontation with the professor which resulted in Walker's being dismissed two months before he was due to graduate.[31]

"I tell you, sir," Ewell continued, "he is as crazy as a March hare. He has gone away, I don't know where, and left me here with instructions to stay until he returns. But Banks's whole army is advancing on me, and I have not the most remote idea where to communicate with General Jackson. I tell you, sir, he is crazy, and I will just march my division away from here. I do not mean to have it cut to pieces at the behest of a crazy man."

Walker, who did not want to remain to hear any more of Ewell's criticism of Jackson, went to see his own brigade commander, Brigadier General Arnold Elzey, who was very much displeased with an order he had received from Ewell. Elzey remarked, "I tell you, sir, General Ewell is crazy, and I have a serious notion of marching my Brigade back to Gordonsville."[32]

Before Walker could make a reply, the scene shifted to a raw conscript, who burst into the room where the two officers were conversing, thrust a paper in front of Elzey, and demanded, "I want you, sir, to sign that paper at once, and give me my discharge. You have no right to keep me here, and I mean to go home!"

Elzey, a West Pointer, was flabbergasted. After looking at the intruder, he sought his pistols. As soon as he had located them, he quickly grabbed them, but not before the conscript realized what was about to happen and had taken refuge in flight. Elzey managed to get off two shots, which missed their mark because of the rapid movement of the intended target. Athough the general undertook pursuit, he was unsuccessful in hitting his quarry, and returned to resume his conversation with Walker, "I should like to know, Colonel Walker, what sort of men you keep over at the Thirteenth Regiment? The idea of the rascal's demanding of me, a Brigadier General, to sign a paper! Oh, if I only could have gotten hold of my pistols sooner."

Walker replied to his superior with the remarks, "Well, I don't know what to do myself. I was up to see General Ewell just now, and he said that General Jackson was crazy; I came down to see you, and you say that General Ewell is crazy; and I have not the slightest doubt that my conscript who ran from you just now, will report it all over camp that General Elzey is crazy; so it seems I have fallen into evil hands and I reckon the best thing for me to do is to turn the conscripts loose, and march the rest of my regiment back to Richmond."[33]

After his unsuccessful pursuit of Milroy, Jackson returned to the Valley to deal with Banks who, meanwhile, had retreated northward to Strasburg. There the Federal commander erected a fort on a high eminence overlooking the town and surrounding countryside. On May 20, Jackson, having been joined by one of Ewell's brigades, arrived at New Market. The remainder of Ewell's division was in the Luray Valley, but one brigade was dispatched to join Jackson in the Main Valley in order to deceive the enemy. This one was commanded by Brigadier General Richard Taylor, the son of former President Zachary Taylor, who, although not a graduate of a military academy, had learned much of the art of war from books. Consequently, he had organized a very efficient brigade. He had overcome the bane of army officers—straggling—by constant exertion on his own part. When his 3,000 Louisianians marched past the camp of Jackson's men, they were an impressive sight. They were dressed in fresh clothing of gray with white gaiters and were led by bands playing martial airs. Even though they had marched twenty-six miles, they maintained their column organization and did not have any stragglers. When Jackson asked Taylor about the road and distance the brigade had marched that day, he was told, "Keezletown road, six and twenty miles." The general commanding the Valley Army then remarked, "You seem to have no stragglers." Taylor's reply was that he never allowed straggling. Jackson was so impressed that he requested, "You must teach my people; they straggle badly."[34]

Confederate hopes at this particular time had been dashed by a series of disasters, particulary in the West. In April, 1862, the

Federals had won an important victory at Shiloh and had caused the death of one of the South's highest-ranking generals, Albert Sidney Johnston. Several weeks later they captured the important port of New Orleans. In the East, Norfolk had been evacuated, the ironclad *Virginia* blown up by Confederates to prevent its capture, and McClellan was pushing up the peninsula with a vastly superior army to try to capture Richmond. Clearly a great victory in the Shenandoah Valley would go a long way in boosting Southern morale.

Stonewall Jackson saw his opportunity and took advantage of it. Federal forces numbering over 60,000 men were scattered throughout the countryside under the commands of Generals Frémont, Banks, Shields, and McDowell, respectively. Jackson had about 17,000 to confront this host, but he enjoyed one of the few advantages the South possessed in the war—interior lines of operation. He was at the hub of the military wheel, while his opponents occupied the rim or perimeter. He was thus in a position to use his geographical advantage to unite his forces and strike at his enemies in detail. With the wounding of General Edward Johnson at McDowell and the retirement of Milroy, Jackson could add Johnson's troops to his own and Ewell's. Quick, decisive action was necessary and he proved equal to the task.

In Washington, where War Secretary Stanton was personally directing the various armies in Virginia, expectations were high. The Federal authorities regarded Jackson's costly victory at McDowell as a minor affair and felt relieved that he was no threat to the capital. On May 26 McDowell was under orders to leave Fredericksburg in order to join McClellan on the Peninsula and President Lincoln and Secetary Stanton were preparing to review McDowell's troops before they left camp.

On May 21 Jackson marched northward from New Market, and his men supposed that they were headed down the Main Valley to Strasburg in order to strike at Banks. Great was the surprise of the Southern army when the van turned to the right and headed eastward through the New Market Gap in the Massanuttens to Luray, where it was joined by Ewell's division. They were now in the Luray or Page Valley. The next day they continued the northward march straight down the Valley toward Front Royal, where there was a small Federal garrison under Colonel John R. Kenly.[35] The addition of Ewell brought the Second and Sixth Virginia Cavalry, which, together with Ashby's force, gave Stonewall about 17,000 men and 50 guns.

While the Confederates were marching northward down the Luray Valley toward Front Royal, Shields's division was heading eastward toward Fredericksburg to join McDowell. Jackson's exploits at this time delayed the latter's efforts to reinforce McClellan again.

Although Ashby's troopers were not always at hand under his immediate command, he enjoyed the reputation of having a high percentage of them reporting for duty. This was not true of many commands. One reason was their love and respect for their intrepid commander, but perhaps another was their fear that they might be transferred out of the cavalry to the infantry. A group of Maryland foot-soldiers whose enlistments had expired and whose request to transfer to the cavalry had been denied swore they would fight no longer and had to be disarmed and placed under guard. One account that has survived to this day is the way that Dr. Thomas Lee Settle, Ashby's personal physician, solved the problem of having too many men report for sick call. When they would enter the doctor's tent to complain of some ailment, they were told, "You go look under my cot and there are two large jugs; get one of them and take yourself a couple of good swigs." As many of these cavalrymen were hard drinkers, they thought that the physician meant they could get a good drink of hard liquor. As a result, they turned the jug upside down and gulped down a big swallow of the contents before they could stop. Much to their suprise, they found that they had been drinking castor oil. They were so embarrassed at the way in which they had been outwitted that they told no one; however, they never answered sick call again unless they were so incapacitated that they had to be carried to Dr. Settle's tent by their stretcher-bearers. No wonder Turner Ashby's command experienced small numbers of men reporting sick![36]

Turner Ashby's Narrow Escape from Capture

Courtesy of The Library of Congress

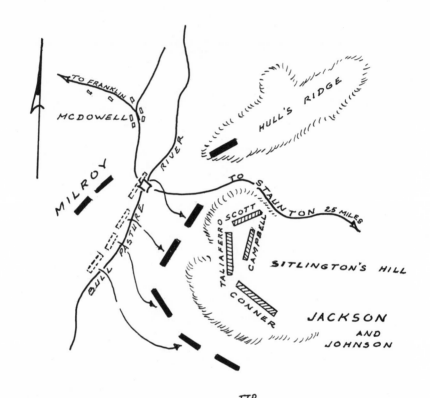

BATTLE OF MCDOWELL
MAY 8, 1862
0 ___ ½ MILE
SCALE
NOTE: ASHBY ON
DUTY IN UPPER
VALLEY

CHAPTER VIII

JACKSON SURPRISES BANKS

When Richard Taylor of Ewell's division rejoined his former comrades at Luray, he may be forgiven if he entertained reservations about Stonewall Jackson's sanity. It will be recalled that he had been ordered to leave the rest of the division where it was encamped at Swift Run Gap in the Luray Valley to join Jackson at New Market in the Main Shenandoah Valley. Using the Keezletown road, he proceeded in a northwestwardly direction to effect the junction. The good impression which his Louisianians made upon the discerning Jackson particularly because they had no stragglers has already been related. When Taylor had seen the eccentric general for the first time, he was surprised to find the army commander sitting on the top rail of a fence sucking a lemon. He described his superior as possessing "a pair of cavalry boots covering feet of gigantic size, a mangy cap with visor drawn low, a heavy dark beard, and weary eyes—eyes I afterward saw filled with intense but never brilliant light."[1] Taylor was mystified as to where Jackson obtained the ever-present lemons, when such luxuries were scarce in the South during the Civil War, but no one ever enlightened him on the source. When Jackson later visited Taylor at his campfire, he informed the brigade commander that the army would move at dawn. As was usually his custom, he did not give his subordinates the slightest indication of their destination.

Great was Taylor's surprise when he perceived the head of the column turn to the right at New Market and march through the gap in Massanutten Mountain until Jackson reached Luray. As this town was in the Luray Valley about twenty miles north of Ewell's camp, Taylor wondered why he had been ordered to take a circuitous route involving three long marches to return to the same Valley from which he had originally departed. He was even more perplexed when Ewell brought the remainder of the division in a straight line to effect a junction with Jackson's army at Luray. Taylor indulged in the following musing, when he remarked, "I began to think that Jackson was an unconscious poet, and, as an ardent lover of nature, desired to give strangers an opportunity to admire the beauties of his Valley."[2] Jackson, of course, had ordered Taylor to join him in the Main Valley so as to deceive the enemy.

When Ewell joined him, Jackson had a concentration that gave him a unified command of about 17,000 men. Besides Ewell's infantrymen, he also brought along two regiments of cavalry, the Second Virginia commanded by Colonel Thomas Munford and the Sixth Virginia led by Colonel Thomas Stanhope Flournoy, which would share with Turner Ashby the scouting, picketing, and fighting required of the mounted arm of service.

With Ashby heading the advance, the Southerners marched northward toward Front Royal, where there was a small Federal force under Colonel John R. Kenly. It was stationed there to protect the bridges and communications of the Manassas Gap Railroad. Ashby remained with the main army until he reached a road to the left, which crossed the South Fork of the Shenandoah at McCoy's Ford and led to Buckton Station on the railroad. This was about midway between Front Royal and Strasburg. Ashby's task was to disrupt communications between these two towns by cutting the telegraph line and burning the railroad bridge. Buckton was protected by two companies of Federal infantry numbering about 140 men.[3] As General Banks had fortified himself at Strasburg with his main force, Ashby was expected to intervene so as to prevent him from reinforcing his outpost at Front Royal or to intercept any Federals seeking to escape entrapment at Front Royal by fleeing westward the twelve miles to Strasburg.[4]

After fording the river, Ashby and his cavalrymen rode around the north end of Massanutten Mountain toward Strasburg. When he reached Bell's Mill, he ordered Sergeant Richardson of Company E and four other troopers to perform vedette duty at Water Lick Station on the railroad.

The cavalry commander took Companies A,B,E,F, and G by Warren Springs to Buckton Station. When he reconnoitered the Federal position, he discovered that the enemy had fortified themselves in the brick depot and another nearby building.[5] They were infantrymen from Wisconsin and Indiana and, as Ashby subsequently learned, were good fighters.

Upon his return to his command, the cavalry leader formed his troopers for a charge. Although he had the advantage of surprise, Ashby met a fire so effective that he had to retire. A second attempt was more successful, as he was able to drive the bluecoats from the station to a strong position at the western end of the railroad bridge behind an embankment. After firing the depot and cutting the telegraph line, Ashby formed his men for a third charge. His eagerness to destroy the railroad bridge caused him to take additional risks. Leading his men, he exhorted them with the challenge, "Forward, boys! We will get every mother's son of them."

Although the Confederate horsemen responded by dashing forward recklessly over fences, rough ground, and numerous other obstacles up to the embankment, they met such a withering fire that they were checked by the hard-fighters from Wisconsin. Still determined to destroy the enemy communications by burning the railroad bridge, Ashby prepared for a fourth attack. Before he could get his men in position, he noted that an enemy bullet had torn off the ear of his black charger. He quieted his horse by speaking a few soft words and then addressed one of his horseless men who had asked the cavalry leader if he didn't think the position was too exposed. Ashby replied, "Oh, no, that was only a stray ball but you'd better see to yourself. Go to your company and get one of the boys to take you up behind him; we must leave here."[6] Ashby was influenced in his decision to break off the engagement and head toward Front Royal by the loss of two of his best captains, George Sheetz and John Fletcher, who had been mortally wounded by the fierce Federal fire.

Meanwhile, another cavalry force moved against the railroad west of Front Royal. Led by Lieutenant Colonel Flournoy of the Sixth Virginia, who was supported by companies from the Second Virginia, these troopers completed the interruption to rail communication between Front Royal and Strasburg.[7]

Another display of Confederate cavalry activity was made farther west in front of Banks's fortified position at Strasburg. Three of Ashby's companies, commanded by Captains Sam Myers, E.H. McDonald, and William Harness, respectively, demonstrated so successfully in front of Banks that the Federal general was firmly convinced that Jackson's army was directly south of Strasburg—in the Main Valley. Even when a courier from Front Royal eluded the encircling Southern troopers and rode the twelve miles to Strasburg to inform Banks that Jackson was in the Luray Valley, the Federal commander refused to believe him. He continued to delude himself with the idea that the Confederates at Front Royal were only a raiding body of cavalry. Ashby's men strengthened this conviction when they drove in Federal pickets and erected breastworks on the hills near Strasburg, in full view of Banks and his army. Captain Myers created the impression that his force was much larger than it actually was, for he deceived the enemy by moving his men from point to point. Even after hearing from fugitives who had fled from Front Royal to Winchester,

Banks did not retreat from Strasburg until he had sent a cavalry force toward Woodstock and learned that there was no strong Confederate army south of his position.[8]

In the capital city of Washington on the night of May 22, optimism prevailed as the war seemed to be drawing to a successful conclusion. McClellan was still threatening Richmond with his overwhelming numbers; and although he was still clamoring for reinforcements, the threat to the Confederate capital was very real. Federal pickets only nine miles away could easily see the spires of the prominent buildings on Church Hill. Frémont had escaped from Jackson after the defeat of part of his army at McDowell and, presumably, was gathering his forces for a return to the fighting. Banks was strongly fortified at Strasburg, and McDowell had crossed the Rappahannock at Fredericksburg and was planning to leave for Richmond on the 26th. Victory was so taken for granted that recruiting offices were closed in Washington. In anticipation of a successful attack on the Confederate capital, President Lincoln and War Secretary Stanton had left Washington to review McDowell's corps before he left Fredericksburg.[9]

Although Banks's command had been reduced to 10,000 men, he did not seem to fear the approaching Confederates. He had 4,500 infantry, 2,900 cavalry, and 16 guns at Strasburg, while at Winchester there were 850 infantry and 600 cavalry. As has been related in connection with Turner Ashby's engagement at Buckton Station, the railroad post was defended by two companies of infantry. East of the Blue Ridge twelve miles from Front Royal Brigadier General John Geary had an independent command of 2,000 Federal infantry and cavalry. The defense of Front Royal itself, as has been noted, had been entrusted to Colonel John R. Kenly, who had 1,000 men and 2 guns, with most of the men belonging to the First Maryland (U.S.) Infantry.[10]

Unfortunately for the Federals, Front Royal was as indefensible as Harpers Ferry and for the same reason. The town is located on low ground and is completely at the mercy of an enemy located on much higher terrain all around. To add to the defenders' difficulties, the North and South Forks of the Shenandoah unite about a mile and half north of the town and then proceed to Harpers Ferry, where the Potomac joins the Shenandoah. The principal turnpike from Front Royal to Winchester crossed both forks. Obviously the possession of their two bridges was of tremendous importance.

Turner Ashby's Charge at the Battle of Middletown

Courtesy of the Virginia State Library

As Jackson approached Front Royal from Luray on the morning of May 23, in order to confuse the Federals, he left the main road and took a lesser one to the right. The route bore the unusual name of Gooney Manor road. He so surprised the Federal defenders that he was able to approach within 1½ miles of the town before he was discovered. About 2:00 P.M. his advance encountered enemy pickets and sent them running toward town. Since Jackson was not aware of the enemy's strength, he halted his columns on a hill overlooking the town and pondered his next move. At this point the Confederates observed the thin figure of a woman running toward them and frantically waving a bonnet in order to attract their attention. When the Southern officers saw the approaching figure, Stonewall detached the youngest member of his staff, Henry Kyd Douglas, to find out what she wanted.

Douglas had not advanced far before he heard someone call his name, and he immediately recognized the approaching visitor as Belle Boyd, who later became, perhaps, the most famous woman spy of the Confederacy. As his home town of Shepherdstown is only eight miles from Belle's home in Martinsburg, he had known her from her earliest girlhood and knew her to be a daredevil. Thus he was not surprised when he learned that the bold woman had miraculously escaped Federal bullets as she made her hazardous journey to Confederate lines from Front Royal, where she had been living with a relative.[11] She brought important information about the enemy to the Confederate leaders.

This was not the first time Belle Boyd had risked her life to aid the Confederate cause nor was it destined to be the last. Over a week earlier she had spied on Federal officers holding a conference in her aunt's Front Royal home known as the Strickler House. This hotel had been converted into a Federal headquarters. Belle listened to the officers' conversation, then rode a thirty-mile round trip at night and gave the information to Ashby, who relayed it to Jackson.[12]

A week later, although breathless from her sortie across fields, through weeds, and across fences, and on the verge of exhaustion, Belle gasped to Douglas, "I knew it must be Stonewall, when I heard the first gun. Go back quick and tell him that the Yankee force is very small—one regiment of Maryland infantry, several pieces of artillery, and several companies of cavalry. Tell him I know, for I went through the camps and got it out of an officer. Tell him to charge right down and he will catch them all. I must hurry back. Good-bye. My love to all the dear boys—and remember if you meet me in town you haven't seen me today."[13]

Having fulfilled her mission of apprising the Confederates of Kenly's strength and dispositions at Front Royal, Belle Boyd returned to the town in order to cheer the men in gray. She was particularly pleased when the Stonewall Brigade swept through the town, for her father, Benjamin R. Boyd, was a member of the Second Virginia Infantry Regiment. Since the Stonewall Brigade had the responsiblity of defending Jackson's rear guard, it did not participate in the Front Royal fight.[14] It remained for the Louisiana Brigade, the First Maryland Infantry (C.S.A.), and the Sixth Virginia Cavalry regiments to do most of the fighting with Kenly's Federals.

Belle Boyd's information proved to be remarkably accurate. Acting on it, Taylor's Louisiana Brigade led the Confederate skirmish-line, passed through the town, and engaged the Federals, who had taken refuge on the west bank of the Shenandoah and whose batteries commanded the wagon bridge. Noticing that the railroad bridge downstream was safer, Taylor ordered his Eighth Louisiana Regiment to cross on it. Although the men encountered some difficulty walking on the ties, they were able to gain the opposite bank. A few unfortunates fell into the murky, swollen waters below. As soon as the Confederates got across, the enemy set fire to some combustibles previously placed on the wagon bridge. Taylor's men, realizing the importance of saving this structure for the bulk of the army to use, rushed into the flames and threw brands into the river. In doing so, many burned their hands severely.[15] Sufficient damage had been done, however, to delay the Confederate crossing.

As the Northern artillery was delaying Jackson's advance, the Southerners brought up some of their own pieces to blast the way ahead. Great was the disappointment of Lieutenant Colonel Stapleton Crutchfield, late of the Virginia Military Institute , whom Jackson had made his chief of artillery, when he discovered that his first artillery pieces on the field had too short a range. Delay ensued until long-range guns could be brought up.

While the fight was raging, a Federal supply train steamed in from the east. Before the hapless engineer could reverse his locomotive, it was boarded by some of Major Roberdeau Wheat's Louisiana Tigers. Whether it was the same train used by the Confederates to indulge in an amusing prank is not clear, but in all probability it was. The Tigers helped themselves to the large quantities of arms, ammunition, clothing, tents, wagons, and commissary stores that the departing enemy had abandoned. The troops from New Orleans even put on some of the blue uniforms

Courtesy of Jac Holland Bushong

Sergeant Edward Mark Bushong, the author's grandfather, a Scout in
Company E, Twelfth Virginia Cavalry, Laurel Brigade

left behind. Then they got on the cars and steamed to the little village of Markham, where a Federal garrison had not heard of the loss of Front Royal. The bluecoats at Markham accepted the invitation of the bluecoats on the train to "take a ride up the road a little ways." Great was the chagrin of the trainriders when their trip ended in Front Royal in the midst of thousands of Confederates![16] Thus their ride ended with their being made prisoners of the enterprising Tigers.

It is interesting to note that at the Battle of Front Royal, the First Maryland Infantry Regiment of the Confederate army met and defeated the First Maryland Infantry Regiment of the Union army.

Colonel Crutchfield waited impatiently for the arrival of his long-range rifled artillery pieces so he could effectively knock out the enemy's guns. Unfortunately he was the victim of one of the shortcomings of the Confederate military organization at this time. Instead of having the work of orderlies performed by a picked company of men who were selected for their intelligence and courage and permanently attached to army headquarters, it was customary to detail a temporary company of cavalry to do the job. By using this system, the organization of the cavalry regiments was broken up and the general had no evidence of their special fitness for the responsible service expected of them. On the day of the Front Royal fight, one of Ashby's least disciplined companies had been detailed to serve as couriers at Jackson's Headquarters. Many of them were raw youths who had just been recruited and, consequently, had never been under fire. The youth entrusted with Jackson's order to his rear units of infantry and artillery to advance into Front Royal by the most direct route panicked and fled. As a result, the message was never delivered.Thus instead of marching only three miles by direct route, the Confederates covered seven or eight miles by using the Gooney Manor road. This delayed them so much that it was nightfall when they reached the town.[17]

When Colonel Kenly withdrew from Front Royal across both forks of the Shenandoah, he took position on a commanding ridge known as Guard Hill. Although the burned-out North Fork wagon bridge might be utilized by infantry walking across in single file, it was too hazardous for Confederate cavalry. Lieutenant Colonel Thomas Flournoy of the Sixth Virginia discovered a practicable ford and soon Companies A,B,E, and K of about 250 troopers, accompanied by Jackson, were splashing across the river. Kenly, realizing that his position on Guard Hill was untenable in view of the swarming numbers of Confederates all around him, ordered a retreat northward. He tried to make a stand at the little village of Cedarville, about three miles in his rear. Scarcely had he taken position when he found himself attacked by overwhelming numbers.

When Flournoy's troopers gained the Cedarville side of the two rivers, Jackson joined them in a relentless pursuit of the retreating Federals. Captain George A. Baxter of Company K from Loudoun County was greatly exasperated when he found his advance impeded by two riders in front of him who were moving at a slower pace. The elder was described as "wearing a dingy gray coat and an old military cap pulled well forward and rode a raw-boned sorrel horse, while on his right rode a youth who was more neatly dressed." Not recognizing either of them and believing them to be disassociated with the company ahead, Baxter in strong language commanded them to "get out of the way of my men." One can well imagine Baxter's consternation when the younger rider, motioning toward his companion, replied, "This is General Jackson." Recovering quickly from his mistake, Baxter waved his hat and led three hearty cheers for General Jackson.[18]

Even though his artillery and reinforcements were not at hand, Jackson ordered the Sixth Virginia to press the advance. When Kenly's New York cavalry was unable to check the Southern horsemen, he ordered his infantry to defend the newly-established line at Cedarville. The Confederate troopers had some difficulty spreading out into the fields, as the turnpike to Winchester was bounded by rail fences on both sides of the highway. The New York cavalry in its haste to escape the hotly-pursuing Virginia troopers dashed through the ranks of the Federal infantrymen and unnerved them considerably. Jackson ordered Captain Baxter to take his command and Company A to assail the enemy on the right of the turnpike while the other two companies maneuvered to the left and up the middle of the highway. Giving the order, "Left into line," Baxter led his men at a gallop. Urging them to follow his lead and charge into the midst of the defending Federals, the brave cavalry leader succeeded in breaking the enemy line. It was a Pyrrhic victory, however, as he was killed by a musket shot fired at close range. Kenly and his officers made gallant efforts to stem the tide of hard-charging graycoats but all to no avail. The brave Federal colonel himself was cut down with a dreadful wound. The intensity of the hand-to-hand combat was such that one man in Company B was pierced with fourteen bullets. Another, Lieutenant George F. Means of Company K, had the misfortune of seeing his horse being killed with bayonets and in falling pinning his rider to the ground and rendering him helpless. Before the hapless Confederate could be dispatched by the enemy using clubbed muskets, he was rescued by a Sergeant Fout of his company.[19]

The crowded masses of panic-stricken infantry were completely at the mercy of the hard-charging gray troopers who fell upon them with saber and revolver before they could even fix bayonets. Although the first fusillade of the defenders emptied many saddles, the attackers continued to press on. The Southern horsemen surrounded one of the artillery gun crews and literally cut the gunners to pieces. The other gun crew managed to escape but abandoned its gun on the wild flight to Winchester. When a fresh Confederate squadron appeared on the scene, the Federal defense disintegrated completely. Hundreds laid down their arms. Companies D and I of the Sixth Virginia arrived in time to join in the pursuit. The other companies of the Sixth and those of the Second Virginia were delayed by the difficulty in crossing the rivers at Front Royal and thus missed most of the fighting at Cedarville. The Confederate victory was complete. 250 gray-clad troopers, sensing success and charging at the right moment, followed their bold leaders with a devotion that was typical of Turner Ashby and the Seventh Virginia who were seeing action in another part of the field. Flournoy's men captured over 600 Federals, including 20 officers and a complete section of artillery. In addition, the defeated force lost 32 killed and 122 wounded. Confederate casualties were much less, for they were reported as 11 killed and 15 wounded. A Federal colonel was so impressed by the sudden and well-delivered attack that he estimated the Confederates to number 3,000 men.[20]

Colonel Kenly was also grealty impressed with the Confederate success. He had a Confederate cousin, T.M.C. Paxson, who was a member of Company K. When Paxson was detailed to accompany the wounded prisoners to Winchester the day following the Cedarville fight, the wounded Kenly, lying in an ambulance, recognized him and called to him. After talking for a few minutes, the Federal colonel asked his cousin to what regiment he belonged and when he learned that it was the Sixth Virginia, he commented, "Do you know that you men made the greatest cavalry charge yesterday on record?" He added the information that he had organized his men so as to repel the attack, and they had maintained their position until the Confederate troopers had overrun them. He ventured the opinion that history nowhere records an instance where so small a force of cavalry had charged and overcome so greatly superior a force of infantry supported by cavalry and artillery.[21]

Jackson's actions at Front Royal and Cedarville had succeeded beyond all expectations. Ashby's two companies under Captains G.W. Myers and Edward McDonald had kept General Banks so confused that he believed that Jackson had a division south of Strasburg on the Valley pike.[22] As has been related, Ashby himself had cut the telegraph and rail communications between Strasburg and Front Royal by his attack on the Union garrison at Buckton. Jackson's main force had deceived Banks by using the Massanutten Mountain as a screen and by marching northward in the Luray Valley instead of the Main Shenandoah Valley. He had captured Front Royal with its vast quantities of supplies of all kinds, had made prisoners of most of the Federal garrison, and was now threatening Banks's main supply depot at Winchester. He had accomplished all of this with the loss of about 100 Confederates.

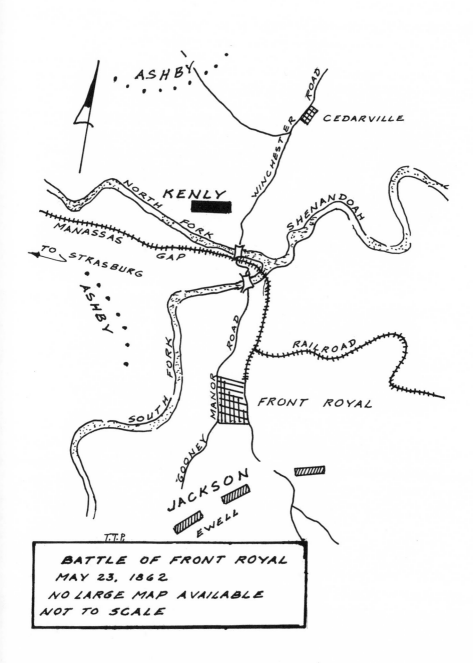

ASHBY

CEDARVILLE

WINCHESTER ROAD

KENLY

NORTH FORK

SHENANDOAH

MANASSAS

GAP

TO STRASBURG

ASHBY

SOUTH FORK

GOONEY MANOR ROAD

RAILROAD

FRONT ROYAL

JACKSON

EWELL

T.T.P.

BATTLE OF FRONT ROYAL
MAY 23, 1862
NO LARGE MAP AVAILABLE
NOT TO SCALE

CHAPTER IX

WHERE IS THE CAVALRY?

While all these events were transpiring to the east of him, General Banks seemed unperturbed at Strasburg. Having no knowledge of the overall situation, he minimized the importance of what was happening on May 23 and seemed to think he had plenty of time to make and execute his plans. Jackson's attack began at 1:00 P.M., but three hours elapsed before Banks was apprised of the reverse at Front Royal. He remained firm in his conviction that Jackson was still at Harrisonburg, sixty miles away. When a panting courier brought him news of Kenly's misfortune, Banks was inclined to dismiss it as a Confederate raid. To the disgust of one of his brigade commanders, Colonel George H. Gordon, he remained unconvinced of any threat to his army or his supply base at Winchester. When Gordon persevered with his entreaties to at least send northward the sick and wounded, to say nothing of the immense supplies, Banks replied, "I must develop the force of the enemy. By God, sir, I will not retreat! We have more to fear, sir, from the opinions of our friends than the bayonets of our enemies!"[1] Except for dispatching a regiment and two guns to Buckton, he did nothing until 3:00 A.M. on the morning of May 24 when he sent his sick and wounded to Winchester. His division left the fortifications at Strasburg about the middle of the morning of the 24th and had not progressed more than a few miles along the Valley Pike when it was struck by Confederates coming from the east. Considering the fact that either Banks or one of his chaplains had described Strasburg as the "dirtiest, nastiest, meanest, poorest, most shiftless town I have yet seen in all the shiftless, poor, mean, nasty, dirty towns of this beautiful valley,"[2] the federal general showed a great reluctance in leaving. Truth to tell, General Banks was afraid of being thought afraid.

When Stonewall Jackson made his battle plans after the capture of Front Royal, he had no easy task. He did not have accurate information about the strength of Banks at Strasburg, which was about 8,000. As far as the Confederates knew, it could have been from 12,000 to 15,000 men. Once Banks learned of the Confederate success at Front Royal, Jackson had no way of determining what his opponent would do. Banks could withdraw north-

133

ward down the Valley Pike to his main base at Winchester or he could, perhaps, cut in behind Jackson and march eastward through Front Royal, cross the Blue Ridge Mountains, and join Federal forces east of the mountains; or, he might march westward from Strasburg and unite with Frémont in the Alleghenies. Jackson, therefore, worked out a plan of battle that he hoped would deal with all the contingencies.

Jackson decided to send Ashby with his Seventh Cavalry toward Strasburg and a staff officer, supported by Taylor's Louisianians, toward Middletown about five miles north of Strasburg and hence nearer to Winchester. The staff officer was ordered to make frequent reports to his chief about what was taking place in the Middletown area. The other cavalry regiments, the Second and Sixth Virginia, temporarily commanded by Brigadier General George "Maryland" Steuart, were sent to Newtown, five miles south of Winchester also on the Valley Pike. Jackson ordered Ewell to move to Nineveh, a small village two miles north of Cedarville on the Front Royal-Winchester Turnpike. What was left of Stonewall's force was to remain at Cedarville preparatory to heading for the Valley Pike at Middletown.[3] In his official report, which was written almost a year later, Jackson stated:

> In the event of Banks leaving Strasburg he might escape toward the Potomac, or if we moved directly to Winchester he might move via Front Royal toward Washington city. In order to watch both directions, and at the same time advance upon him if he remained at Strasburg, I determined, with the main body of the army to strike the turnpike near Middletown, a village 5 miles north of Strasburg and 13 miles south of Winchester.[4]

Obeying Jackson's orders to watch the Front Royal-Strasburg road until he was sure of the route of Banks's retreat, Ashby posted vedettes on his left and with his main force headed toward Middletown. He sent Major Funsten to strike the Valley Pike farther north, in the vicinity of Newtown. Although Banks and most of his infantry had passed the point of contact when the Confederates reached the Valley Pike, Funsten struck a Federal wagon train with its escort and forced the enemy to seek safety by trying to take another route to Winchester. This was known as the Back Road or Cedar Creek Road and is located west of the Valley Pike. The Confederates pursued so closely, however, that the bluecoats set fire to their wagons and scattered through the fields. This dispersion caused the Southerners to scatter in order to capture them.[5]

After skirmishing with Federal reconnoitering parties, Ashby came up with the rear elements of Banks's army at Middletown. Although his command had been greatly depleted by companies detailed to picket duty and other types of work reserved for horse-soldiers, he gathered what few men he could muster and led them in riding among the enemy teamsters and stragglers. Leaping over stone fences, he and his men rode among the enemy's teamsters and their escorts, overturning wagons, setting fire to others, and capturing many prisoners. Crying out to his men to charge the enemy, Ashby led the way and was so impetuous that his recklessness sometimes caused him to be separated from his followers. When some of the Federals, despairing of advancing northward, tried to go back to Strasburg, they encountered the cavalry of Captain Sam Myers. They escaped into the South Branch Valley, going by way of Wardensville and Capon Springs.

The main body of Federals, however, continued their hasty retreat to Winchester. At Newtown an artillery officer managed to hold off the pursuing graycoats until darkness came to his rescue. Ashby brought up Chew's and Poague's guns in reply, but Federal sharpshooters behind cover picked off his gunners. In order to end this needless loss of life, Ashby ordered his artillerymen to cease firing while he led a charge that drove the annoying sharpshooters away. Night ended most of the fighting except for occasional out-bursts.[6]

Ashby's effectiveness in attacking the wagon train and its cavalry escort was mitigated by the fact that he had so few of his troopers on hand. His command had been reduced so much by detached groups that he had hardly enough men left to operate ef-fectively. Ten of his companies had accompanied Jackson in the McDowell Campaign and upon its conclusion most of these men had been sent to the gaps in the North Mountain to keep an eye on Frémont. Four companies under Captain Sam Myers were sent to Strasburg to watch Banks and to make him think that Jackson's army was in the Main Valley. Another company was watching Shields, who was marching toward Front Royal from the east. Two companies were left at Front Royal to assist the Twelfth Georgia Infantry in guarding the prisoners and supplies captured at Front Royal and Cedarville. One other company was detailed on scout duty near Strasburg. When Ashby had to send other men to guard the prisoners captured at Middletown, it is understandable that he had only about one hundred men left under his immediate command.[7]

In Jackson's official report of the operations at Middletown he commented:

I accompanied the movement of the main body of the army to Middletown. Upon arriving there we found the Valley turnpike crowded with the retreating Federal cavalry, upon which the batteries of Poague and Chew, with Taylor's infantry, promptly opened, and in few moments the turnpike, which had just before teemed with life, presented a most appalling spectacle of carnage and destruction. The road was literally obstructed with the mingled and confused mass of struggling and dying horses and riders. The Federal column was pierced, but what proportion of its strength had passed north toward Winchester, I had no means of knowing. Among the surviving cavalry, the wildest confusion ensued, and they scattered in disorder in various directions, leaving, however, some 200 prisoners, with their equipments, in our hands. A train of wagons was seen disappearing in the distance toward Winchester, and Ashby, with his cavalry, some artillery, and a supporting infantry force from Taylor's brigade, was sent in pursuit.[8]

As part of Jackson's overall plan to strike at the Federals along the Valley Pike, General George H. Steuart had been ordered to take the Second and Sixth Virginia Cavalry Regiments to Newtown, five miles south of Winchester. When he arrived there, before noon on the 24th, he discovered the road filled with a long line of wagons. A few shots threw everything into confusion. Teamsters fled in all directions, wagons were overturned and plundered, and the Confederates continued the work of destruction until Banks sent forward a regiment of cavalry and a brigade of infantry. These Federal reinforcements drove off the attacking Confederates, and what was left of the wagon train continued its northward march.[9]

Meanwhile Banks proved himself very skillful in retreat. Realizing that the Confederates must have been without food for some time, he decided to try to delay their pursuit of his retreating army by discarding wagons and supplies in hopes they would yield to the temptation to help themselves. He was not disappointed, for both infantry and cavalry abandoned their main objective in order to treat themselves to articles that they had not seen in a long time. Ashby's ill-disciplined troopers, many of whom had just volunteered to join his command, were particularly susceptible to this trick. Even Jackson indulged in the luxury of dismounting, helping himself to a dirty, hard cracker found in an overturned wagon, and attempting to eat it. Although he seemed able to get along without much nourishment and rest, he remembered that he had not eaten anything since early morning.[10]

According to Henry Kyd Douglas, "Ashby's cavalry, having given themselves up, in their hunger, to plundering wagons were so reduced in numbers that they were virtually inefficient. That the defeat of Banks was not his destruction is due to the failure of the cavalry at the critical moment, and General Jackson never ceased to lament and condemn that costly want of discipline."[11]

James B. Avirett, Ashby's chaplain, was very resentful of the criticism directed against his chief because most of Banks's army had escaped to Winchester. In this connection he asserted:

> No one will pretend to say that the plundering after the initial success at Middletown was entirely confined to the infantry. Colonel Ashby was too busily engaged with the important duty of keeping up the panic and preventing the enemy from getting artillery in position to play upon the pursuers, to attend to or prevent it, and regretted extremely that any member of his command should have so forgotten his duty on this occasion. The charge, however, that the plundering was for the most part confined to the cavalry is as untrue as it is unkind. That body of noble patriots known first as the Ashby Cavalry, and afterwards, under William E. Jones and Rosser as the Laurel Brigade, which still preserves with lofty pride the memory of such men as Sheetz, Fletcher, Marshall, Myers, Magruder, Jamie Thomson, and the gallant Coyner, shall not be branded with impunity as stragglers and plunderers, *par excellence,* while a grateful people retain the recollection of what was accomplished by them under the lead of Ashby.[12]

Banks was also aided in his escape to Winchester by the skill and ingenuity of Colonel George H. Gordon, who had charge of the rear guard. He organized defense after defense and, in the absence of pursuit beyond Newtown, was successful in saving a large part of the Federal army.

Apparently it became quite a joke among the Confederates in the Valley about the fact that Jackson got so many of his supplies from the Federals. At Front Royal he had captured about $300,000 worth of all kinds of things needed by an army and this amount was augmented by what was gained in the attack at Middletown. It was even surmised that the ever-present lemons which Jackson enjoyed so much and which were scarce in the Confederacy because of the Union blockade came from the enemy. Since Banks was one of Jackson's chief suppliers, he was known as "Commissary" Banks. According to an account that has survived in the files of the *Confederate Veteran,* there were two large wagon manufacturers in Wheeling, West Virginia, that made wagons for the Federal army. One, Messrs. Bodley Brothers, turned out wagons for the Army of the Potomac, while the other, Messrs. Moffatt and McKnabb, likewise supplied Banks's army. The writer who was the source of this episode attended to most of the latter's fire insurance after the war and reports that

Mr.McKnabb informed him that his firm generally shipped from 50 to 75 wagons to the Valley every Monday morning and that Jackson's cavalry was in the habit of capturing every one of the wagons before the next shipment. One morning McKnabb brought to his insurance agent's office a letter which he had received from General Jackson and which had been sent him by a paroled Federal soldier. It read:

> Messrs. Moffatt and McKnabb, Wheeling, Va.
> Dear Sirs:
> I have just received your last consignment of wagons. I like them very much; but hereafter please make their *tongues a little stronger*, as many of them are broken off when turned over to me.
> T.J. Jackson[13]

When Banks finally reached Winchester, he thought he was safe. After reassuring his superiors in Washington, he obtained a comfortable place for his headquarters and indulged in the luxury of a leisurely bath. Although he felt confident that Jackson would not attack him in Winchester, he was disturbed by the sounds of small-arms fire to the south. By midnight he realized that the Confederates were indeed approaching the city and he, therefore, sent his military train through Martinsburg to the safety of the Potomac. When dawn arrived on Sunday, May 25, Jackson's gray-coated "foot cavalry" were entering the city's southern outskirts.

Jackson had continued to press the Federals retreating from Middletown and Newtown, even though his men were in no condition to do so. Many of them had marched eighteen miles on May 24, had fought numerous skirmishes with the enemy, and had not eaten since dawn. The demanding Confederate general was anxious to continue the pressure on Banks so that he could not take advantage of the high ground near the city for defense purposes. However, several ambushes and the exhausted condition of his men convinced the reluctant Stonewall to order a few hours' rest.[14]

Although Jackson's wagon trains were far behind, impeded by a bad road in the Luray Valley, his ammunition conveyances were nearer at hand. When he expressed surprise at this situation, his chief quartermaster, Major John A. Harman, informed him that since the ammunition wagons were ahead of the other vehicles, he had brought them through by doubling the teams. General Taylor of the Louisiana Brigade observed of Jackson, "Without physical wants himself, he forgot that others were differently constituted, and paid little heed to commissariat; but woe to the man who

failed to bring up ammunition! In advance, his trains were left far
behind. In retreat, he would fight for a wheelbarrow."[15]

While the Confederate officers and soldiers gathered a few hours
of sleep, Jackson and Ashby stood silent sentinels. To keep awake,
they walked up and down the Valley Pike. As soon as dawn arrived, Jackson prepared to put his battle plan into execution. While
Ewell attacked along the Front Royal pike and moved against
Banks's left flank, part of Jackson's force would hold the Federal
center. The major thrust would be against the Federal right flank.
Banks had taken possession of the range of hills southwest of the
town and was prepared to fight.

As soon as dawn appeared, Jackson attempted to take advantage of a morning mist as cover and advanced the Stonewall
Brigade. As the Confederates advanced, they noticed the enemy in
possession of a long ridge southwest of Winchester. As this hill
commanded the road, Jackson ordered General Winder to occupy
it.[16] When the Stonewall Brigade marched toward the hill, it met
no resistance, for the Federals had abandoned it and withdrawn
toward Winchester. At the same time Ewell's division advanced
down the Front Royal road, toward Winchester. One of his
regiments, the Twenty-first North Carolina, advanced so far that it
penetrated the enemy's lines. A surprise volley from Federal infantry behind a stone fence decimated their ranks. Ewell then sought
to outflank the enemy. The Stonewall Brigade, having taken its
objective, found the position untenable because of devastating artillery fire from the enemy. Winder's men fell back to take refuge
in ravines and other places where they could find some protection.
Jackson ordered Captain Poague to bring up his batteries to
answer the Federal challenge. Before the Confederate artillery
could fire a shot, it suffered frightful casualties at the hands of an
enemy battery. When Jackson noticed Federal infantry marching
into position behind a stone wall in order to support the guns, he
ordered Carpenter's Battery to the aid of Poague.[17] It was eventually necessary for Poague to fire solid shot into the stone wall in
order to end the murderous fire of sharpshooters behind it. This
had the desired effect as far as the infantry was concerned, but
Poague's gunners were so outranged by the Federals that they
continued to suffer serious losses. When Winder found that he
could not make any headway against the Federal artillery, he requested Jackson to send infantry to turn the right flank of the
bluecoats.

Jackson agreed with his brigadier general. He lost no time in
ordering eleven regiments to turn the right flank of the stubborn

Courtesy of John W. Gott

Private Bladen Dulany Lake, Company A, Seventh Virginia Cavalry

Federals who had been holding up his advance for three hours. With Dick Taylor's Louisiana Brigade, supported by those of Taliaferro, Scott, and Elzey leading the advance, the Confederates charged up the hill and caused the enemy to withdraw in the wildest confusion. A Federal cavalry attack against Wheat's Louisiana Tigers was stopped dead in its tracks, with many empty saddles testifying to the unerring accuracy of the infantrymen.

The Confederates' assault had not been without great losses. As they approached the enemy lines, infantry and artillery fire tore great holes in their ranks. They did not falter but closed up ranks and marched on as if on dress parade. Once when Taylor observed some of his Louisianians attempting to duck shells that were whistling overhead, he demanded, "What the hell are you dodging for? If there is any more of it, you will be halted under this fire for an hour."[18] The sound of their commander's voice, which they grealty respected, produced the desired effect for the men looked as if they had swallowed ramrods.

One of the Confederates who fell in battle that day was Lieutenant Charles Marshall Barton of the Newtown Artillery. Lieutenant Barton's home was in Winchester.[19]

Meanwhile, the other Confederate troops met with success. On their right, Ewell sent Brigadier General Isaac Trimble to roll up the left flank of Banks's defense line. Winder continued on the Valley Pike. The encircling movements on both of their flanks, plus the pressure from the center, were too much for the embattled Federals, who seemed to have but one objective—put as much distance as possible between themselves and the victorious Confederates. They streamed throught the streets of Winchester in utmost confusion and vied with each other in their efforts to reach the Martinsburg Pike on the northern side of town. Occasionally, some braver than the others attempted to make a stand in the streets of the town but their efforts were in vain. As the Southern infantrymen pursued as best they could in their exhausted and famished condition, Federals surrendered by the hundreds. Even the townspeople showed their displeasure at the Federal occupation of their town, for they added to the discomfort of the bluecoats by throwing rocks, pouring scalding water, and even firing shotguns and flintlocks at the retreating enemy. In vain did Banks and his fellow-officers attempt to stem the panic which, according to one account, was comparable to that displayed by the Federals at the First Battle of Bull Run.

"My God!" General Banks shouted at a mob of fleeing soldiers. "Don't you love your country?"

"Yes," came a reply from some unknown soldier," and I am trying to get back to it as fast as I can!"[20]

In their effort to prevent huge amounts of all kinds of military supplies from falling into the hands of the Confederates, the Federals set fire to the buildings in which they were stored. Townspeople assisted soldiers in putting out some of the fires, with the result that Jackson captured badly-needed medical supplies, all kinds of food, guns, ammunition, horses, and wagons.

With Banks's army in full retreat toward Martinsburg and Williamsport on the Potomac, Jackson followed with vigor. Here was an ideal situation to be climaxed by a relentless pursuit by the cavalry. One of Jackson's principal maxims of war was his firm belief that an army commander should mystify, mislead, and surprise the enemy so as to cause him to flee and then continue the pursuit as long as possible. He felt that Banks, even though heavily outnumbered and in command of a demoralized army, should not be allowed to make a stand but should be pushed as rapidly as possible. The Confederate infantry and artillery had conducted themselves with great credit, but they were too exhausted to apply as much pressure on the Federals as Jackson wanted. Obviously this was a situation made to order for Confederate cavalry. Jackson looked in vain for his troopers to charge into the mass of panic-stricken enemies with pistol and saber and not allow time to regroup and make a stand so the bulk of the army could escape.

When General Taylor asked his chief, "Where is the cavalry?" Jackson was so disgusted that he could only glower and remain silent. He remembered that he had not seen Ashby since before daybreak and that "Maryland" Steuart, in charge of Ewell's troopers, was not in evidence. Steuart commanded the Second and Sixth Virginia Regiments which had performed so creditably at Cedarville. Stonewall dispatched his aide-de-camp, Lieutenant Sandie Pendleton, to find Steuart and give him an order "to move as rapidly as possible and join me on the Martinsburg turnpike, and carry on the pursuit of the enemy with vigor."[21] After much hard riding Pendleton had located the object of his search about three miles east of Winchester with his troopers taking it easy while their horses refreshed themselves in a clover field.

In response to Jackson's order, Steuart, a West Pointer who was a stickler for details, refused and maintained that he could not move until he had received orders from his immediate superior, General Ewell. No amount of remonstrance on the part of Pendleton could budge the pedant from his stand. Imploring him to the last and emphasizing the urgency of quick action by the cavalry, the aide rode off to find Ewell. When "Old Bald Head" heard about Steuart's failure to obey Jackson's orders, he exploded with a variety of oaths and gave Steuart the necessary command. Unfortunately for Jackson, two hours had elapsed before Steuart's 600 troopers reached the Martinsburg Pike and Banks had made good his escape. Steuart pursued as far as Martinsburg, where he captured a number of prisoners and some supplies, but he could not catch up with the fast-retiring Federal army before it reached the Potomac at Williamsport.[22]

Where was Turner Ashby? When the cavalry chief finally rode up to Jackson with a few troopers after the Battle of Winchester, Ashby explained that he had moved to the enemy's left in order to cut off a portion of his force.[23] According to a recent appraisal:

> Ashby had squandered one of the finest cavalry opportunities of the war, and it was a blunder which could not be remedied. Ashby and Steuart finally combined at least 800 sabers, but they were too late for decisive action. Banks had been handed the time he needed to regroup. He pulled some artillery into line outside Martinsburg, and the rebels backed away. The Federals were safely across the Potomac by sundown.[24]

This same study of the Valley Campaign also refutes the statement that Ashby's attack on Banks's wagon train at Middletown was made less effective because so many of the Confederate troopers had been detailed elsewhere for scouting and picketing. In this connection the author relied on the word of Captain Harry Gilmor that his company alone had been left to watch Frémont after the Battle of McDowell. It will be recalled that Ashby's chaplain, in attempting to defend Ashby's command from the plundering charge at Middletown, had said that ten companies had been left behind in the mountains. Gilmor is supported by Trooper Bill Wilson, who wrote in his diary for May 22: "That portion of Ashby's cavalry which has been camped for the last three or four weeks at Mt. Crawford, Lacey Springs and this place [New Market] together with ten companies just returned from accompanying Jackson on his expedition to McDowell received marching orders." These directed them to cross the Massanutten Mountain with Ashby. "It is true that one or two companies were detached from Ashby's immediate control to act as scouts and couriers for Headquarters, while four companies were deployed above Strasburg; but even deducting all of the detachments cited by Avirett which were not specifically refuted by Gilmor and Wilson accounts for only eight companies of a command which Avirett numbered at twenty-six companies."[25]

Major Robert L. Dabney, Jackson's assistant adjutant general, whose biography of his chief provided many details about the eccentric commander, was also very critical of Ashby's Cavalry. Referring to the Middletown affair he wrote:

> Nearly the whole of Colonel Ashby's cavalry present with him, and a part of the infantry under his command had disgracefully turned aside to pillage; so that their gallant commander was compelled to arrest the pursuit. Indeed, the firing had not ceased, in the first onset upon the Federal cavalry at Middletown, before some of Ashby's men might have been seen, with a quickness more suitable to horse-thieves than to soldiers, breaking from their ranks, seizing each two or three of the captured horses, and making off across the fields. Nor did these men pause until they had carried their illegal booty to their homes, which were, in some instances, at the distance of one or two day's journey. That such extreme disorders could occur, and that they could be passed over without a bloody punishment, reveals the curious inefficiency of officers in the volunteer Confederate army.[26]

While this breakdown of discipline cannot be condoned under any circumstances, one should be reminded that the Confederate troopers had to supply their own horses and received no compensation for their loss by disease or capture. This might partly explain the troopers' eagerness to appropriate as many of the enemy's horses as they could obtain.

Major Dabney was also critical of Ashby's actions after the Battle of Winchester had been won and Banks's defeated army was retreating to Martinsburg. After the war, Dabney wrote that on the morning of May 25, the troopers were so scattered that Ashby could collect only a handful of them and with these "he had undertaken an independent enterprise, to cut off a detachment of Federalists on their left; and passing around the scene of action he joined in the pursuit many hours after, at Bunker Hill..."[27]

Ashby's men could not allow these accusations to remain unchallenged. They were quick to rise to the defense of their idol and, as a result, there has come down to posterity another one of those unfortunate controversies so characteristic of the Civil War, especially among the Confederates. As might be expected, one of Ashby's most outspoken defenders was Chaplain Avirett, who rarely criticized anything done by his chieftain. In giving a detailed account of Ashby's movements on the day of the Battle of Winchester, Avirett wrote:

> Ashby's advance led him across the Northwestern Grade a little west of the town. As soon as he saw the complete success of the Confederate arms, he swooped down upon the flying masses of the enemy, which, rushing wildly forward, sought every avenue

of escape, crowding the roads, and even fields leading to Pughtown and the North Mountain, as well as the more direct turnpike leading to the Potomac. Along the left of the enemy's main line he was busy in capturing squads of them and sending them to the rear. Those who stood in the court-house yard in Winchester, where the prisoners were guarded, will remember that he was sending in squads of prisoners during the entire day. The reader will bear in mind, as we have said before, that Banks's men retreated by no one particular line; but that to the north-northeast and northwest of the town the fields as well as roads were literally blue with the retreating foe. Of the 3,000 prisoners captured during this movement, nearly all, except the 700 found in the hospitals, were taken in small squads, seldom exceeding fifteen or twenty. It is needless to follow Ashby along his whole ride to Bunker Hill;—suffice it to say that, in proportion to his force no officer contributed more to swell the spoils of victory. It is true that "when Jackson issued into the open ground again at the Martinsburg turnpike," the movements of his faithful cavalry officer did not come within range of his eye as it eagerly swept over the fields, "dark with a confused multitude of fugitives utterly without order or thought of resistance." But the un-tiring Ashby was at work behind the hills which shut out the crowds of fugitives who sped along their western bases in wild dismay. And if, when he reached Bunker's Hill, he had by his side but a "handful" of his tired troopers, he had sent many handfuls of the enemy back to the rear under guard of his men, thus from time to time reducing his little band. Doctor Dabney is both unjust and ungenerous towards the unfaltering soldier...[28]

In his biography, Avirett continued to exonerate Ashby from the charges made against the cavalry leader. In order to clarify his position concerning what actually happened at Middletown and Winchester, he wrote someone who should have known, Lieutenant Colonel Roger Preston Chew, the youthful commander of Chew's Battery, whose horse artillery was attached to Ashby's Cavalry. It is interesting to note that although the State of West Virginia was formed in 1863 and the artilleryman's letter was written in 1867, like many residents of his home county, Jefferson, he stubbornly refused to admit that he was living in the new state. This delusion lingered among Jefferson's residents until 1871 when the United States Supreme Court by a vote of 6 to 3 awarded the disputed area to West Virginia.[29] Colonel Chew replied to Avirett in a lengthy letter, part of which reads as follows:

Charlestown, Va., January 18th, 1867

Mr. Avirett,
Dear Sir: I have the pleasure to acknowlege the receipt of yours through Mr. White, this evening. With reference to the affair referred to by Dr. Dabney, I will give you a statement of the facts as far as my observation and knowledge extend. General Ashby follow-

ed the infantry of General Jackson with a detachment of his
cavalry, (a portion of it having been sent down the Shenandoah
Valley to confront the enemy at Strasburg). I accompanied him
with my guns. He diverged from the Front Royal and Luray road
and struck the railroad as you know at Buckton. I was not with
him, until I rejoined the head of the army near Cedarville. Here
General Ashby, with his cavalry, my battery, two guns of
Poague's battery, and some infantry skirmishers, left the turnpike
and pushed for Middletown. When he arrived in sight of the place,
we discovered the enemy in the town, and immediately opened on
them with artillery. General Ashby detached his cavalry, and sent
them, under Major Funsten, to strike the turnpike at some point
between Middletown and Newtown, with a view of cutting off the
enemy in his front from retreat to Winchester. After a short delay,
to enable this force to reach its destination at the proper time, he
formed his skirmishers and advanced rapidly across the fields to
the lower portion of the town. Here he encountered a considerable
force of cavalry, and running up his artillery to within a hundred
yards, opened on the Yankees with artillery and small arms. The
enemy, crowded in the turnpike, gave way and retreated in all
directions. Ashby dashed in among them, and, pistol in hand,
captured himself many prisoners. Major Funsten in the meantime
had reached the turnpike below Middletown, perhaps two miles,
and forced the retreating Yankees towards the Back Road, besides
capturing a large wagon-train. It was here that the cavalry
became dispersed, and the reasons why Ashby failed to have his
cavalry in hand the next morning, as I always understood them
were these:—The cavalry we defeated at Middletown retreated
towards North Mountain and Winchester, scattered, in fact completely routed. Major Funsten prevented those retreating towards
Winchester from pursuing their retreat in that direction, and forced them to retreat across the hills, as I said before, towards the
Back Road. Our cavalry, of course, pursued, and of necessity in
pursuing a scattered foe, became dispersed themselves. Ashby
pursued with my guns towards Winchester, and, when we reached the point where Funsten struck the turnpike, we threw the
guns into position, and Ashby, with about forty men, charged a
line of the enemy's infantry between us and Christman's house.

Gen. Ashby had started from New Market with but a portion of
his cavalry. They had marched until the horses were exhausted—without rest day or night; and when the enemy became
dispersed and fled in the greatest confusion, our cavalry pursued
and *scattered in pursuit* of the enemy. Major Funsten had but a
very small detachment when we reached him, and we had passed
the wagon-train where the plundering was reported to have occurred, and the cavalry were not there, and unless they returned
after we passed, the infantry and not the cavalry got the benefit of
the spoils. This has, at any rate, always been my impression. Gen.
Ashby pushed the enemy with this small force of cavalry and my
guns, through Newtown, and until dark, when we went into camp
to feed our exhausted horses—having pursued the enemy at a

gallop from hill to hill between Middletown and Newtown. Gen. Jackson now pushed forward, and evening found him before the enemy at Winchester. Our cavalry had pursued the enemy until dark, and the whole army pressing forward, *prevented them from reassembling, and, the day following, Gen. Ashby was almost without a command.* [Italics supplied by author of this book.] Gen. Ashby was with Gen. Jackson on the morning of the battle of Winchester, while the latter was engaged in planting his batteries. I know nothing of his subsequent action until after the battle. I overtook him below Stephenson's depot, dashing upon the enemy whenever an opportunity offered, with a handful of men. I was never aware of any *independent enterprise* of Gen. Ashby's, nor do I believe he was anywhere but at the front of the army with a small force of his cavalry. The rapidity of Gen. Jackson's movements, added to the confusion attending the march of a large army, prevented our cavalry from re-forming after they were scattered. *I always believed that the matter was misrepresented to Gen. Jackson, and hence his severe criticism upon the cavalry* [italics supplied by author of this book]. It was certainly unfortunate for Ashby, as well as the cause, that his men were not with him on that day, as an excellent oportunity was afforded for the employment of cavalry. Yet I do not believe he was to be blamed with their absence. It was then popular to say Gen. Ashby exercised no control over his men beyond personal influence, that there was no discipline in his command. It was boasted that his successes were gained, not by skillful manoeuvre [sic], but by reckless dash and courage of himself and men; but I will do him the justice to say that he could always command more men for duty from the same muster-rolls than any cavalry commander under whom I have since served. While he was not possessed of brilliant intellect, his complete self-possession under all circumstances, and that absence of fear or regard for personal security, enabled him at all times to exercise a cool and clear judgment. I have served at different times during the war with almost all the prominent cavalry leaders of Virginia, and I have never seen one who possessed the ability to inspire troops under fire with the courage and enthusiasm that Ashby's presence always excited. His modesty, combined with his gentleness, rendered him agreeable to all who came in contact with him. He was always bold in his operations with cavalry, and believed in charging the enemy whenever opportunity afforded. He adopted in the beginning of the war the tactics with cavalry by which later in the war other cavalry commanders could only secure success—namely, always meeting the enemy by bold and determined charges, and when defeated, to press them with the utmost vigor. I have always believed his audacity saved Gen. Jackson's army from *total destruction* at the battle of Kernstown...[30]

While the present writer does not wish to belabor this point indefinitely, he does feel that the serious criticism of Ashby's actions requires the inclusion of any evidence that might throw additional

Courtesy of the Library of Congress

Lieutenant Colonel Thomas L. Kane, Commander of the Pennsylvania
Bucktails Who Three Times Saved the Life of Turner Ashby

light on the matter. At the risk of boring the reader unnecessarily, he includes the following extract from Chaplain Avirett's book:

>...the writer has been informed by Lieut. Joseph Wood and Private Alfred Tanquary, Company C, Twelfth Virginia Regiment of Cavalry, Laurel Brigade, that Ashby, at the head of his troopers, accompanied by Maj. Funsten, charged *through the town of Winchester* with drawn sabres, taking Braddock Street first where it is entered by Water from the west. They say, furthermore, that Ashby *in the advance* continued to drive the enemy, not allowing them time to form until with about 400 cavalry they made a short stand at the "Yellow House," 8 miles north of Winchester. The pursuit was energetically continued beyond Darksville that night. Lieut. Wood remembers that this was the only time he ever saw Gen. Ashby run his horse. These gentlemen both live in the vicinity of Winchester, and went through the Confederate struggle with honor to themselves. They concur with the writer in saying that there is no ground for Dr. Dabney's expression of an "independent enterprise" on the part of *Gen. Ashby,—who was at no time during the pursuit over a mile west of the Martinsburg turnpike.* [italics supplied by author of this book]. They say he had not a large force of cavalry...[31]

General Richard Taylor, whose Louisiana Brigade had performed so brilliantly in turning Banks's right flank in the attack, south of Winchester, was, like Jackson, greatly disappointed in the failure to capture the bulk of the enemy's retreating army. Like Jackson, he put the blame on the cavalry and in his interesting book entitled *Destruction and Reconstruction* he wrote:

>Past the town [Winchester], we could see the Federals flying north on the Harper's Ferry and Martinsburg roads. Cavalry, of which there was a considerable force with the army, might have reaped a rich harvest, but none came forward. Raised in the adjoining region, our troopers were gossiping with their friends, or worse. Perhaps they thought that the war was over...
>
>Here I will "say my say" about Confederate cavalry; and though there were exceptions to the following remarks, they were too few to qualify their general correctness. The difficulty of converting raw men into soldiers is enhanced manifold when they are mounted. Both man and horse require training, and facilities for rambling, with temptation to do so, are increased. There was but little time, and it may be said less disposition, to establish camps of instruction. Living on horseback, fearless and dashing, the men of the South afforded the best possible material for cavalry. They had every quality but discipline, and resembled Prince Charming, whose manifold gifts, bestowed by his sisters, were rendered useless by the malignant fairy. Scores of them wandered about the country like locusts, and were only less destructive to their own people than the enemy. The universal devotion of Southern women to their cause led them to give indiscriminately to all wearing the gray. Cavalry officers naturally desired to have as

large commands as possible, and were too much indulged in this desire. Brigades and regiments were permitted to do work appropriate to squadrons and companies, and the cattle were unnecessarily broken down. Assuredly our cavalry rendered much excellent service, especially when dismounted and fighting as infantry. Such able officers as Stuart, Hampton, and the younger Lees in the east, Forrest, Green, and Wheeler in the west, developed much talent for war; but their achievements, however distinguished, fell far below the standard that would have been reached had not the want of discipline impaired their efforts and those of their men.[32]

Jackson himself, in his official report of the engagements at Middletown and Winchester which was written almost eleven months later, was also very critical of his cavalry. In referring to the fight at Middletown, he wrote:

From the attack upon Front Royal up to the present moment every opposition had been borne down, and there was reason to believe if Banks reached Winchester, it would be without a train, if not without an army; but in the midst of these hopes I was pained to see, as I am now to record the fact, that so many of Ashby's command, both cavalry and infantry, forgetful of their high trust as the advance of a pursuing army, deserted their colors, and abandoned themselves to pillage to such an extent as to make it necessary for that gallant officer to discontinue farther pursuit. The artillery, which had pushed on with energy to the vicinity of Newtown, found itself, from this discreditable conduct, without a proper support from either infantry or cavalry...[33]

In the same report, referring to the fight at Winchester on May 25, Jackson voiced his disappointment again with his cavalry. In this connection he wrote:

The Federal forces, upon falling back into the town, preserved their organization remarkably well. In passing through its streets they were thrown into confusion, and shortly after, debouching into the plain and turnpike to Martinsburg and after being fired upon by our artillery, they presented the aspect of a mass of disordered fugitives. Never have I seen an opportunity when it was in the power of cavalry to reap a richer harvest of the fruits of victory. Hoping that the cavalry would soon come up, the artillery, followed by infantry, was pressed forward for about two hours, for the purpose of preventing, by artillery fire, a reforming of the enemy, but as nothing was heard of the cavalry, and as but little or nothing could be accomplished without it in the exhausted condition of our infantry, between which and the enemy the distance was continually increasing, I ordered a halt, and issued orders for going into camp and refreshing the men.
...
There is good reason for believing that, had the cavalry played its part in this pursuit as well as the four companies had done

under Colonel Flournoy two days before in the pursuit from Front
Royal, but a small portion of Banks's army would have made its
escape to the Potomac.[34]

With all the conflicting evidence, it is very difficult to determine
who was to blame for the cavalry's alleged gross dereliction of duty. As has already been mentioned, Major Dabney's biography of
his hero, Stonewall Jackson, puts most of the blame on Turner
Ashby. Other biographers of Jackson, especially G.F.R. Henderson and John Esten Cooke, share the same opinion. On the other
hand, Ashby's defenders are legion, especially those who served
under him. They include, besides Colonel Chew, Chaplain Avirett,
and Lieutenant Wood, Captain William N. McDonald, and a
surgeon on Ashby's staff, Dr. Thomas L. Settle. Practically all
agree that Ashby's troopers were relatively few both at Middletown and Winchester. While Jackson in his report was critical
of Ashby's troopers for their pillaging at Middletown, he does not,
unless by inference, blame his colonel for not having them under
better control. He devotes more space to the failure of General
Steuart to obey his order to begin the pursuit immediately.
Jackson and Ashby had spent part of the night of May 24-25 in
each other's presence and if Jackson gave his cavalryman specific
orders to be executed on the 25th, they cannot be found. It is
unlikely that if Jackson had done so, Ashby would have undertaken the "independent enterprise" to which Major Dabney referred. Since Ashby was later made the Chief of Cavalry in the Valley, it
would appear that Stonewall Jackson must not have been too
displeased with his service several days before. In the reorganization
of the cavalry which followed, Steuart was transferred to the infantry
and his two regiments were placed under Ashby.

In spite of Jackson's disappointment that Banks had managed
to escape across the Potomac with the bulk of his army, Jackson
could be very proud of his victories at Middletown and Winchester. He had driven Banks out of the Valley into Maryland, had
inflicted 3,500 casualties on his opponent, had captured 9,000
small arms, 2 cannon, medical supplies, cattle, sheep, and many
wagons. All of this had been accomplished at a cost to himself
of only 400 men, 329 of whom were wounded, 68 killed, and 3
missing.[35]

As for the unfortunate General Banks, after he had reached the
safety of the Maryland shore of the Potomac at Williamsport, he
tried to preserve what was left of his reputation as an army commander in his official report of the fighting at Front Royal, Middletown, and Winchester. It makes amusing reading:

It is seldom that a river-crossing of such magnitude is achieved with greater success. There were never more grateful hearts in the same number of men than when at midday of the 26th we stood on the opposite shore. My command had not suffered an attack and rout, but had accomplished a premeditated march of near 60 miles in the face of the enemy, defeating his plans and giving him battle wherever he was found.[36]

Banks fooled no one.

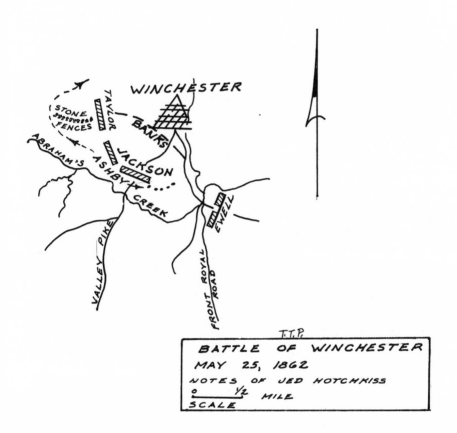

CHAPTER X

ESCAPING THE TRAP

Stonewall Jackson's victories at Front Royal, Middletown, and Winchester had dispelled much of the optimism that had formerly prevailed in Union circles. It will be recalled that McDowell had been preparing to leave Fredericksburg in order to reinforce McClellan at Richmond. On the very day of the Winchester engagement, May 25, McClellan bombarded Confederate lines in the Richmond suburbs; and three days later Joseph E. Johnston was preparing an offensive before McDowell could bring his reinforcements. Rumors of impending disaster poured into Washington.

President Lincoln and Secretary of War Stanton sent out calls for more troops to protect the capital city. The governors of thirteen states were requested to call out their militia, and troops were sent from Washington and Baltimore to reinforce Brigadier General Rufus Saxton, the commander of the Federal garrison at Harpers Ferry. Lincoln wired McClellan either to launch a vigorous attack on Richmond or else to return to the defense of Washington. Patriotism was running so high that on one day almost half a million civilians volunteered their services. McDowell was ordered to send about half of his corps, consisting of Shields's and Ord's infantry divisions and Bayard's brigade of cavalry, numbering over 21,000 officers and men, to retrieve Federal fortunes in the Valley. At the same time Frémont was commanded to lead his force from Franklin to Harrisonburg.[1]

Realizing that he had his opponents confused and wishing to capitalize to the fullest upon his victories, Jackson rested his army and then sent the Stonewall Brigade, with Poague's and Carpenter's guns to Harpers Ferry. This would give the Washington authorities additional cause for alarm in view of the fact that the Ferry is only sixty miles from the capital. Lincoln's concern was not lessened when he received word from Brigadier General John W. Geary, who was stationed east of the Blue Ridge, that Jackson with 20,000 troops was moving through Ashby's Gap and Aldie toward Centreville.[2] Although Geary's information proved to be utterly without foundation, the President did not know this at that time.

155

Another reason for Jackson's thrust to Harpers Ferry was his desire to give his chief quartermaster, Major John A. Harman, time to collect enough wagons to move southward the huge quantities of supplies that had been captured. These were considerable and it taxed all of Harman's ingenuity to meet the challenge. When he had assembled all of his wagons, surreys, Conestogas, etc., he estimated their length to be eight miles. One shortcoming which he had that disturbed the straight-laced Stonewall was his liberal use of profanity. Perhaps this was a holdover from the days when Harman had operated a stage line. On one occasion when Jackson was critical of his quartermaster for allegedly not working hard enough, Harman attempted to resign. When the army commander realized that he had gone too far, Harman joined Ashby in becoming one of the few men to make Jackson back down.[3] According to General John D. Imboden, Major Harman was the only man who could swear before Jackson with impunity. Apparently the devout Jackson felt that swearing was a necessary qualification for anyone who tried to work with balky horses and mules, and he was willing to condone its use by such a person.[4]

On May 28, the Stonewall Brigade met an enemy detachment at Charles Town and after a fight of twenty minutes drove it back to Bolivar Heights, a low ridge which defended Harpers Ferry from the southwest. Ewell and Jackson followed in support of Winder, and on the 29th most of the Valley Army went into position near Halltown and Harpers Ferry. The Louisiana Brigade occupied Berryville, and the Twelfth Georgia Regiment remained in Front Royal to guard the prisoners and military stores that had been captured from Colonel Kenly. Turner Ashby and his troopers were posted on the Wardensville road, west of Strasburg, so they could keep a close watch on Frémont. One of the regiments from the Stonewall Brigade, the Second Virginia, crossed the Shenandoah River and ascended Loudoun Heights.[5] Since there was no bridge over the river where they wanted to cross, the infantrymen solved the problem by having each man grab hold of the tail of a horse, while its owner swam his animal across.

Meanwhile, Lincoln and Stanton planned an ambitious trap that included a junction at Strasburg of three Federal armies for the purpose of cutting off Jackson's retreat southward along the Valley Pike. As has been stated, Frémont had been ordered to move from Franklin across the Alleghenies to Harrisonburg.[6] After making a half-hearted attempt to carry out these orders, he found the road blockaded and changed his plans to march northward to Moorefield, and then eastward so as to enter the Valley at

Strasburg. Shields's division, leading McDowell's advance from, Fredericksburg, passed through Manassas Gap on the way to Front Royal. At Stanton's insistence Major General E.O.C. Ord's division would proceed to Alexandria by water so as to protect Washington and then march to the Valley.[7] A reinforced Banks was expected to close the pincers by moving southward up the Valley Pike. As these Federal armies totaled about 64,000 men and Jackson had but 16,000, it is obvious that his exposed position in the Lower Valley portended ill for the Confederates. To complicate his problem further, Stonewall had left at Winchester his captured prisoners and supplies.

Both McClellan and McDowell had protested very vigorously against Lincoln and Stanton's plan to interrupt the projected reinforcement of McClellan's army with McDowell's corps but all to no avail. They felt that Shields and Ord could not reach the Valley in time to cut off Jackson's retreat and that Frémont's threat should be enough to cause Jackson to fall back, but according to Lieutenant Colonel Matthew F. Steele, whose textbook on military tactics and strategy has been used at West Point for years, "...Mr. Stanton was directing this campaign; it was he who was pitted against Lee and Jackson in the game of strategy. He would listen to no advice or protests from McDowell and McClellan, and by his obstinacy and his ignorance of the science of war he probably set back the fall of Richmond and the Confederacy just three years."[8]

Before Jackson left Winchester to advance to Bolivar Heights, he had received alarming news about the Federal threat to his little army. His aide, Sandie Pendleton, had been awakened during the night of May 27-28 at Jackson's Headquarters at the Taylor Hotel. When Sandie met the cause of the interruption to his sleep, he discovered an elderly gentleman who was insistent that he was the bearer of information vital to the safety of the Valley Army. He stated that he had ridden a great distance in order to forewarn Stonewall. He revealed further that the Washington authorities feared that Jackson was strong enough to cross the Potomac into Maryland and might be able to capture Washington. The informer stated that he had observed a column of Shields's division that by forced marches was within a day's travel to Front Royal.[9] Although Stonewall realized the calamitous results that could come if the Federal strategy were successful, he continued his plans to march to Harpers Ferry. He wanted to frighten Lincoln all he could and draw McDowell as far as possible from Richmond.

While at Charles Town, General Jackson was a guest at the home of Major Wells J. Hawks, his chief commissary. Although

Hawks was a native of Massachusetts, he entered business in the South and established a carriage factory in Charles Town. It is interesting to note that when Jackson was dying, in his delirium he said, "Tell Major Hawks..." However, he left the sentence unfinished but later cried, "Let us cross over the river and rest under the shade of the trees." After Jackson's death Hawks served on the staffs of Generals Richard S. Ewell, Jubal A. Early, and for a short time, Robert E. Lee.[10]

As Jackson and his staff were returning to Hawks's home for dinner, a young cavalry lieutenant rode up and asked, "General, are the troops going back?"

He received the reply, "Don't you see them going?"

Not satisfied with this answer, the lieutenant asked, "Are they all going?"

Jackson turned to Colonel Abner Smead and said, "Colonel, arrest that man as a spy." The offending officer could hardly believe his ears but was rescued from his dilemma when Turner Ashby intervened and informed Jackson that his fellow-trooper did not have much sense.[11]

Having remained at Harpers Ferry as long as he felt it was prudent, Jackson decided to retire to Winchester, collect his prisoners and captured supplies, and retreat up the Valley before Lincoln and Stanton's offensive to capture him could be consummated. Before he left his Halltown headquarters, he called his friend, Colonel Alexander R. Boteler, before him and requested the latter to undertake an important journey to Richmond. Citing the need for reinforcements, Stonewall informed Boteler of the growing Federal efforts to cut off his retreat. He stated that his present force was probably strong enough to baffle the existing enemy armies and to send off the prisoners and supplies; however, the Confederate leader was confident that if his command could be increased to 40,000 soldiers, he could invade Maryland, raise the siege of Richmond, and transfer the fighting from the banks of the James River to the banks of the Susquehanna.[12]

Jackson told Boteler to take a train at the Charles Town station and proceed immediately to Winchester, where Major Harman would provide transportation to Staunton. Although Boteler made good time on the trip to Charles Town, he had hardly reached the station before Jackson arrived with Sandie Pendleton. The army commander, after leaving word for his men to follow, had decided to go by rail to Winchester so as to arrive there before his troops. As soon as he had gotten aboard, Jackson fell asleep and remained asleep most of the journey. His rest was interrupted when Boteler

THOMAS L. ROSSER

Major General Thomas L. Rosser, Commander of the Laurel Brigade,
Successor to Ashby's Cavalry

recognized a Confederate horseman who was furiously riding across the fields near Summit Point in a desperate effort to flag the engineer and stop the train. Realizing the apparent urgency of the rider's mission, Boteler awakened Jackson who ordered the train stopped. The horseman proved to be a courier with a dispatch which revealed the alarming news that Shields had already reached Front Royal, had driven out Colonel Z.T. Conner's Twelfth Georgia Regiment of Infantry, and had captured some prisoners, as well as supplies the Confederates were unable to destroy. Unperturbed, Jackson tore up the paper, ordered the conductor to resume the journey, and went back to sleep.[13]

Unfortunately for the Confederates, this bad news turned out to be remarkabley accurate. In fairness to the Georgians, it should be pointed out that the Twelfth Georgia Regiment, which had belonged to Edward Johnson's command, was a fine fighting unit. When Shields's men burst through the Blue Ridge at Front Royal on May 30, they apparently caught Conner by surprise. The regimental commander lost his head and hastened toward Winchester. His second in command, a major, thinking escape was impossible, wanted to surrender but the enlisted men refused to do so. Encouraged by a 60-year-old captain, William F. Brown, who assumed command, the regiment made good its escape to Winchester. In this disaster the Southerners had to destroy supplies and stores worth $300,000 and to leave behind six officers and 120 men.[14]

After Jackson had reached his hotel headquarters in Winchester he allegedly sent for Colonel Conner and had the following conversation with him: "Colonel, how many men did you have killed, Sir?"

"None," Conner replied.

"How many wounded?"

"None, Sir," said he.

"Do you call that much of a fight?" Jackson retorted and then he ordered the colonel placed under arrest.[15]

While Jackson was preparing the papers he desired Boteler to take to Richmond, the Confederate Congressman visited his only son, a youth in his teens who had received two serious wounds in the battle on the 25th. He was then lying disabled at the home of a Winchester friend. Boteler not only saw his son but also his wife who had managed to reach the bedside. He then returned to the hotel late at night and ordered two whiskey toddies to be sent to his room. Thinking that Jackson needed some stimulant to carry him through the critical days ahead, Boteler offered one of the

glasses to Jackson who at first refused to imbibe and then began
the following conversation exchange:

> "No, no, colonel, you must excuse me; I never drink intox-
> icating liquors."
> "I know that, general," said Boteler, "but though you habitual-
> ly abstain, as I do myself, from everything of the sort, there are oc-
> casions, and this is one of them, when a stimulant will do us both
> good, otherwise I would neither take it myself nor offer it to you.
> So you must make an exception to your general rule and join me
> in a toddy tonight."
> Jackson again shook his head, but, nevertheless, began sipping
> some of the tumbler's contents. After a few drinks, he put the con-
> tainer on the table and resumed the conversation:
> "Colonel, do you know why I habitually abstain from intox-
> icating drinks?" Receiving a negative reply he continued:
> "Why, sir, because I like the taste of them, and when I
> discovered that to be the case, I made up my mind at once to do
> without them altogether."[16]

After Boteler had left for Richmond in his effort to obtain reinforcements for the Valley Army, Jackson turned his attention to
the more immediate problems facing him. There was no doubt but
that his position was becoming more serious with each passing
hour. He had to reach Strasburg ahead of his opponents, for the
Valley Pike was the only escape route over which he could send
his captured prisoners and supplies. Shields had captured Front
Royal, twelve miles east of Strasburg, while Frémont was approaching the junction point from Wardensville to the west. When
the Valley Army, with the exception of the Stonewall Brigade still
at Halltown, reached Winchester, it was eighteen miles north of
Strasburg. On Saturday, May 31, Jackson instructed Jed Hotchkiss to go to Charles Town, contact General Winder, and help to
bring up the Stonewall Brigade. As Charles Town is twenty-two
miles northeast of Winchester, not a moment could be lost.
Jackson had told Hotchkiss to try to bring off the Stonewall
Brigade through Winchester but that if the engineer discovered
that the enemy occupied the town, he was to use a route through
the mountains and join the rest of the army at Strasburg.
Although Jed, the topographer, got lost en route to Charles Town,
he eventually contacted Winder.

Winchester, which is estimated to have changed hands seventy-
two times during the Civil War, is referred to as the "Bandy Ball."
Although the Battle of Kernstown was sometimes called the Battle
of Winchester by some Northerners, it is generally known by the
former name. However, there were three other engagements
known as the Battle of Winchester. On May 25, as has been

related, Jackson drove Banks out of the town. On June 14, 1863, General Ewell defeated Major General Robert Milroy, and on September 19, 1864, Major General Philip H. Sheridan bested General Jubal Early in the most decisive contest of the three. The town and county records of Winchester were sent to Luray for safekeeping in the war. During its occupancy by the Federals some of Banks's men discovered in the museum of the Winchester Medical College some papers identifying a corpse as having been that of one of John Brown's sons. At the time of the Harpers Ferry raid in October, 1859, some of the medical students had gone to the river town and had found a corpse of one of the raiders near the bank of the Shenandoah River. Realizing the need for bodies to be used for dissection, they obtained a box and brought their find back to Winchester. When this fact was revealed to General Banks, he ordered that the college buildings be burned.

Another Winchester landmark that was destroyed by the Federals was *Selma*, the home of former United States Senator James M. Mason. The senator had been a prominent politician in the history of the Old Dominion and, after the formation of the Confederacy, had been appointed Minister to England. Along with John Slidell, who had been appointed to represent the South in France, the two politicians had been seized by a Federal warship from the English vessel, the *Trent*. England was outraged by this insult to her flag and war talk was heard, but the situation was eased when Lincoln released his controversial prisoners. Since the Trent Affair, as the incident was called, had taken place a few months before, it is believed to have instigated the destruction of the Mason home. [17]

Early in the morning of May 31, the Valley Army left Winchester in an effort to reach Strasburg ahead of the encircling Federals. The march was slowed by the miles of wagons carrying off the captured supplies. According to Jed Hotchkiss, the wagon train was eight miles long, although other estimates say it stretched for seven miles, two wagons abreast. Then came the prisoners, 2,300 of them, guarded by the Twenty-first Virginia Regiment under the capable command of Lieutenant Colonel R.H. Cunningham. Next were the thousands of infantrymen, who were followed by hundreds of stragglers. Many of the latter were given assistance by being taken up behind the saddles of Flournoy's and Munford's cavalrymen.[18] As the graycoats were spread out for fifteen miles along the Valley Pike, there was an excellent opportunity for enemy cavalry to strike. Shields had sent a capable cavalry officer, Brigadier General George D. Bayard, to take his brigade to the aid of Frémont, but the Southerners were not molested on the route to Strasburg. Great was their relief when the Valley Army reached the environs of Strasburg, and they found it unoccupied by the enemy! Some fighting occurred that day between a Confederate outpost and Federal brigade about halfway between Front Royal and Strasburg.[19] Although Frémont was getting close from the west, the escape route was still open.

When Jackson reached Strasburg with most of his army, he went into camp just north of town. He sent his trains on ahead through the town and along the Valley Pike southward. He ordered Ewell to leave at dawn, move on the Wardensville road, and check Frémont who was only three miles away. The Stonewall Brigade was not yet on the scene but was expected the next day. General Winder, who had been waiting at Halltown for his Second Regiment to rejoin him from Loudoun Heights, had left at dawn on May 31 in a pouring rain, marched through Winchester, and had gone into camp at Newtown. Thoroughly exhausted, the men sought shelter from the relentless rain and went to sleep without benefit of food. Four of their regiments had covered twenty-eight miles that day and the Second Virginia had marched thirty-five miles and had not eaten for two days.[20]

In the retreat from Winchester the Valley Army straggled badly. Private John O. Casler of the Thirty-third Virginia Infantry Regiment has left us an interesting account of the activities of his unit as seen by a man in the enlisted ranks. In his book entitled *Four Years in the Stonewall Brigade* he estimated that 500 of his fellow- soldiers had remained behind in Winchester after the Confederate withdrawal. After leaving the Charles Town vicinity and marching until dark, the men learned that because of the danger threatening their retreat route, they would have to undergo a forced march. Not desiring to comply, they decided to spend the night with some of their Winchester friends and rejoin their comrades the next day. Some of them found convenient quarters, where they enjoyed the luxury of comfortable beds and good meals. When they arrived in Newtown, they encountered Confederate cavalry with the alarming news that the enemy had cut them off from the Valley Army. The horsemen suggested that the foot-soldiers leave the Valley Pike, move into the mountains on their right and, under the protection of the friendly Alleghenies, move southward until they could rejoin their commands. This they did, although they were not able to effect a junction until they reached Harrisonburg.[21]

Turner Ashby's Last Fight

General Turner Ashby's troopers had been busily engaged in observing Federal troop movements and reporting to General Jackson. When the cavalry commander reached Winchester on May 30, he was instructed to take his cavalry and artillery on the Front Royal road and engage any hostile force found there. Because of some mixup in Federal plans, Shields's men, upon leaving Front Royal, had taken the road to Winchester instead of the one to Strasburg. When the mistake was finally discovered, much valuable time had been lost, and the troops disgustedly retraced their steps. Encountering a body of Federal infantry at Cedarville, Ashby's troopers, with the assistance of Chew's Battery, sent the bluecoats back to Front Royal. He then went to Middletown, where he was relieved to find Winder's Stonewall Brigade. As one of Winder's aides rode up to him, Ashby asked, "Is that General Winder coming up?" When the aide replied in the affirmative, Ashby answered "Thank God for that!" After Winder put in his appearance, Turner resumed, "General, I was never so relieved in my life. I thought that you would be cut off and had made up my mind to join you and advise you to make your escape over the mountain to Gordonsville."[22]

Ashby continued to watch the approaching Federals and sent several companies to watch Shields, as well as others to observe Frémont. He ordered his men to report any troop movements to Jackson's Headquarters on Hupp's Hill just north of Strasburg. With the remainder of his command he escorted the Stonewall Brigade to Strasburg.

Jackson visited Dick Taylor around the latter's campfire and seemed unusually communicative. He apparently needed someone with whom he could share his thoughts. He gave the Louisianian the latest information he had received. Shields had abandoned the attempt to close his part of the pincers on the embattled Confederates, for,. instead of marching from Front Royal to link up with Frémont, he was moving southward up the Luray Valley. Unless something was done to upset his plan, he might march to Luray and then turn eastward, cross the Massanutten Mountain, and reach the Valley Pike at New Market. If these plans materialized, he could cut in south of Jackson and thus bar his escape. Or he could move southward from New Market and capture the Confederate wagon train at Harrisonburg. Jackson told Taylor that Frémont was only three miles to the west of Strasburg and had to be met and checked the next morning. Jackson felt that the immense trains, filled with captured stores, were so important that he was going to give their defense his personal attention. As for

Frémont, he entrusted the capable Ewell with the job of keeping him at bay. Some of Taylor's men expressed the belief that Jackson's anxiety about the wagons was because of the lemons among the stores![23]

Early on the morning of June 1, "Old Bald Head" Ewell's division engaged the advance of "the Pathfinder," General John C. Frémont. As the Stonewall Brigade had not yet reached the main army, Ewell's orders were to check the enemy's advance but not to commit himself too far. Several miles west of Strasburg, he established contact with Frémont and exchanged artillery and musket fire. When he went out to his skirmishers, he saw a large number of bluecoats; but the enemy did not advance. Taylor suggested that he move his Louisiana Brigade so that it would be at right angles to the Federal front and would be in position to develop the enemy's intentions. When he reached their flank, he forced its retirement. According to his own statement, "Sheep would have made as much resistance as we met." Although both he and Ewell wished to pursue their advantage, they had their orders not to bring on a general engagement and their familiarity with Stonewall convinced them that he was not to be disobeyed. When the fighting had practically ended, Jackson ordered his infantry commanders to resume the southward trek along the Valley Pike. He designated Taylor's Brigade to protect the western flank and Ashby's Cavalry to serve as the rear guard.[24]

Stonewall Jackson had performed a miracle. By hard work, fast marching, constant scouting, forceful leadership, and military sagacity, he had escaped the trap that Lincoln and Stanton had laid for him. He had had a very narrow escape from a noose that could have dealt him a serious setback. Of course he was aided by the timidity and fear displayed by his opponents, but the chief credit for his success was due to his own leadership and that of his officers, as well as the stamina of his "foot cavalry." Several weeks later when Colonel Boteler asked Jackson what he would have done if Shields and Frémont had united their forces at Strasburg so as to have prevented his retreat up the Valley, he replied," I should have fallen back into Maryland for reinforcements."[25]

CHAPTER XI

ASHBY'S LAST CHARGE

The Valley Army had escaped the Federal trap at Strasburg, but there was no time to relax. Frémont had 15,000 troops, while Shields had 10,000 with more on the way. Back along the Potomac, Banks and Saxton had been reinforced until they had 15,000 soldiers. To oppose these forces, Jackson had but 16,000 men. Obviously if the enemy armies were to unite and march rapidly after the retreating Confederates, the bluecoats might redeem their tarnished reputation as fighting units. Fortunately for Frémont, Shields had sent him General George D. Bayard's cavalry brigade, which proved to be a big improvement over the troopers to which Frémont had been accustomed. Bayard was a West Pointer later mortally wounded at Fredericksburg.

The danger threatening Jackson's escape route was that Shields might advance rapidly up the Luray Valley and then turn westward to intercept Stonewall at New Market, where the Luray-New Market road met the Valley Pike. To accomplish this, Shields would have to cross the South Fork of the Shenandoah near Luray and then ascend Massanutten Mountain. In other words, he could retrace the route that Jackson had taken before he surprised Kenly's Federals at Front Royal.

Jackson was equal to meeting this new threat. When he discovered that Shields had been in possession of Front Royal for forty-eight hours and had not effected a junction with Frémont at Strasburg, he suspected that the Federal officer was attempting to get in his rear at New Market.[1] Without losing any time, he dispatched some of Ashby's Cavalry to destroy the Columbia and White House bridges across the South Fork of the Shenandoah. This was accomplished successfully. Although the South Fork contains many fords and is not a formidable obstacle before its junction with the North Fork near Front Royal, unusually heavy rains in May and June, 1862 had swollen its waters considerably. Thus topography aided Jackson in his effort to keep the two enemy commanders from joining forces.

As soon as he could get his army in motion for the southward march, Jackson left Strasburg on the evening of June 1. Even though his men had not rested sufficiently from the arduous

167

marching of the previous week, he kept them moving all night. With Frémont following and Shields attempting to intercept him, he had no time to lose. Confusion reigned everywhere. Many of the units were hopelessly intermingled; and generals and colonels were wandering about in an effort to locate their commands. With each delay in getting started, Stonewall became more and more impatient. He was so exasperated with an officer whose brigade was divided into two or three parts that he upbraided him in the following conversation: "Colonel, why do you not get your brigade together, keep it together, and move on?"

"It's impossible, General; I can't do it."

"Don't say it's impossible. Turn your command over to the next officer. If he can't do it, I'll find someone who can, if I have to take him from the ranks."[2]

During the night of June 1-2 the Federal cavalry, emboldened by Jackson's withdrawal, pressed the Confederate rear guard, which was defended by Ashby and Steuart. Ashby had gone into camp near Tom's Brook, four miles north of Woodstock. In order to gain an advantage over the Southern troopers, some of the enemy succeeded in a ruse. Riding up to the Confederates, they said they were Ashby's Cavalry, and before their true identity was discovered, they had wreaked havoc. As some of Ashby's men were on patrol and the night was dark, it is understandable why the Federals were not identified earlier. They were able to get very close and succeeded in scattering the graycoats. Colonel Flournoy's Sixth Virginia, being nearest the enemy, fled in confusion and communicated their panic to Colonel Munford's Second Virginia. When these cavalrymen fled in all directions, they uncovered the Louisiana Brigade. General Taylor managed to end the rout by having his infantrymen make a stand.[3]

The rain continued to come down in torrents and did not make any distinction in regard to rank. Jackson and his staff were preparing to try to find shelter where they could spend the night in some degree of comfort. Before they were able to relax, a courier rode up to Stonewall with a note from Turner Ashby. The cavalry leader informed his superior that the Federals were pressing him vigorously and that unless he received infantry support, he might lose some of his artillery. Without losing a minute, Jackson ordered his staff to ride to Ashby. As it continued to rain hard and most of the staff were without overcoats or gum blankets, it was a most uncomfortable night ride of three miles to find the cavalryman. When they arrived at his side, they marveled at his unperturbability. He was protected by his innumerable gum blankets and capes and seemed as unconcerned as if there was not an enemy within fifty miles. When Jackson inquired about the Federals, he was told that they had stopped for the night and had not been active for several hours. Wondering about the urgency mentioned in the note, Jackson showed it to him. Ashby explained that he had sent the note at 8:00 o'clock in the morning when the enemy was pressing him hard and that he had been surprised that Jackson had not come to his aid. Left to his own resources, Ashby had succeeded in repulsing the attack. Apparently the courier to whom Ashby entrusted the message had carried the dispatch all day and then had given it to an unsuspecting colleague for delivery.[4]

Near Woodstock, Ashby incurred Jackson's displeasure for some irregularity and was relieved from the responsiblity of acting as rear guard.[5] Unfortunately careful research has failed to discover the details. According to Jed Hotchkiss, Ashby was "somewhat in disgrace." General Steuart mismanaged an enemy cavalry attack on the rear guard with the result that some of his men fled in panic. The resulting confusion caused the Twenty-seventh Virginia to mistake the Second Virginia Cavalry for Federals and to fire into them. Although he was not in charge, Ashby rallied a number of straggling infantrymen behind a thicket; and when the Federal attackers appeared, the Confederates emptied a number of saddles. The cavalry leader then mounted his stragglers on captured horses and at their head rode up to Jackson's Headquarters in Woodstock. Jackson complimented him and again placed him in command of the rear guard.[6] General Steuart's performance had so exasperated Colonels Flournoy and Munford that they went to Ewell and requested him to transfer their regiments to Ashby's command. When Ewell relayed this request to Jackson, he agreed and put Ashby in command of all the cavalry in the Valley.[7] Steuart returned to the infantry in Ewell's division and was placed in charge of one of the brigades formerly in Allegheny Johnson's force.

Stonewall Jackson's complimenting Turner Ashby and placing him in command of all the cavalry in the Valley seems all the more remarkable in view of the fact that he had opposed Ashby's promotion to brigadier general as has been noted earlier in a letter to Colonel Alexander R. Boteler dated May 6, 1862.[8] When the Richmond authorities felt different about the matter and promoted Ashby anyway a few weeks later, there was nothing Jackson could do but acquiesce. However, he did not have to place Ashby in charge of all his cavalry unless he felt, deep down, that his cavalryman's leadership qualities outweighed his disciplinary deficiencies.

Jackson's infantrymen began to realize that with General Ashby protecting their rear they were not likely to be overridden by Bayard's hardcharging troopers. Consequently, when they recognized his familiar figure riding among their columns, they responded with resounding cheers. Major William Goldsborough of the First Maryland Infantry Regiment related an interesting incident concerning Ashby's popularity with the infantrymen of his command. As the Marylanders were moving along the turnpike, they were overtaken by a swarthy Confederate officer who was sporting a long black beard. Goldsborough told his men, "Come, boys, yonder comes Ashby; let's give him a welcome." As a result, they responded all along the line with hearty cheers. However, when the officer saw Goldsborough, he drew rein and said, "Major, you have made a mistake. I am Major John Shack Green, of the Sixth Virginia Cavalry—a cousin of General Ashby." When Goldsborough related the experience to Turner Ashby a day later, the cavalry leader appreciated the joke and replied: "Never mind, Major, the cheers were given a very gallant officer."[9] When it is recalled that Turner Ashby's mother was Dorothea Green and the Greens were distinguished by dark hair and dark complexion, Major Goldsborough and his men can be forgiven for making a natural mistake.

Jackson's main problem was to move his trains and prisoners as rapidly as possible to Staunton and then try to defeat his foes separately before they could unite at Harrisonburg. Heavy rains that had fallen in the Valley made the fords impassable. Destruction of the Columbia and White House bridges across the South Fork prevented Shields from coming to the aid of Frémont. As the Massanutten Mountain ends in the Harrisonburg vicinity, it was possible to get to the Main Valley from the Luray Valley by going around its southern extremity. Since Shields had no pontoons and the roads in the Luray Valley were much worse than those in the Main Valley, his southward progress would, of necessity, be slow. The Valley Pike was macadamized.

In spite of the admonition which Sandie Pendleton had given Turner Ashby when he handed him the promotion at Winchester, Ashby failed to heed it. Pendleton, like most of the officers and men of the Valley Army, realized that continued reckless exposure of Ashby's person to the enemy guns would eventually end disastrously. Hence he had expressed the hope that the newly appointed brigadier general would be more careful. The Federals were likewise impressed with the bravery of the cavalry commander and were lavish in their praise. One of them, Colonel Marcy of the First Connecticut Cavalry in Frémont's command, was so struck by Ashby's bravery that he wrote:

> I have been in advance with my regiment most of the time from Strasburg, and the horse of General Ashby is a familiar object to us all, as he daily superintends the movements of Jackson's rear guard. As we see him on the outposts, he affords an excellent mark for our flying artillery as he is descried upon the hill in advance of us, seemingly never out of sight or absent from his post of duty. He is always the last man to move on after satisfying himself as to the movements of our forces. Many and many a time on this advance have I seen the rifled field-piece brought to bear upon him, and the solid shot go shrieking after him, striking within a few feet of him, throwing up clouds of dust over him, or else go singing over his head, dealing destruction to his men behind him.[10]

In order to delay Frémont's advance, Jackson hurried his command across the bridge over the North Fork of the Shenandoah just above Mt. Jackson and then ordered Ashby to destroy the structure. Although Frémont had pontoons, the river was rising rapidly and it would be difficult to prevent the bridge from being swept away by the swift current. On June 3 Ashby's men brought dry wood, gunpowder, and artillery shells and placed them on the covered wooden structure. When the combustibles were ignited, they burned furiously until the bridge was completely destroyed. Frémont did succeed in laying pontoons across the stream but was unable to keep them in place because of the swift waters. [11] As there had been a widespread downpour, the stream rose twelve feet in four hours. Some Federal cavalry got across before the pontoons became unusable. In some skirmishing, Ashby's fine gray stallion was mortally wounded but managed to walk a short distance above New Market, where he died. Ashby, himself, narrowly escaped with his life. The destruction of the North Fork bridge by Ashby delayed Frémont for twenty-four hours.

Another casualty of the Valley Campaign of 1862 was a rooster which belonged to Pete, the cook of the officers' mess of the Liberty Hall Volunteers. This bird had always enjoyed riding with his master on the officers' wagon, and Pete had boasted that it had whipped every rooster from Harrisonburg to Winchester. However, in the retreat of the Confederates up the Valley in the early days of June, 1862, the gamecock had come off second best at the spurs of a rival bird. Pete was so shaken by the setback to his pet that he consigned it to the pot with the explanation that "no chicken dat kin be whipped shall go 'long with General Jackson's headquarters [wagon]."[12]

Jackson was very anxious for his sick and ambulatory wounded to reach Staunton where they might be hospitalized. If the Federals approached too close to this important town in the Upper Valley, the convalescents could take the cars of the Virginia Central Railroad to Richmond. At Mount Crawford, south of Harrisonburg, the Valley Pike crosses North River, but the bridge had been destroyed. Jackson sent Captain J.K. Boswell to see if the structure could be repaired quickly, but he had to be content with a negative report because of the high waters. The problem was solved when the sick were transported across the stream in small boats.

No doubt Jackson wished for his expert bridge-builder who was called "Old Miles." It was said that this important figure could construct a bridge in the time it would take another man to take the measurements. On one occasion when Jackson wanted a bridge across the Shenandoah, he called Old Miles to his side and said, "You must put all your men to work, Miles, and must keep them at it all night for I've got to have a bridge across this stream by morning. My engineers will draw up the plans for you."

When Jackson, very much worried, met Old Miles early the next morning, he asked, "See here, how about that bridge? Did the engineer give you the plans?"

Old Miles, after taking a cigar from his mouth and flicking the ashes off, replied with a sneer, "General, the bridge is done! I dunno' whether the picter is or not."[13]

Since Jackson was still committed to the strategy of keeping the two Federal armies from uniting, he had to keep in mind the importance of the bridge across the South Fork of the Shenandoah at Conrad's Store. Possession of this crossing would enable Shields to round the southern end of the Massanutten and join forces with his Federal colleague. Accordingly, Jackson sent a cavalry force which destroyed it. In order to keep watch on Shields's movements, Jackson on June 4 sent for Jed Hotchkiss and directed him to take a signal operator with him and proceed to the top of the Peaked Mountain at the southern end of the Massanutten. From this position he could send reports of Shields's progress in the Luray Valley. When the two Confederates reached the top, they observed the head of Shields's column encamped two miles north of Conrad's Store near Big Spring. Having accomplished the object of their ascent of the mountain, they returned to Harrisonburg, where they learned that Jackson's command had taken the road to Port Republic.[14]

Still determined to keep his Federal opponents from joining forces, Jackson sent troops to Port Republic to gain possession of the bridge across the South Fork. This village is fifteen miles south of Conrad's Store. The North River and South River join at Port Republic to form the South Fork of the Shenandoah. The only way by which Shields could join Frémont at this location was to use the bridge across the North River. Although Port Republic was a small village, it lay astride the shortest road over the Blue Ridge Mountains through Brown's Gap to the tracks of the Virginia Central Railroad. If Jackson were ordered to join Lee in the defense of Richmond, this artery was of the greatest importance. Unfortunately for Jackson's plans, the road from Harrisonburg to Port Republic was not paved and because of the recent heavy rains was almost impassable. Jackson passed through Harrisonburg on the morning of June 5 and took the road to Port Republic. He found it so muddy that he ordered a commissioned officer to assign forty men to help each brigade train to get through. As a result of these conditions, progress was necessarily slow.[15] By nightfall, all of the prisoners and some of the wagons had reached the Port Republic vicinity. Since the bulk of the army was between Harrisonburg and Cross Keys, Jackson established his headquarters a mile from Harrisonburg.

When Brigadier General Turner Ashby went into camp near Harrisonburg on the night of June 5, he reflected on what the morrow might bring. As chief of cavalry in the Valley, he now commanded 1,000 horsemen and had the responsibility of trying to hold back the pursuing Federals long enough to enable Jackson to move his wagons loaded with captured supplies over the muddy road to Port Republic. To add to his problems, in General Bayard he had an adversary worthy of his tactical skill. It seemed as if the Federal cavalry commander could not be shaken off. Even the slow-moving Frémont, whose campaigning had been anything but distinguished, showed unaccustomed energy in pursuing the retreating Southerners. Ashby found it difficult to sleep; and pacing before his campfire, he planned his actions for the morrow.

In sharp contrast to the cloudy skies and heavy rainstorms that had plagued the Valley Army during most of its retreat southward, the morning of June 6 appeared bright and sunny. The beautiful country around Harrisonburg appeared in all its splendor. Ashby's rear guard duties required him to guard the east flank of the army from any advances that Shields might make as well as to protect Jackson's rear from any thrust by Frémont. He was kept busy skirmishing with the ubiquitous Federals during the morning but was not heavily engaged. He fell back through the town and, when the pressure eased, allowed his men to dismount and the horses to graze about two miles south of Harrisonburg.[16]

As Ashby was passing through town, he stopped at a large white house that stood at the end of a long street. Its owner, Colonel Douglas Gray, though a Union sympathizer, was his personal friend. Some of the Confederate troopers had dismounted to converse with a group of sweethearts and cousins and also to share some of the Grays' food that was available on short notice. Colonel Gray was approached by Ashby with the greeting, "How do you do today, Colonel Gray? Will you tell the young men that the enemy is advancing and to rejoin their commands at once?"

His host replied, "Certainly, General Ashby," and then repeated the order to a young girl on the porch who had been conversing with a few young troopers gathered around her. Instantly the men obeyed their commander. Before they said good-byes to their girl friends, the horsemen were allowed to fill their haversacks with provisions not available on the battlefield.[17]

General Ashby partook of a glass of milk, which was brought to him by one of the girls named Nellie. Leaning down so that only Nellie and the young captain with her could hear, Ashby said, "I suspect that fellow of trying to get through the lines to obtain information a little more frequently than is necessary; and if the Yankees catch my best scout, I shall know who is to blame." The soldier, Captain Charles Hilary, laughed and then mounted his horse in order to follow his chieftain. About that time Ashby noted a column of bluecoats marching down the long, wide street, whereupon he shouted: "Look! there is the head of the enemy's column. Ride at a quick trot, four abreast. We are leading to an ambush, they suspect, and will not follow too closely. As soon as over the hill, gallop to the command."[18] About two miles south of Harrisonburg, when the pressure eased, Ashby allowed his men to dismount and their horses to graze.

Suddenly there appeared a body of enemy cavalry coming down the road from the town. At Ashby's command, "Mount and form," the Confederate troopers got on their horses. As was Ashby's custom, he was preparing to meet a charge with a counter-charge. His plan of battle was very simple. He set an ambush for the advancing Federals and ordered some of his men into the woods on both sides of the road. After the unsuspecting enemy had passed, he proposed to charge them with the remainder of his command.

Fight of the Pennsylvania Bucktails at The Battle of Harrisonburg

Ashby's leadership qualities so impressed a member of his infantry escort that Private James Baumgardner, Jr., of Company A, Fifty-second Virginia Infantry, gave us this eyewitness account:

> ...The regiment to which I belonged was lying in the road a short distance in the rear of the line of cavalry. My attention was aroused by a sharp command given by General Ashby to the cavalry in the field on the south side of the road, and immediately afterwards I saw General Ashby gallop up to the high stake-and-rider fence between the field and the road. The splendid stallion on which Ashby was mounted leaped the fence and landed in the road a few feet in front of me, then leaped over the fence into the field on the north of the road. General Ashby galloped to the center and front of the cavalry there and gave the command to move forward. The cavalry started forward, first in a walk, then in a trot, then in a gallop, and then disappeared from my sight as they entered the woods on the slope of the hill, and next was heard his ringing voice as he commanded the charge. For a few minutes the supporting infantry in the road heard wild yells and shouts, the cracking of pistols, and the clanking of sabers, and then all was quiet.[19]

The First New Jersey Cavalry Regiment was approaching the Confederates. Its commander was one of the most interesting of all the foreigners involved in the American Civil War. He was an English soldier of fortune named Sir Percy Wyndham, who had seen service in the Revolutions of 1848-1849, as an ensign in the French Navy, the British Artillery, the Austrian Lancers, and, in 1860, in the Italian forces of Garibaldi. Two years later, he received a commission as colonel in the Federal forces. When he heard about what a gadfly General Turner Ashby was, he requested that he be sent to the Valley where, he boasted, he would "bag Ashby." His appearance was somewhat ludicrous. He was a large man sporting huge mustaches, and he seemed to be wearing every ornament permissible under regulations. He had low-topped boots with gold tassels hanging in front and spurs worthy of a caballero. His slouched hat with its plume did not improve his appearance.[20]

Ashby met this threat with a charge followed by a withdrawal. Wyndham was sure that the Confederate was retreating and, fearful that his quarry was escaping, he led a charge. He thought that his command was supporting his impetuous attack, when, much to his chagrin, he saw the Confederates closing in behind him. Before he knew what was happening, he and sixty-three of his fellow-horsemen were cut off and made prisoner. The remainder of the First New Jersey troopers turned around and rode furiously back to their infantry support. The Confederate cavalryman who captured the foreign adventurer was Captain Holmes Conrad of

Winchester who later became a major and served as assistant adjutant general on the staff of Major General Thomas L. Rosser.[21] As the first bluecoated prisoner, a private, was brought to the rear, he was questioned about what had happened. His reply was, "Percy Wyndham met the man he had so long sought, and I didn't think he'd care about seeing him soon again, for we've been smashed all to flinders."[22]

Greatly chagrined at the turn of events, Colonel Wyndham trudged to the Confederate rear on foot because his horse had been shot in the fighting. He was in a foul humor and was very resentful toward his own troops who, he felt, had started with him and then deserted him in the most cowardly manner. Suddenly he heard someone exclaim, "Percy! Old boy!" As he looked to see who was addressing him, he espied Major Chatham Roberdeau Wheat, commander of the Louisiana Tigers, who had served with him under Garibaldi in Italy. Exclaiming, "Why, Bob!" he embraced his former companion-in-arms before rejoining the prisoner ranks.[23] Wyndham's ridiculous appearance caused much laughter to his captors and one of them called out, "Look yonder, boys; there is a Yankee colonel." The Britisher exploded and exclaimed, "I am not a Yankee, you _____ Rebel fool!" Swearing profusely, the bragging foreigner found himself a prisoner of a group of ragged, shabby-looking Confederates.[24]

After the capture of Colonel Wyndham along with part of his command and forcing the remainder to retreat to their infantry support, there was a lull of several hours before the Battle of Harrisonburg was resumed. Late in the afternoon, Ashby noticed some of Frémont's infantry moving toward him. Hoping to repeat the successful ambush of Wyndham's cavalry regiment, he asked General Steuart for some infantry support. Steuart, having been transferred back to the infantry, refused the request until ordered by Ewell to cooperate with Ashby. Although Ewell was somewhat apprehensive of the success of this plan, he sent two regiments of infantry, the Fifty-eighth Virginia commanded by Colonel Samuel H. Letcher and the First Maryland led by Colonel Bradley T. Johnson. Ashby left Colonel Thomas Munford in charge of his cavalry and gave him the support of two guns from Chew's Battery. Ashby then retraced his steps toward Harrisonburg and rode into the woods on his right. He, himself, led the Virginia infantrymen, while he sent the Marylanders to attack the Federal flank. Although the Fifty-eighth Virginia was small in numbers, Ashby did not hesitate to lead them against the enemy, who were protected by a heavy rail fence. From this vantage point the Federals poured a destructive fire into the advancing Confederates.

Ashby's plan was to let Munford and the cavalry lure the enemy along the Harrisonburg road and then to use his infantry to attack the left flank of the bluecoats from their hidden position in the woods to the right.

Frémont's force in this encounter consisted of the Pennsylvania Bucktail Rifles, who were commanded by Lieutenant Colonel Thomas L. Kane, a brother of the famous Arctic explorer, Elisha Kent Kane. The Bucktails, as this regiment was commonly called, were crack companies of hunters and woodsmen who were from the mountainous region of Pennsylvania and who wore a bucktail in their cap. They were supported by two other regiments, the First Pennsylvania Cavalry and the Sixtieth Ohio.[25]

Ashby found his plan of flanking and surprising the enemy thwarted as the Bucktails had beaten him to the wooded area. The Confederates were now in an ambush. They kept firing at the enemy, but the protection afforded by the rail fence minimized the effect. Seeing his infantrymen falling on all sides from the murderous fire of the Bucktails, Ashby ordered his men to stop firing and to charge the enemy with the bayonet. He waved his hand toward the enemy and shouted, "Virginians, charge!" At this time his horse, a bay or cream-colored one, fell mortally wounded, and he had to lead his men on foot. Incidentally, this horse which had been loaned to the cavalryman by Lieutenant James Thomson of Chew's Battery, had been ridden by Stonewall Jackson at the First Battle of Bull Run. When Ashby saw his men begin to waver, he cried out again, "Men, cease firing! Charge, for God's sake, charge!" and he advanced several paces ahead. On the left was heard the hot fire of the Marylanders, who were rapidly advancing to turn the Bucktails' flank. The Pennsylvanians lived up to their reputation and continued to fire on the Virginians in their front and the Marylanders on their flank. While leading his last charge, Turner Ashby received a bullet wound in the heart and died instantly in the arms of his close friend, Lieutenant James Thomson.[26]

Ashby's sacrifice had not been in vain. He had encouraged his men so much that they continued the charge and finally drove the stubborn Bucktails from the field. The enemy lost 55 out of 125 that went into action. Among those left behind wounded was the gallant Colonel Kane, who was taken to the rear, as a prisoner. His admiration for Turner Ashby has been cited at the beginning of this book. When he later learned of the death of his brave adversary, he remarked to a person writing about the war, "Deal justly with the memory of Ashby. He must have been a noble fellow, a brave soldier, and a gentleman." [27] The Battle of Harrisonburg ended when the Federals retired to Harrisonburg. Ashby's last charge had gained enough time for Jackson to save his army, prisoners, and trains.

General Ewell was so impressed with the performance of his men, especially the First Maryland Regiment, that he complimented its commander, Colonel Bradley T. Johnson, and authorized a captured bucktail to be affixed to the color staff.[28]

Turner Ashby's men could hardly believe their ears when they heard that he had been killed. They were so accustomed to his reckless exposure when leading charges against the enemy that they believed the enemy bullet had not been molded that could end his life. Grief was widespread throughout the army and not even the Confederate victory on the field could compensate for the loss. In fact, one Confederate soldier even expressed himself as believing that all the successes of the Valley Campaign did not compensate for the loss of an officer as valuable as Ashby. Another said that he never saw a more sincere grief in the army except when Stonewall Jackson died.[29] Veterans who had never been known to break down emotionally could not refrain from shedding tears when they saw their fallen hero. Lieutenant James Thomson, who later transferred from the Horse Artillery to the cavalry, never afterwards mentioned Ashby's name without a sigh.[30] Thomson rose to the rank of major and was killed at the Battle of High Bridge just a few days before Lee's surrender at Appomattox.

So many different versions have arisen as to who was responsible for General Ashby's death that no biography would be complete without mentioning them. As has been related above, he was shot by a member of the Pennsylvania Bucktails while the Confederate cavalry officer was leading an infantry charge. He had penetrated to a point within twenty-five or thirty yards of the enemy's defense line and when one remembers that the Bucktails were a regiment of picked sharpshooters, it does not seem possible that one of them could escape responsibility for the fatal act. Major W.W. Goldsborough of the Maryland infantry stated unequivocally that Turner Ashby died at the hands of a member of the Pennsyvania Bucktail Regiment, and the general consensus seems to uphold this view.[31]

However, Frederick Trullender, who was a member of Company E, First New Jersey Cavalry, claims it was he who killed Turner Ashby. He says that he was on picket duty when he observed a

Confederate officer, whom he shot and killed. He said that he did not know until the next day that his victim had been Ashby. Major Goldsborough refutes this version by pointing out that the First New Jersey Regiment commanded by Sir Percy Wyndham had been so badly beaten by Ashby earlier that it did not participate several hours later in the fight which cost Ashby his life.[32]

Three different writers have left statements that Ashby was accidentally shot by his own men. One of them, Thomas Green Penn, wrote, "...[I] suppose it is most probable that he [Ashby] was killed by the Maryland Regiment which fired into his cavalry when they were returning from the pursuit of the enemy's pickets, which were driven in day before yesterday evening by our troops."[33] Jed Hotchkiss wrote, "... Ashby directed them to cease firing and went forward to reconnoitre; just at that time he was shot, it is supposed by one of our men mistaking him for a Yankee. So fell the gallant General Turner Ashby; a loss irreparable..."[34] Finally, Private Winfield Peters of the First Maryland Infantry asserted, "As a member of 'Jackson's Foot Cavalry' and in sound of the battle in which the *beau sabreur* Ashby fell, I was cognizant, somewhat, of attendant circumstances. My information was that Ashby went into the action afoot, and against the remonstrance of General Ewell, in the lead of their troops. It was an accepted fact that getting between the enemy and our own troops he fell under fire of our own men."[35]

In spite of these statements, James B. Avirett, Ashby's chaplain and biographer, sought to set the record straight by writing:

> I have often heard that Turner Ashby received his death-wound from a shot fired by one of his own men. This is altogether a mistake. He died by the hand of an enemy. I visited the spot about a year afterwards, and carefully examined the ground. It is on the edge of the wood, three or four hundred yards to the left of a little school-house, on the Port Republic road going from Harrisonburg, and, as before stated, about two miles from the latter town.[36]

The confused circumstances surrounding the tragedy will probably prevent the actual truth from being positively known, but the author is inclined to credit the generally accepted version. In taking this view, he has many supporters.

The members of the household at Colonel Douglas Gray's white house in Harrisonburg had been listening to the sound of musketry on the Port Republic road. They had seen the Pennsylvania Bucktails marching past, and they waited with eager anticipation for the news that the bluecoats had walked into an ambush. Soon they saw riderless horses and later Federal stragglers

Courtesy of Ben Ritter

Monument over the Graves of Turner and Dick Ashby

limping to receive treatment at the improvised hospital in a deserted schoolhouse. Colonel Gray asked news of the fight from Federal soldiers who stopped by for something to eat. After offering them buttermilk, he invited them to stay for supper. The guests told their host about the fight, their retreat, the capture of Colonel Wyndham, and the death of the Confederate cavalry leader. One of them frankly stated: "Mere men could not resist them. We can stand as much as most men, but demons were too much for us. We had to back down this time, anyhow."[37]

Although Colonel Gray did not agree with the cause for which General Ashby fought, he regarded the Southerner as a true friend. Yet he was skeptical and answered, "The report of Ashby's death follows every skirmish." A Major Pankin replied, "I fear you will find it is true this time, Colonel Gray, for at every house we passed this afternoon we heard weeping."

After the Federal officers had taken their departure, the younger members of the household, who had remained conspicuously absent, asked Colonel Gray what stories the "horrid old Yankees" had repeated. When they were informed of the truth, they refused to believe it. It was incredulous that Ashby was dead. They waited for more news of the battle. After dark the girls heard a tap at the back door and upon opening it, they saw Captain Hilary and his faithful servant. After embracing and feeding the hungry Confederate officer, the girls listened with eager ears as he spoke of Ashby's last charge:

> You must listen quietly and be very brave. Walls have ears. If you cry out, they will suspect you; and even if we escape, they will burn your house if they think you have harbored us. They are rather sore over this evening's fight, anyway. Ashby was killed while leading a wavering regiment to victory. We did not dare at first let the men know the leader they thought invincible was dead, and so we covered his face at once. But we need not have been afraid. When the men found it out each man fought like ten. Right well we avenged his death, but a thousand lives could not be worth to us as much as his—no, no one can fill his place in the hearts of his men or to our cause. After the fight was over we had his picture taken as he lay there—beautiful as if carved in marble, only there was a dark spot above the heart.[38]

The photograph referred to, a gruesome reminder of the gallant Turner Ashby, has been preserved for posterity in the files of the Chicago Historical Society.

With the end of the day's fighting after Ashby's death, the Confederates took the body of their hero into the village of Port Republic, where it was placed in a house owned by Frank Kemper.

They stationed an honor guard nearby. The remains were visited by Stonewall Jackson who spent some time paying his last respects to the former cavalry chief. He had been conversing with Sir Percy Wyndam when he received news of the tragedy. Telling an aide to get rid of his prisoner, he left headquarters to see the fallen Ashby's body. All during the night there was a procession of Confederates to the house in Port Republic to see their idol for the last time. Many could not refrain from giving vent to their sorrow by bursting into tears. Through their sobs could be heard the refrain, "Noble Ashby! Gone! Gone!" One of them, Private Richard Black of Company B, who was one of Ashby's scouts, remained for some time in the presence of his chief. Finally, when he prepared to leave, he lamented: "We shall miss you mightily, General. We shall miss you in the camp! We shall miss you as we go out on the scout! But we shall miss you most, General, when we go out to..." Black was so overcome with emotion that he could not finish his tribute as he broke down and left Ashby's presence, sobbing convulsively.[39]

Jackson's official report of the engagement which cost him the services of his cavalry leader showed that, although he had had his differences with Ashby, he still retained a great deal of respect for his character and services. Jackson wrote:

> ...
> An official report is not an appropriate place for more than a passing notice of the distinguished dead but the close relation which General Ashby bore to my command for most of the previous twelve months, will justify me in saying that as a partisan officer I never knew his superior; his daring was proverbial; his powers of endurance almost incredible; his tone of character heroic, and his sagacity almost intuitive in divining the purposes and movements of the enemy.[40]

In a note to General John D. Imboden [then a captain] which was written with pencil on a newspaper, Jackson concluded: "Poor Ashby is dead. He fell gloriously...I know you will join with me in mourning the loss of our friend, one of the noblest men and soldiers in the Confederate army."[41]

Lieutenant Colonel Matthew F. Steele in his textbook used at West Point referring to Ashby wrote, "The death of no other man, save Jackson only, could have caused so great a loss to the Army of the Valley."[42]

Even many of the Federals displayed their respect for the fallen Ashby. It has already been related that Colonel Kane saved his life three times and thought that the cavalry leader was too brave to be shot down. General Frémont in his official report of the Battle of

Harrisonburg wrote: "On their part, the enemy in this sharp affair suffered still more severely, losing among the killed General Ashby, who up to this time had covered their retreat with admirable audacity and skill."[43] One of Frémont's officers was even more lavish in his praise:

> Our men advanced cautiously to the spot where the cavalry under Wyndham had been repulsed, and there met a body of infantry, and quite a heavy engagement ensued. I get this information from one of the Bucktails. The enemy were led by an officer who made himself very conspicuous by the daring exposure of his person and by the wonderful influence he exerted over his men. He afforded at the same time an excellent mark, and a number of muskets were evidently aimed and fired at him. He soon fell, mortally wounded. This man, the next day, we found to be General Ashby, the brilliant leader of the enemy's cavalry, a man worth to them regiments, a blast upon whose bugle-horn was worth a thousand men. When we found the brave Ashby was slain, there was no rejoicing in our camps, though by it we had gained a great advantage, and I have not yet heard an unkind or injurious word by either officers or soldiers of our forces, but on the contrary they seem to abide faithfully by the motto, *Nihil de mortuis dicere nisi bonum* [To speak nothing of the dead except good].[44]

Fully cognizant of the depressing effect that Turner Ashby's death had upon the soldiers, Stonewall Jackson, accompanied by his full staff, on June 7 rode through the Confederate camp. He hoped that his presence would help encourage them to continue to fight for the cause that Ashby held so dear.

Ashby's friends decided to give him a temporary burial-place in the cemetery of the state university in Charlottesville because the Federal troops were in possession of his home in Fauquier County. His grief-stricken mother, who had given up her third and last son to the Southern cause, was greatly disappointed that his remains were not brought back to his home. With Company A, the original Ashby command, as escort, the funeral procession left Port Republic on Saturday, June 7. As it passed a group of Federal prisoners captured at Winchester, the bluecoats showed their respect for their fallen foe by uncovering their heads. When the body reached Waynesboro, it was placed on a train of the Virginia Central Railroad which carried it to Charlottesville. After appropriate church services which were witnessed by many persons, Turner Ashby was buried on Sunday, June 8. The services were conducted by the devoted chaplain, James B. Avirett, assisted by the Reverend G.H. Norton. Ashby's body remained in the Charlottesville cemetery until October, 1866, when it was given a permanent resting-place, along with his brother Richard, in Stonewall Cemetery, Winchester.[45]

Meanwhile the Shenandoah Valley Campaign of 1862 wound toward a close. Jackson's main strategy continued to be an effort to keep the two Federal armies apart. If Frémont could unite his 15,000 men with Shields's 10,000, they could pose a serious threat to Jackson who had but 16,000 troops. Jackson could easily have escaped by burning the bridge across the South Fork of the Shenandoah at Port Republic, crossing the Blue Ridge at Brown's Gap, and taking the Virginia Central cars to Richmond. Such was not his plan, however; he wanted to defeat Shields and Frémont in detail. After giving the bulk of his army two days' rest, he prepared for battle. He wanted to hold Frémont in check at Cross Keys with Ewell's division, while he overwhelmed Shields whose forces were strung out for twenty-five miles in the Luray Valley. Then he could fall upon Frémont with his entire army. Since the latter Federal general had a stronger force than Shields, Jackson wanted his victory to be complete.[46]

The Battle of Cross Keys began about 8:30 o'clock in the morning of June 8 when Frémont attacked Ewell with his superior force. The Union general had 10,000 infantry, twelve batteries, and 2,000 cavalry, while Ewell could muster but 6,000 infantry, five batteries, and 500 cavalry. Jackson's main force was at Port Republic, four miles to the rear. Fortunately for the Confederates, Frémont did not know where Shields was and thought that Jackson's entire army was facing him. He had shown much energy in pursuing Jackson's army in retreat but once the graycoats stood at bay and confronted him, Frémont's natural timidity reasserted itself. Although he had twenty-four regiments on the field, he attacked with only five. They assaulted Ewell's right but were repulsed. His subordinates, Milroy and Schenck, who had given a good account of themselves at the Battle of McDowell, began to attack the Confederate left but were recalled by the cautious Frémont. The Battle of Cross Keys ended with the two hostile forces bivouacking within sight of each other.[47]

Two of Shields's brigades, commanded by Brigadier General Erastus B. Tyler and composed largely of Ohio and West Virginia regiments, were near Port Republic. The remainder of the division was far to the rear. Thus Shields ignored valuable advice given by General McDowell, which was to keep his force closed up so that Jackson could not strike parts of it with overwhelming numbers. Tyler's 4,000 men had a strong defense line from the Shenandoah River to a group of hills a mile to the east. When Jackson sent the Stonewall Brigade against this line, it met fierce resistance. To add to the discomfiture of the Confederates, they discovered that they were subjected to a destructive enfilading fire from a six-pounder battery located in some coal diggings in the hills on the Union left. Although the Stonewall Brigade was forced to fall back, it was saved from further destruction by the arrival of Dick Taylor's Louisianians, who, after a fierce hand-to-hand fight, captured the battery. When Ewell's men arrived on the field, Jackson threw his entire force against the outnumbered enemy and caused it to fall back. Tyler had held up the Confederate attack for four or five hours, but eventually he had to retreat. The Confederates pursued nine miles but gave up the chase when they discovered they would have to fight Shields's whole force.[48] The graycoats had had enough fighting for one day. Frémont, who might have been expected to come to the aid of Shields, had marched cautiously and slowly to Port Republic only to find that the bridge there had been burned by the retreating Southerners. Consequently, he could only stand on the west side of the river and watch his colleague being defeated, unable to render any kind of assistance.

The Battle of Port Republic ended the Shenandoah Valley Campaign of 1862. Jackson went into camp in the hills near Weyers Cave in the Blue Ridge, where he remained until June 17, when he crossed the mountains at Brown's Gap and left to join Lee in the defense of Richmond. Shields, who wanted to repeat his Kernstown victory, hoped that Frémont would join him in a united effort to catch Jackson. However, his hopes were dashed to pieces when he received orders to return to Fredericksburg. Frémont retreated to Harrisonburg and then to Strasburg. When the Federals did not know where Jackson would strike next, they remained in the Valley. It wasn't until June 20 that McDowell's two divisions left the Valley to join McClellan and then it was too late.

In summary, Jackson's Valley Compaign, taken as a whole, was most remarkable. In twelve weeks, besides skirmishing almost daily, he had fought five battles and defeated three armies, those commanded by Frémont, Banks, and McDowell. Marching his "foot cavalry" over 550 miles, he had captured 4,000 to 5,000 prisoners and immense stores. Besides this, he had immobilized 60,000 troops which might have been used by the cautious McClellan against the Southern defenders of Richmond. As has been related, on three occasions McDowell's 40,000 men were ordered to join McClellan and on three occasions the orders were rescinded. These times were first after Kernstown, then after Banks's defeat at Winchester, and, finally, after Jackson's army disappeared into the Blue Ridge after Port Republic. When it is remembered that Jackson never had more than 17,000 troops at any one time, his accomplishments appear all the more remarkable.

In trying to account for Jackson's successes, it should be pointed out that, although his opponents outnumbered him generally, he had numerical superiority at the point of contact where the actual fighting took place. In other words, to repeat the expression credited to General Nathan Bedford Forrest, "he got there fustest with the mostest." Jackson's knowledge of the terrain and his intelligent use of that knowledge gave him a tremendous advantage over his opponents. We have already commented on his use of Massanutten Mountain, the various rivers, and lesser hills to screen his movements and confuse his opponents. Many of the Confederate troops were from the Valley and were familiar with every little cowpath. Jackson's Cromwellian discipline, especially in marching, enabled him to cover ground at an astounding pace. No wonder his infantrymen earned the name of "foot cavalry."

This ability to move quickly from place to place enabled Jackson to carry out the two principles of war which he believed every military commander should observe. One is to mystify, mislead, and surprise the enemy so as to cause him to flee and then continue the pursuit as long as possible. In this way one could capitalize to the fullest upon his opponent's panic. The other rule is to avoid fighting against superior numbers if it is possible to maneuver and fight part of the enemy's force. We should also mention the skill with which Jackson employed the cavalry commanded by General Turner Ashby. Even General Robert E. Lee allowed his cavalry to go off on spectacular, though useless, marches and thus he was deprived of his "eyes and ears" at a time when he needed them most. The proper roles of the cavalry were to scout for information about the enemy, to screen one's own movements, and to follow up an infantry victory and harass the panic-stricken foe.

Undoubtedly the incompetence of Jackson's opponents contributed greatly to his success. They remained so persistently separated that one might get the impression this was what the Washington authorities wanted. This policy of dispersion violated one of the most important principles of war. Secretary of War Edwin Stanton should have been able to unite the various Federal armies and defeat Jackson easily. Unfortunately for the Union, he did not do so, and Lee and Jackson were able to keep the Federal armies apart and defeat them one at a time. The enemy commanders in the Valley usually waited for Jackson to seize the initiative. It apparently never occurred to them to do so. With the exception of the cavalry, their troops were as good as Jackson's, hence we must put the blame for their failures on their leaders. However, we should not allow the incompetence of his opponents to detract from Stonewall Jackson's accomplishments. He merely capitalized upon their mistakes and aided by his brilliant cavalry leader, Turner Ashby, he conducted one of the most remarkable campaigns in military history.[49]

Foot Cavalry Chronicle[50]

by

Hard Cracker

1. Man that is born of woman and enlisteth in Jackson's army is of few days and short rations.

2. He cometh forth at reveille, is present also at retreat, and retireth, apparently, at taps.

3. He draweth his rations from the commissary, and devoureth the same; he striketh his teeth against much hard bread, and is satisfied; he filleth his canteen with water, and clippeth the mouth thereof upon the bung of a whiskey barrel, and after a little while goeth away rejoicing at the strategy.

4. Much soldiering hath made him sharp; yea, even the sole of his shoe is in danger of being cut through.

5. He fireth his Minie rifle in the dead hour of night, and the camp is aroused and formed in line, when to his mess he cometh bearing a fine porker, which he declareth so resembled a Yankee that he was compelled to pull the trigger.

6. The grunt of a pig or the crowing of a cock waketh him from the soundest sleep, and he sauntereth forth in search of the quadruped or biped that dareth to make night hideous; and many other marvelous things doeth he; and lo! are they not already recorded in the morning reports of Jackson's "Foot Cavalry?"

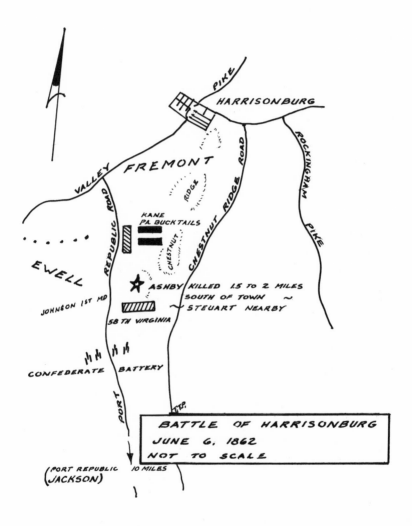

KANE
PA. BUCKTAILS

ASHBY KILLED 1.5 TO 2 MILES
SOUTH OF TOWN ~
STEUART NEARBY

JOHNSON 1ST MD

58 TH VIRGINIA

CONFEDERATE BATTERY

BATTLE OF HARRISONBURG
JUNE 6, 1862
NOT TO SCALE

(PORT REPUBLIC 10 MILES
(JACKSON)

CHAPTER XII

EPILOGUE

The death of General Turner Ashby left a vacuum that was not easy to fill. His command had grown to include twenty-six companies and was too large to continue efficiently without proper organization. After the Battle of Port Republic, there was a period of inactivity in the Upper Valley and thus it was a favorable time to attend to this important task. The cavalry was reorganized into a brigade at Swift Run Gap on June 15 and 16, 1862.[1]

Since most brigades in the Confederate army assumed the names of their commanders, Thomas L. Rosser's brigade, which had been Ashby's Cavalry, was unique in that it became known as the Laurel Brigade. Rosser called it the Laurel Brigade as he was influenced by his admiration of the brigade's prowess, pride of commandership, and a desire to increase its *esprit de corps*.

The Laurel Brigade was different not only in name but also in the way it grew. Most of the time brigades resulted from an arbitrary combination of different bodies of troops into a single group by the army's commanding general. The beginning of the Laurel Brigade was a few companies which later developed into a regiment and then into a brigade. As new companies were added to the original ones, the number of troopers grew considerably. Turner Ashby's old company was the nucleus of the Laurel Brigade.[2]

After Ashby's death,the temporary command of his brigade was given to the senior colonel, Thomas T. Munford, an able officer and Virginia Military Institute graduate who had headed the Second Virginia Regiment. When Confederate authorities decided the cavalry needed a more thorough brigade organization, including the imposition of proper discipline, they replaced Munford with a West Pointer, Brigadier General Beverly Robertson, late Colonel of the Fourth Virginia Cavalry. The brigade consisted of the original ten companies called the Seventh Virginia and ten companies belonging to the Twelfth Virginia Cavalry. Five companies of the Ashby command were formed into the Seventeenth Virginia Battalion, which later received an additional five companies and was reorganized into the Eleventh Virginia Cavalry. Four companies were later organized into the Thirty-fifth Virginia

Cavalry, known as White's Battalion. Chew's Battery continued to remain an important part of the brigade.[3]

Robertson's efforts to improve the discipline of the command did not endear him to the troopers, who regarded the imposition of needed discipline as a reflection upon their fighting qualities. The men felt that Robertson was more interested in drilling than in fighting. Consequently, there was no great shedding of tears when on September 4 it was announced that General Robertson was being transferred to North Carolina to organize some cavalry troops. Colonel Munford again assumed temporary charge of the brigade until November 8 when Brigadier General William E. "Grumble" Jones succeeded him, and the command became known as the Second Brigade. General Jones, who was also a West Pointer, utilized his spare time to drill and instill discipline in the brigade. This greatly increased its efficiency.[4]

Unfortunately for the cavalrymen, General Jones and General J.E.B. Stuart had a personality conflict which resulted in Jones's being court-martialed, relieved of his brigade, and assigned to duty in southwestern Virginia. Jeb accused him of using disrespectful language to a superior officer and preferred charges against him. Even though Jones had not at first been popular with his troopers, who regarded him as a martinet, he had gradually won them over and in the incompatibility clash, they sided with him and felt he had been sacrificed to the animosity of Stuart. The vacant leadership position was then given to Colonel Oliver R. Funsten of the Eleventh Regiment. In October Brigadier General Thomas L. Rosser assumed the command and retained it until he was wounded at the Battle of Trevilian Station in June, 1864. The temporary headship devolved upon Colonel Richard H. Dulany. General Rosser returned in August and led the brigade until October when he was promoted to major general. Dulany succeeded him again but was wounded shortly after at Woodstock. Colonel Funsten returned to head the brigade until he was succeeded by Brigadier General James Dearing, who was mortally wounded at High Bridge. The last commander of the Laurel Brigade was Colonel Elijah V. White, who, refusing to surrender at Appomattox, cut his way out and made it to Lynchburg, where he disbanded the organization.[5]

After the successful defense of Richmond against McClellan's efforts to capture it, one of Turner Ashby's friends suggested to Stonewall Jackson that the bodies of Turner and Dick Ashby should be returned to the Shenandoah Valley for a permanent resting-place. Jackson agreed and promised that if he survived the war, the reinterment would be made. When hostilities ceased and Jackson had given his life in the conflict, the same friend approached some ladies in Winchester about the project. When they approved, they sought and obtained permission from the dead heroes' sisters. Although the residents of Romney, where Dick Ashby had been buried, and Charlottesville were not enthusiastic about the transfer, they yielded their precious possessions to the committee in charge of the project.[6]

The ladies of Winchester realized the desirability of collecting the remains of many other soldiers who had been buried on the battlefield or in unmarked graves in the Lower Valley. With very little money but with much personal effort and devotion, in the spring of 1866 they set in motion the project which resulted in the establishment of the Stonewall Cemetery in Winchester. By October 25, 1866, they had made so much progress that they were ready to dedicate the new resting-place. A few weeks earlier the body of General Ashby was disinterred and brought to Charles Town, where it was placed in a vault pending the completion of a suitable coffin. When all was ready for the trip to Winchester, the procession started. Four white horses pulled the hearse, and sixty mounted men of the Ashby Brigade formed a suitable escort. In Berryville, a stop was made so that the people of Clarke County could pay their respects, and the body was placed in the Grace Episcopal Church for a few hours. When the procession reached Winchester, the coffin was carried into the Episcopal Church. It was joined there by three others containing the remains of Captain Dick Ashby, Lieutenant Colonel Thomas Marshall, and Captain George Sheetz. During the night the church was visited by hundreds of mourners.[7]

There was considerable interest in the coffins, especially the one containing the remains of General Ashby. The funds for its construction were raised by patriotic ladies in Charles Town, and the work on it was done by a local undertaker, George W. Sadler. Made of black walnut, it was covered with black cloth and was elaborately adorned with silver mountings. At the head and foot were three silver stars denoting General Ashby's rank. Upon the lid of the coffin were thirteen silver stars, while over the breast was a heavy silver plate bearing the inscription:

General Turner Ashby
Born October 23, 1828,
Killed in a Heavy Skirmish Near Harrisonburg
June 6, 1862

Ashby's pallbearers were the following: Colonel R.W. Baylor, Colonel J.S. Mosby, Colonel R. Preston Chew, Colonel T.B. Massie, Lieutenant Colonel Dan Hatcher, Major Ed McDonald, Captain D. Humphreys, Captain Philpot, Captain Benjamin Crampton, and Captain William Turner.[8]

The coffin containing the remains of Captain Richard Ashby was placed in the same grave with his brother Turner.

The story of Turner Ashby ends on an unfortunate note, for his estate was involved in financial difficulties. This was not unusual in the post-war era, as Confederate money and securities were worthless. Destruction of private property, seizure of personal possessions, and the taking of fence rails for campfires had impoverished the Southern people. This was especially true in those areas that had seen considerable fighting. Turner Ashby was no exception to this situation. When he bought his land in western Fauquier County, he had signed a promissory note for $1,166.67 payable on or before December 25, 1858, to Richard W. Herndon. Apparently the future Confederate general had engaged in mercantile pursuits, in addition to farming, with disastrous results. On May 24, 1860, five merchants had gone to the County Court of Fauquier County and obtained judgments totaling $1,492.90 against Ashby. There the matter stood until the end of the Civil War.

When hostilities ended, the litigation began anew. Since Turner Ashby was no longer alive, on November 27, 1865, Edward C. Marshall, Jr., was appointed administrator of the deceased cavalryman's estate. On September 7, 1867, a number of creditors, most of whom were merchants, were ordered by the Circuit Court of Fauquier County to present their claims on December 30. This was done and on June 28, 1869, special commissioners sold the Ashby tract of forty-six acres near Markham at public auction for $3,000.00. Thus was realized enough to pay the debts of the unfortunate cavalry leader, with a little remaining for his heirs.[9]

Since Turner Ashby was one of the first heroic generals to die in Virginia, it is not surprising that poets joined in the efforts to glorify his name. Some of the more typical verses that were written to honor his memory are as follows:

ASHBY[10]
by John Oliver Crown

A wail swells o'er thy valley,
　　Virginia, deep with woe;
Thy noble sons and daughters
　　In mournful grief bend low,
　　In mournful grief bend low,
Above that fallen brave,
　　The high-souled, gallant Ashby,
Who sleeps in Glory's grave.

His clarion voice is silent
　　That stirred his band to dare
The front and shock of battle
　　When cannon rent the air
　　When cannon rent the air,
And armies met in strife,
　　Advancing or recoiling
Before the tide of life.

Amid the war-storm's thunder
　　A battle god he moved;
But in the hour of victory
　　Stern death relentless proved,
　　Stern death relentless proved,
As he pressed down the foe
　　That came in mocking triumph
To lay Virginians low.

Virginia, with thy glory
　　Will live his endless fame!
The Shenandoah's waters
　　Will chant his deathless name.
　　Will chant his deathless name.
And every rill will tell
　　And every breeze will whisper
How, fighting, Ashby fell.

With his proud name we linger
　　Like some bright dream that's fled,
And scarce our hearts can echo—
　　He sleeps among the dead,
　　He sleeps among the dead,
But, oh, his deeds live on,
　　That speak in battle's language—
Strive on till victory's won!

　　　　　　　　　—Baltimore Sun

Courtesy of the Chicago Historical Society

Turner Ashby in Death

ASHBY[11]
by Arthur Louis Peticolas

Silver clear above the river,
  Hear the bugle calling!
Through the forest by the river,
O'er the hills and o'er the river,
  Shades of night are falling;
While the dusky echoes waking,
Airy, fairy music making—
  Ashby's bugle calling!
Matchless horseman of the Valley!
Knightly horseman of the Valley!
  Ashby's bugle calling.

Wakeful pickets by the river,
  Keeping watch and ward;
Soldiers sleeping by the river,
By the rapid, rushing river,
  On the velvet sward;
'Neath the stars of midnight gleaming,
Stonewall's army peaceful dreaming,
  Ashby's keeping guard!
Matchless horseman of the Valley!
Knightly horseman of the Valley!
  Ashby's keeping guard.

Loud and clear above the river,
  Hear the rifles ringing!
Flaming guns that set aquiver
All the echoes by the river,
  Songs of death are singing;
Through the raging fight, and after,
Hears the foe, like mocking laughter,
  Ashby's bugle ringing!
Matchless horseman of the Valley!
Knightly horseman of the Valley!
  Ashby's bugle ringing.

Well the Valley, well the river,
  Knew the silver tone;
Knew the steeds whose hoof beats ever
Woke the echoes by the river.
  White, and black, and roan
Were the steeds of valiant mettle,
Were the three that bore to battle
  Ashby's self alone!
Matchless horseman of the Valley!
Knightly horseman of the Valley!
  Ashby's self alone.

But no more beside the river
    Ashby's steeds career;
And no more the rushing river,
Hill and vale and rushing river,
    Ashby's bugle hear;
Nevermore in charge or rally
Wakes the echoes of the Valley
    Ashby's bugle clear!
Matchless horseman of the Valley!
Knightly horseman of the Valley!
    That we loved so dear.

In a sunshine guilded meadow
    Fell that battle day;
Ashby formed us in the shadow
Of a wood; below the meadow
    Flower spangled lay;
While beyond, with pomp and daring,
Wyndham came with trumpets blaring,
    Charging to the fray!
Futile all his pomp and daring,
Futile all his trumpets blaring,
    Proved that fatal day.

Three fierce volleys, then a tempest
    Set the echoes ringing!
Sweetly clear a silver tempest,
Deadly clear a silver tempest—
    Ashby's bugle singing!
Down we charged on Wyndham's squadrons,
Charged on Wyndham's reeling squadrons,
    All our sabers swinging!
Charged, and broke, and rode them over,
Stained with blood the meadow clover,
    All our sabers swinging!

Riflemen beside the meadow
    Swept the volleyed field;
From the copse beside the meadow,
Volleyed woodland by the meadow,
    Back our footmen reeled!
Ashby spurred to lead them, crying;
"Charge!" They charged, but he was lying
    Dead upon the field!
Matchless horseman of the Valley!
O loved horseman of the Valley!
    Dead upon the field!

Sadly sweet the bugle's calling
    Over Ashby's bier!
Soft and low the bugle's calling

As the shades of night are falling,
  But he does not hear.
Stilled forever by the river,
In the Valley, by the river,
  Ashby's bugle clear!
Matchless horseman of the Valley!
Knightly horseman of the Valley!
  That we loved so dear.

DIRGE FOR ASHBY[12]
by Mrs. M.J. Preston

Heard ye that thrilling word—
  Accent of dread—
Fall, like a thunderbolt,
  Bowing each head?
Over the battle dun,
Over each booming gun—
Ashby, our bravest one!
  Ashby is dead!

Saw ye the veterans—
  Hearts that had known
Never a quail of fear,
  Never a groan—
Sob, though the fight they win,
Tears their stern eyes within—
Ashby, our Paladin,
  Ashby is dead!

Dash, dash the tear away—
  Crush down the pain!
Dulce et decus, be
  Fittest refrain!
Why should the dreary pall,
Round *him* be flung at all?
Did not our hero fall
  Gallantly slain?

Catch the last words of cheer,
  Dropt from his tongue:
Over the battle's din,
  Let them be rung!
"Follow *me*! follow *me*!"
Soldier, oh! could there be
Paean or dirge for thee,
  Loftier sung?

Bold as the lion's heart—
    Dauntlessly brave—
Knightly as knightliest;
    Bayard might crave;
Sweet, with all Sydney's grace,
Tender as Hampden's face,
Who now shall fill the space,
    Void by his grave?

'Tis not one broken heart,
    Wild with dismay—
Crazed in her agony,
    Weeps o'er his clay!
Ah! From a thousand eyes,
Flow the pure tears that rise—
Widowed Virginia lies
    Stricken today!

Yet charge as gallantly,
    Ye, whom he led!
Jackson, the victor, still
    Leads at your head!
Heroes! be battle done
Bravelier, every one
Nerved by the thought alone—
    Ashby is dead!

TURNER ASHBY[13]
by John R. Thompson, of Virginia.

To the brave all homage render,
    Weep, ye skies of June!
With a radiance pure and tender,
    Shine, oh saddened moon!
    "Dead upon the field of glory,"
    Hero fit for song and story,
Lies our bold dragoon!

Well they learned, whose hands have slain him,
    Braver, knightlier foe
Never fought with Moor nor Paynim—
    Rode at Templestowe;
    With a mien how high and joyous,
    Gainst the hordes that would destroy us,
Went he forth we know.

Never more, alas! shall sabre
  Glean around his crest:
Fought his fight, fulfilled his labor,
  Stilled his manly breast:
    All unheard sweet nature's cadence,
    Trump of fame and voice of maidens—
Now he takes his rest.

Earth that all too soon hath bound him,
  Gently wrap his clay;
Linger lovingly around him,
  Light of dying day:
    Softly fall the summer showers,
    Birds and bees among the flowers
Make the gloom seem gay.

There, throughout the coming ages,
  When his sword is rust,
And his deeds in classic pages:
  Mindful of her trust
    Shall Virginia, bending lowly,
    Still a ceaseless vigil holy
Keep above his dust.

Turner Ashby High School, Dayton, Va.

Courtesy of Turner Ashby High School

FOOTNOTES
Chapter I
Background

1. James B. Avirett, *The Memoirs of General Turner Ashby and his Compeers*, p. 233.
2. Thomas A. Ashby, *Life of Turner Ashby*, pp. 16-17.
3. John W. Wayland, *Stonewall Jackson's Way*, p. 33; Letter from John K. Gott to author, August 29, 1979.
4. Ashby, *Turner Ashby*, p. 20.
5. Millard K. Bushong, *Historic Jefferson County*, p. 23.
6. Ashby, *Turner Ashby*, pp. 23-24.
7. Frank Cunningham, *Knight of the Confederacy: General Turner Ashby*, p. 6.
8. Ashby, *Turner Ashby*, p. 26.
9. Lee Fleming Reese, *The Ashby Book*, Vol. 1, p. 260.
10. Ashby, *Turner Ashby*, pp. 27-28.
11. *Ibid.*, pp. 32-33.
12. Avirett, *Memoirs*, pp. 20-21.
13. Bushong, *Jefferson County*, pp. 170-171.
14. Fauquier County Bicentennial Committee, *Fauquier County, Virginia, 1759-1959*, p. 271.
15. Emily G. Ramey and John K. Gott, *The Years of Anguish, Fauquier County, Virginia, 1861-1865*, p. xxi.
16. Avirett, *Memoirs*, pp. 23-24.
17. *Ibid.*, pp. 24-25.
18. *Confederate Veteran*, Vol. XXIII, No. 5, (May, 1915), p. 209.
19. Avirett, *Memoirs*, pp. 43-44.
20. Ashby, *Turner Ashby*, p. 45.
21. *Ibid.*, pp. 46-49.
22. Avirett, *Memoirs*, pp. 44-46.
23. *Ibid.*, pp. 46-47.

Chapter II
John Brown

1. Bushong, *Jefferson County*, pp. 177, 183.
2. *Ibid.*, p. 178.

3. Boyd B. Stutler, *Captain John Brown and Harper's Ferry*, p. 15.
4. Bushong, *Jefferson County*, p. 175.
5. *Virginia Free Press*, May 5, 1859.
6. Stutler, *John Brown*, pp. 18-19.
7. Bushong, *Jefferson County*, p. 180.
8. Ashby, *Turner Ashby*, p. 53.
9. *Baltimore Weekly Sun*, Nov. 12, 1859; Dec. 3, 1859.
10. Stutler, *John Brown*, p. 21.
11. *Baltimore Weekly Sun*, Oct. 22, 1859; *The Shepherdstown Register*, Feb. 5, 1886.
12. *John Brown Papers*, Circuit Clerk's Office, Charles Town, W. Va.; *Independent Democrat*, Nov. 1, 1859.
13. *Baltimore Weekly American*, Nov. 5, 1859.
14. *John Brown Papers; Baltimore Weekly American*, Nov. 5, 1859.
15. Bushong, *Jefferson County*, p. 196.
16. *Baltimore Weekly Sun*, Nov. 26, 1859.
17. Bushong, *Jefferson County*, pp. 196-197.
18. *Ibid.*, pp. 199, 201.
19. *Baltimore Weekly Sun*, Dec. 10, 1859.
20. *Ibid.*, Jan 14, 1860; Feb. 4, 1860; Feb. 11, 1860; *Spirit of Jefferson*, July 18, 1929.
21. Oswald Garrison Villard, *John Brown, 1800-1859: a Biography Fifty Years After*, p. 555.
22. Avirett, *Memoirs*, pp. 63-64.
23. Letter n.d. from Wallace W. Phillips to author.
24. Avirett, *Memoirs*, p. 66.

Chapter III
Hostilities Begin

1. Millard K. Bushong, *Old Jube: a Biography of General Jubal A. Early*, Second Printing, p. 10.
2. Mark M. Boatner, III, *The Civil War Dictionary*, p. 26.
3. Avirett, *Memoirs*, p. 70.
4. *Ibid.*, p. 73.
5. Charles H. Ambler, *West Virginia: the Mountain State*, p. 320.
6. Bushong, *Jefferson County*, p. 207.
7. *Ibid.*, pp. 208-209.
8. *Ibid.*, pp. 209-210.

9. *Ibid.*, p. 210.
10. Ashby, *Turner Ashby*, pp. 63-64.
11. R.U. Johnson and C.C. Buel (eds.), *Battles and Leaders of the Civil War*, Vol I, pp. 123-124. Hereinafter cited as *Battles and Leaders*.
12. Avirett, *Memoirs*, pp. 395, 399.
13. *Ibid.*, p. 399.
14. *Ibid.*, pp. 98-99; William N. McDonald, *A History of the Laurel Brigade*, p. 21.
15. McDonald, *Laurel Brigade*, p. 22.
16. Cornelia McDonald, *A Diary with Reminiscences of the War and Refugee Life in the Shenandoah Valley, 1860-1865*, pp. 20-21.
17. Letter from Captain John Q. Winfield to his wife, June 30, 1861, in *Laura Virginia Hale Papers*.
18. Avirett, *Memoirs*, pp. 106-110; Hu Maxwell and H.L. Swisher, *History of Hampshire County, West Virginia* (reprint, 1972), p. 555.
19. Avirett, *Memoirs*, pp. 110-113; Seldon W. Brannon, (ed.), *Historic Hampshire, A Symposium of Hampshire County and Its People, Past and Present*, p. 323.
20. Avirett, *Memoirs*, pp. 114-115.
21. *Ibid.*, p. 116.
22. Ashby, *Turner Ashby*, p. 87.
23. *Battles and Leaders*, Vol. I., p. 222.
24. Avirett, *Memoirs*, pp. 116-118, 120.
25. *Confederate Veteran*, Vol.I, No. 4, (April, 1893), p. 104.
26. Avirett, *Memoirs*, pp. 120-121.
27. Festus P. Summers, *The Baltimore and Ohio in the Civil War*, pp. 99-100.
28. Bushong, *Jefferson County*, pp. 231-232.
29. Avirett, *Memoirs*, pp. 123-124.
30. Letter from A.R. Boteler to some unidentified "Phil,", September 1, 1861, *Turner Ashby Papers*, National Archives, Washington, D.C.
31. *The War of the Rebellion: A Compilation of the Official Records of the Union and Confederate Armies*, Series I, Vol. V., pp. 247-248. Hereinafter cited as *Official Records*. All references to Series I unless otherwise indicated.
32. Bushong, *Jefferson County*, pp. 404-405.
33. Clement A. Evans, (ed), *Confederate Military History*, Vol III, pp. 89-90.

Chapter IV
Reorganization

1. *Confederate Veteran*, Vol. IV, No. 1, p. 23.
2. John N. Opie, *A Rebel Cavalryman with Lee, Stuart, and Jackson*, pp. 52-53.
3. John Esten Cooke, *Wearing of the Gray*, pp. 169-170.
4. *Confederate Veteran*, Vol. XXVIII, No. 1, (Jan., 1920), p. 25.
5. *Southern Historical Society Papers*, Volume XXVI (1898), p. 359. Hereinafter cited as *S.H.S.P.*
6. *Confederate Veteran*, Vol. XXVI, No. 8, (Aug., 1918), p. 359.
7. *S.H.S.P.*, Vol XXVI (1898), pp. 360-361.
8. *Official Records*, Vol. V, p. 937.
9. Letter from Ashby to Cooper, November 7, 1861, *Turner Ashby Papers*, National Archives.
10. *Register of Former Cadets, Virginia Military Institute*, Centennial Edition, 1939, p. 31.
11. McDonald, *Laurel Brigade*, pp. 30-32.
12. Bushong, *Jefferson County*, pp. 206-207.
13. *Confederate Veteran*, Vol. XXVII, No. 1 (Jan., 1919), p. 6.
14. *Ibid.*, p. 7.
15. *S.H.S.P.*, Vol. XVI, p. 215.
16. Monroe F. Cockrell (ed.), *Gunner with Stonewall: Reminiscences of William Thomas Poague*, pp. 12-13.
17. *Official Records*, Vol. V, pp. 892-893.
18. *Ibid.*, pp. 919-920.
19. *Ibid.*, Vol. XII, Part 3, p. 880; Letter from Jackson to Ashby, March 14, 1862, *Thomas Lee Settle Papers*, Duke University; Jackson to Boteler, May 6, 1862, *Alexander Robinson Boteler Papers*, Duke University; *Turner Ashby Papers*, Virginia Historical Society, Richmond.
20. Letter from Ashby to J.P. Benjamin, March 17, 1862, *Turner Ashby Papers*, Chicago Historical Society.
21. Averitt, *Memoirs*, pp. 129, 132, 136-137.
22. *Official Records*, Vol. V, p. 390.
23. Cockrell (ed.), *Gunner with Stonewall*, p. 14.
24. Undated letter written by Captain John Q. Winfield to his wife in *Laura Virginia Hale Papers*.
25. *Ibid.*
26. Avirett, *Memoirs*, p. 135.
27. Henry Kyd Douglas, *I Rode with Stonewall*, p. 19.

Chapter V
Bath and Romney

1. Boatner, *The Civil War Dictionary*, p. 432.
2. G.F.R. Henderson, *Stonewall Jackson and the American Civil War*, Authorized American Edition, p. 15.
3. George Baylor, *Bull Run to Bull Run*, pp. 30-31.
4. Robert G. Tanner, *Stonewall in the Valley*, p. 66.
5. Douglas S. Freeman, *R.E. Lee*, Vol. I, p. 550.
6. Tanner, *Stonewall*, p. 67.
7. *Ibid.*, pp. 66-67.
8. James I. Robertson, Jr., *The Stonewall Brigade*, p. 58.
9. Douglas, *I Rode with Stonewall*, p. 20.
10. *Ibid.*, pp. 20-21.
11. Robertson, *The Stonewall Brigade*, pp. 60-61.
12. Avirett, *Memoirs*, pp. 140-141.
13. *Ibid.*, p. 145.
14. Tanner, *Stonewall*, p. 75.
15. *Official Records*, Vol. V, pp. 391-392.
16. John O. Casler, *Four Years in the Stonewall Brigade*, 2nd Ed., pp. 62-63.
17. Tanner, *Stonewall*, p. 78.
18. Avirett, *Memoirs*, pp. 146-147.
19. *Official Records*, Vol. V, p. 393
20. *Ibid.*, pp. 1034, 1039.
21. Frank E. Vandiver, *Mighty Stonewall*, p. 190.
22. *Diary* of Sandie Pendleton under date of January 16, 1862 in *William N. Pendleton Papers*, Southern Historical Collection, University of North Carolina, Chapel Hill, N.C.
23. *Official Records*, Vol. V. p. 1053.
24. *Ibid.*, p. 1042.
25. *Ibid.*, p. 1053.
26. *Ibid.*, pp. 1059-1060, 1062, 1071-1072.
27. Douglas, *I Rode with Stonewall*, p. 26.
28. Cockrell (ed.), *Gunner with Stonewall*, p. 18.
29. Casler, *Stonewall Brigade*, p. 64.
30. Avirett, *Memoirs*, pp. 148-150.

Chapter VI
Ashby Fails Jackson but Later Redeems Himself

1. Matthew F. Steele, *American Campaigns*, Vol. I, p. 106.
2. *Ibid.*, p. 107.

3. *Ibid.*
4. *Ibid.*, pp. 108-109, 114.
5. Henderson, *Stonewall Jackson*, p. 169.
6. Baylor, *Bull Run to Bull Run*, pp. 33-34.
7. Henderson, *Jackson*, p. 170.
8. *Ibid.*, p. 171.
9. *Ibid.*
10. Boatner, *The Civil War Dictionary*, p. 524.
11. *The Advanced Engineer Manual*, Vol. II, 5th Ed., p. 70.
12. Steele, *Campaigns*, p. 107.
13. Henderson, *Jackson*, pp. 174-175.
14. Cooke, *Wearing of the Gray*, p. 74.
15. Avirett, *Memoirs*, p. 156.
16. Robertson, *The Stonewall Brigade*, pp. 69-70.
17. Avirett, *Memoirs*, p. 157.
18. *Official Records*, Vol. XII, Pt. 1, p. 381; Tanner, *Stonewall*, p. 118.
19. *Official Records*, Vol. XII, Pt. 1, p. 380.
20. *Ibid.*, p. 389.
21. *Ibid.*, pp. 381-382.
22. *Confederate Veteran*, Vol. XVII, No. 3 (March, 1909), p. 125.
23. Douglas, *I Rode with Stonewall*, p. 37.
24. *Official Records*, Vol. XII, Pt. 1, pp. 340-341.
25. Tanner, *Stonewall*, p. 124.
26. Douglas S. Freeman, *Lee's Lieutenants*, Vol. 1, pp. 313-314.
27. *Official Records*, Vol. XII, Pt. 1, p. 382.
28. *Battles and Leaders*, Vol. II, p. 307n.
29. Avirett, *Memoirs*, pp. 256-257, 272.
30. *Official Records*. Vol. XII, Pt. 1, p. 383.
31. *Ibid.*, Vol. XI, Pt. 1, pp. 346-347; Robertson, *The Stonewall Brigade*, pp. 76-77n.
32. William G. Bean, *Stonewall's Man: Sandie Pendleton*, p. 57.
33. Henderson, *Jackson*. pp. 188-189.
34. Steele, *Campaigns*, p. 108.
35. *Ibid.*
36. Avirett, *Memoirs*, pp. 163-164.
37. Francis T. Miller, *The Photographic History of the Civil War*. Vol. 4, pp. 170-172.

Chapter VII
Ashby Resigns; Jackson Backs Down

1. Avirett, *Memoirs*, p. 167.
2. *Ibid.*, pp. 167-168.
3. *Ibid.*, p. 172.
4. *Official Records*, Vol. XII, Pt. 3, p. 384.
5. Archie P. McDonald (ed.), *Make Me a Map of the Valley: The Civil War Journal of Stonewall Jackson's Topographer*, pp. xv, xix, xxi.
6. Boatner, *The Civil War Dictionary*, p. 411.
7. Freeman, *Lee's Lieutenants*, Vol. I, pp. 317-318.
8. Douglas, *I Rode with Stonewall*, p. 37.
9. Avirett, *Memoirs*, pp. 173-174.
10. Letter from John K. Gott to author, August 29, 1979.
11. Letter from Wallace W. Phillips to author, November 6, 1979.
12. Tanner, *Stonewall*, pp. 137, 151.
13. *Official Records*, Vol. XII, Pt. 1 p. 386.
14. Baylor, *Bull Run to Bull Run*, p. 37.
15. Freeman, *Lee's Lieutenants*, Vol. I, pp. 337-338.
16. *Ibid.*, p. 338; Tanner, *Stonewall*, p. 151.
17. Avirett, *Memoirs*, p. 176.
18. McDonald, *Laurel Brigade*, p. 50.
19. *Ibid.*, p. 53.
20. Clarence Thomas, *General Turner Ashby: the Centaur of the South*, p. 195.
21. Freeman, *Lee's Lieutenants*, Vol. I, p. 340; *Official Records*, Vol.XII, Pt. 3, p. 880.
22. Tanner, *Stonewall*, p. 149.
23. Edward Hungerford, *The Story of the Baltimore and Ohio Railroad*, Vol. 2, pp. 7-14.
24. Steele, *Campaigns*, Vol. I, p. 109.
25. *Ibid.*
26. *Ibid.*
27. Letter from Jackson to Boteler, May 6, 1862, *Alexander R. Boteler Papers*, Duke Univerisity.
28. Avirett, *Memoirs*, p. 206.
29. Steele, *Campaigns*, pp. 109-110.
30. *Ibid.*, p. 110.
31. *S.H.S.P.*, Vol. 9, pp. 364-365.
32. *Ibid.*
33. *Ibid.*

34. Richard Taylor, *Destruction and Reconstruction: Personal Experiences of the Late War*, pp. 49-50.
35. Steele, *Campaigns*, p. 110.
36. Letter from Wallace W. Phillips to author, November 6, 1979.

Chapter VIII
Jackson Surprises Banks

1. Taylor, *Destruction*, p. 49.
2. *Ibid.*, p. 50.
3. Avirett, *Memoirs*, pp. 186-187.
4. *Official Records*, Vol. XII, Pt. 1, p. 702.
5. *Ibid.*, p. 560.
6. Avirett, *Memoirs*, pp. 188-189.
7. *Official Records*, Vol. XII, Pt. 1, p. 702.
8. McDonald, *Laurel Brigade*, p. 59.
9. Henderson, *Stonewall Jackson*, p. 240.
10. *Ibid.*, pp. 241-242.
11. Douglas, *I Rode with Stonewall*, p. 51.
12. Louis A. Sigaud, *Belle Boyd: Confederate Spy*, pp. 33, 35.
13. Douglas, *I Rode with Stonewall*, pp. 51-52.
14. Robertson, *The Stonewall Brigade*, p. 92.
15. Taylor, *Destruction*, pp. 52-53.
16. Lucy Rebecca Buck, *Diary: Sad Earth, Sweet Heaven*, p. 83.
17. Robert L. Dabney, *Life and Campaigns of Lieutenant General Thomas J. Jackson*, pp. 366-367.
18. *Confederate Veteran*, Vol. XXII, No. 7 (July, 1914), p. 308.
19. *Ibid.*
20. Henderson, *Stonewall Jackson*, p. 244.
21. *Confederate Veteran*, Vol. XXII, No. 7, (July, 1914), p. 309.
22. *Official Records*, Vol. XII, Pt. 1, p. 526.

Chapter IX
Where Is the Cavalry?

1. Henderson, *Stonewall Jackson*, p. 247.
2. James I. Robertson, Jr., "Stonewall in the Shenandoah: the Valley Campaign of 1862," *Civil War Times Illustrated*, May, 1972, p. 25.
3. Henderson, *Stonewall Jackson*, p. 250.

4. *Official Records,* Vol. XII, Pt. 1, p. 703.
5. Avirett, *Memoirs,* p. 193.
6. *Ibid.,* pp. 195-196.
7. *Ibid.,* pp. 198.
8. *Official Records,* Vol. XII, Pt. 1, p. 703. .
9. Henderson, *Stonewall Jackson,* p. 252.
10. Douglas, *I Rode with Stonewall,* p. 55.
11. *Ibid.*
12. Avirett, *Memoirs,* pp. 198-199.
13. *Confederate Veteran,* Vol. XIX, No. 11 (Nov., 1911), p. 520;
    Ibid., Vol.XX, No. 1 (Jan., 1912), p. 58.
14. Robertson, "Stonewall in the Shenandoah: the Valley Cam-
    paign of 1862," in *Civil War Times Illustrated,* May, 1972,
    p. 31.
15. Taylor, *Destruction,* p. 56.
16. *Official Records,* Vol. XII, Pt. 1, pp. 736, 746.
17. *Ibid.,* pp. 761,779.
18. Taylor, *Destruction,* p. 58.
19. Douglas, *I Rode with Stonewall,* p. 60.
20. Robertson, *The Stonewall Brigade,* p. 97.
21. *Official Records,* Vol.XII, Pt. 1, p. 706.
22. *Ibid.*
23. *Ibid.,* pp. 706-707.
24. Tanner, *Stonewall,* p. 233.
25. *Ibid.,* p. 256.
26. Dabney, *Jackson,* p. 373.
27. *Ibid.,* p. 382.
28. Avirett, *Memoirs,* pp. 200-202.
29. Bushong, *Jefferson County,* p. 279.
30. Avirett, *Memoirs,* pp. 269-272.
31. *Ibid.,* pp. 200-201.
32. Taylor, *Destruction,* pp. 59-60.
33. *Official Records,* Vol. XII, Pt. 1, p. 704.
34. *Ibid.,* pp. 706-707.
35. *Ibid.,* p. 708.
36. *Ibid.,* p. 551.

Chapter X
Escaping the Trap

1. Henderson, *Stonewall Jackson,* p. 263.
2. *Official Records,* Vol. XII, Pt. 1, p. 626.

3. Letter from John Harman to his brother, May 18, 1862, *Jedediah Hotchkiss Papers*, Library of Congress, Washington, D.C.
4. Letter from Henry Kyd Douglas to Editor of *The Century Illustrated Monthly Magazine*, May 15, 1885, in issue dated August, 1885, Vol. XXX, No. 4, p. 641.
5. *Official Records*, Vol. XII, Pt. 1, p. 730.
6. *Ibid.*, Pt. 3, p. 219.
7. *Ibid.*, pp. 230, 235.
8. *Ibid*, pp. 220-221; Steele, *Campaigns*, Vol. I, p. 111.
9. Douglas, *I Rode with Stonewall*, pp. 62-63.
10. Bushong, *Jefferson County*, p. 421.
11. McDonald (ed.), *Make Me a Map of the Valley*, p. 49.
12. *S.H.S.P.*, Vol. 40 (Sept., 1915), pp. 164-165.
13. *Ibid.*, pp. 165-166.
14. *Official Records*, Vol. XII, Pt. 1, p. 682.
15. McDonald (ed.), *Make Me a Map of the Valley*, p. 50.
16. *S.H.S.P.*, Vol. 40 (Sept., 1915), pp. 167-168.
17. William Couper, *History of the Shenandoah Valley*, Vol. II, p. 888; Cornelia McDonald, *A Diary*, p. 76.
18. *Thomas Munford Papers*, Duke University.
19. *Official Records*, Vol. XII, Pt. 1, p. 314.
20. Robertson, *The Stonewall Brigade*, pp. 101-102.
21. Casler, *Stonewall Brigade*, pp. 80-81, 84.
22. Robertson, *The Stonewall Brigade*, p. 102.
23. Taylor, *Destruction*, p. 61.
24. *Ibid.*, p. 65.
25. *S.H.S.P.*, Vol. 40. (Sept., 1915), p. 173.

Chapter XI
Ashby's Last Charge

1. *Official Records*, Vol. XII, Pt. 1, p. 711.
2. Douglas, *I Rode With Stonewall*, p. 71.
3. *Official Records*, Vol. XII Pt. 1, p. 711.
4. Douglas. *I Rode with Stonewall*, pp. 72-73.
5. John W. Wayland, *Stonewall Jackson's Way*, p. 136.
6. Letter from Jedediah Hotchkiss to Major Holmes Conrad, October 7, 1898, *Homes Conrad Papers*, Virginia Historical Society Library, Richmond, Va.; *Official Records*, Vol. XII, Pt. 1, pp. 711-712.
7. *Official Records*, Vol. XII, Pt. 1, pp. 712, 731.

8. Letter from Jackson to Boteler, May 6, 1862, *Alexander R. Boteler Papers*, Duke University.

9. Avirett, *Memoirs*, pp. 211-212.

10. *Ibid.*, p. 214.

11. McDonald (ed.), *Make Me a Map of the Valley*, pp. 51-52.

12. William G. Bean, *The Liberty Hall Volunteers: Stonewall's College Boys*, p. 119n.

13. *Confederate Veteran*, Vol.XXV, No. 11 (Nov., 1917), p. 492.

14. McDonald (ed.) *Make Me a Map of the Valley*, pp. 51-52.

15. *Official Records*, Vol.XII, Pt. 3, p. 906.

16. Avirett, *Memoirs*, pp. 217-219.

17. *Confederate Veteran*, Vol. VIII, No. 6 (June, 1900), p. 273.

18. *Ibid.*, p. 274.

19. *Ibid.*, Vol. XXIII, No. 2 (February, 1915), p. 72.

20. *Ibid.*

21. Douglas, *I Rode with Stonewall*, p. 79.

22. Avirett, *Memoirs*, p. 222.

23. Charles L. Dufour, *Gentle Tiger: the Gallant Life of Roberdeau Wheat*, p. 182.

24. *Confederate Veteran*, Vol.XXIII, No. 2, (February, 1915), p. 72.

25. Evans, (ed.), *Confederate Military History*, Vol. III, p. 254.

26. Douglas, *I Rode with Stonewall*, p. 80; Edward A. Pollard, *Lee and His Lieutenants*, p. 584.

27. Douglas, *I Rode with Stonewall*, p. 80.

28. *Official Records*, Vol.XII, Pt. 1, p. 782; *S.H.S.P.*; Vol. XXIX, p. 136.

29. *Samuel D. Buck Papers*, p. 22, Duke University; Letter from Thomas Green Penn to his brother, June 8, 1862, *Green W. Penn Papers*, 1764-1894, Duke University.

30. Douglas, *I Rode with Stonewall*, p. 80.

31. *S.H.S.P.*, Vol. XXI (1893-1894), p. 226.

32. *Ibid.*

33. Letter from Thomas Green Penn to his brother, June 8, 1862, *Green W. Penn Papers, 1764-1894*, Duke University.

34. McDonald (ed.), *Make Me a Map of the Valley*, p. 53.

35. *S.H.S.P.*, Vol. XXIX, 1901, p. 136n.

36. Avirett, *Memoirs*, p. 223.

37. *Confederate Veteran*, Vol. VIII, No. 6 (June, 1900), p. 274.

38. *Ibid.*, pp. 274-275.

39. Avirett, *Memoirs*. p. 226.

40. *Official Records*, Vol. XII, Pt. 1, p. 712.

41. *Battles and Leaders*, Vol. II, pp. 291-292.

Chapter XII
Epilogue

1. McDonald, *Laurel Brigade*, p. 17.
2. *Ibid.*, p. 18.
3. Avirett, *Memoirs*, pp. 261-263.
4. McDonald, *Laurel Brigade*, pp. 90, 105, 109.
5. *Ibid.*, pp. 168-169; Avirett, *Memoirs*, pp. 263-265.
6. Avirett, *Memoirs*, p. 239.
7. *Ibid.*, pp. 243-244.
8. *Ibid.*, pp. 244-245, 248.
9. *Fauquier County Records*, Warrenton, Va.
10. *Notes* belonging to Mrs. Ralph Dorsey of Berryville, Va.
11. *Confederate Veteran*, Vol. XXXIII, No. 1, (Jan., 1925), p. 21.
12. H.M. Wharton, *War Songs and Poems of the Southern Confederacy*, 1861-1865, pp. 152-153.
13. *Ibid.*, pp. 206-207.

Continued from page 213 —

42. Steele, *Campaigns*, Vol. I, p. 112.
43. *Official Records*, Vol. XII, Pt. 1, p. 18.
44. Avirett, *Memoirs*, p. 232.
45. *Ibid.*, pp. 239-243.
46. Henderson, *Stonewall Jackson*, p. 279.
47. Steele, *Campaigns*, Vol. I, p. 113.
48. Henderson, *Jackson*, pp. 288-292.
49. Millard K. Bushong, "Jackson in the Shenandoah," *West Virginia History: a Quarterly Magazine*, Vol. XXVII, No. 2, (Jan., 1966), pp. 95-96.
50. Lizzie Cary Daniel, *Confederate Scrap Book*, p. 55.

APPENDIX
MUSTER ROLL OF THE SEVENTH
VIRGINIA CAVALRY (LAUREL BRIGADE)
ARMY OF NORTHERN VIRGINIA
COMPANY A[1]
Officers

Ashby, Turner, Captain
Ashby, Luther R., Third Lieut.
Fletcher, John, Captain
Glascock, Alfred, Third Lieut.

Hatcher, Daniel C., Captain
Smith, Granville, First Lieut.
Smith, Sullivan, Second Lieut.
Turner, William F., Captain

Enlisted Men

Ashby, Richard
Ashby, Vernon
Anderson, Edward
Anderson, E.W.
Athey, W. Scott
Barnes, Jacob S.
Bayne, C. Milton
Blackmore, Robert
Brent, Hugh
Brent, James A.
Brent, Warren
Brent, William A.
Bruce, Charles
Buckner, Richard C.
Byrne, H. Milton
Carter, Cassius
Carter, George
Carter, J. Pitman
Chancellor, George W.
Clem, A.W.
Cochran, Thomas B.
Coffman, A.
Cornwell, Silas
Crane, Major
Crane, Smith
Darnell, J.B.
Dawson, Nicholas
Dean, Thomas
Diffendaffer, George
Donnelley, John B.
Dufenderfer, J.M.
Eastham, Henry
Engle, Bub

Eskridge, H.R.
Evans, Caswaller
Fletcher, Clinton
Fletcher, Joshua C.
Fletcher, Robert
Flynn, Henry
Flynn, John
Foley, Oswald
Foster, Hunton
Francis, George W.
Gaines, Lucien
Garrison, Albert
Garrison, Bushrod
Garrison, Tip
Geiman, Jesse C.
Gibson, Gurley
Gilmor, Harry
Gilmore, Howard
Gilmore, Richard
Glascock, Robert
Glascock, Samuel
Glascock, Thomas
Graybill, J.C.
Grigsby, Bushrod
Grigsby, Nathaniel
Hackley, James
Harman, Dr. John D.
Harrison, Daniel B.
Hatcher, Harry
Hatcher, William P.
Hathaway, C.H.
Hawbaw, George
Hawks,

Hefflin, John
Henderson, John D.
Herndon, John G.
Hicks, Kimball
Hitt, James W.
Hoffman, Wesley
Holmes, Charles A.
Horner, Richard H.
Hughes, Charles
Hunton, James
Jacobs, L. Thomas
Jeffries, James A.
Jones, Henry
Jones, Philip
Jones, Scott
Jordan, J.H.A.
Keys, James
Kidwell, Evan H.
Kincheloe, Elisha
Kincheloe, John W.
Kirkpatrick, W.S.
Lacy, W.J.
Ladd, John A.
Lake, Bladen D.
Lake, F. Marion
Lake, Luther
Larkin, Richard D.
Lawler, Robert
Lee, William
Leslie, Thomas
Lewis, John
Long, E. Pendleton
Maddox, Weadon

215

Maddox, Webster
Marlow, John
Marlow, Richard
Marshall, James
Marshall, Polk
Marshall, Richard C.
Marshall, Thomas
Martin, Gibson
Martin, Thomas
Massey, Edward
McArthur, Hickerson
McClennahan, S.B.
Melton, H.
Middleton, Campbell
Middleton, Humphrey
Middleton, John W.
Mitchell, James W.
Mitchell, John H.
Mitler, Proff
Morrison, D.B.
Myers, Frank
Noell, J.M.
O'Forton, Dr.
Owens, Cuthbert
Owens, Morgan
Packard, William
Payne, Edward A.
Payne, Hugh G.
Payne, John T.
Payne, Lafayette
Payne, Mason
Payne, Rice W.
Payne, Richard C.
Payne, Robert B.
Payne, Robert J.

Payne, Robert W.
Payne, Thomas H.
Payne, Upton
Payne, Wallace J.
Payne, Wilson V.
Pendelton, David E.
Peyton, Robert E.
Phillips, Charles E.
Phillips, Evan D.
Phillips, John E.
Pickett, Albert
Potterfield, Thomas L.
Potterfield, W.H.T.
Price, James Polk
Price, John H.
Rector, Abner
Rector, Asa H.
Rector, Columbus
Rector, Howard N.
Rector, W.A.
Rector, William F.
Reed, Joseph H.
Roberson, __
Robinson, W.S. (Bear)
Rogers, William S.
Royston, John
Rust, H. Clay
Rust, John R.
Santmyers, R.R.
Scanlon, Dade
Seely, George W.
Selix, Tom
Settle, Dr. T.L.
Shippey, W.D.
Silcott, Landon

Skinner, Charles G.
Skinner, William Jeff
Smith, Golden H.
Smith, Horace
Smith, O'Connell
Smith, R.S.
Smith, Seldon
Smith, Thomas
Stewart, John W.
Strother, John W.
Strother, Lewis
Sutton, James
Taylor, Rufus
Templeman, Dr. James
Templeman, James
Templeman, Robert
Tibbetts, Albert
Triplett, Leonidas
Turner, Hezekiah
Turner, Thomas
Utz, J.J.
Violet, Elijah
Welsh, Bogue
Welsh. F.R.
Welsh, Silvester, M.
Welsh, S.M.
Wigfield, James
Wigfield, William H.
Wigginton, George W.
Wigginton, Isaac
Wigginton, James
Wiggonton, Isaac
Wilson, James
Wilson, William

COMPANY B[2]
Officers

Winfield, John Q., First Captain
Magruder, J.H., Second Captain
Humphreys, D., Third Captain
Liggett, J.N., Lieut.

Jordan, S.B., First Lieut.
Pennybacker, J.S., First Lieut.
Kenon, P.P., Lieut.
Acker, Jacob, Second Lieut.

Enlisted Men

Acker, Isaac
Acker, Peter,
Alger, Harry
Ashby, Richard
Baker, Daniel

Barbe, Daniel
Barbe, Noah
Barbe, Simon
Barglebaugh, John M.
Barks, David

Baxter, Jacob T.
Beam, Jacob
Beam, John
Black, Richard
Bowers, William F.

Bowman, George
Bowman, Michael
Brock, Godfrey
Brock, William
Bull, A.V.
Burkholder, George E.
Burns, Jacob
Bush, Henry
Byrd, Jerry
Carpenter, John
Carpenter, N.H.
Coffelt, J.D.
Coffman, George C.
Cowell, A.J.
Cromer, David R.
Custer, Isaac
Devier, Giles
Devier, H.K.
Duff, W.J.
Dyer, A.W.
Emswiler, J.P.
Emswiler, Noah
Emswiler, Samuel
Emswiler, W.P.
Fetzer, Cyrus
Fitzwaters, Aaron
Frank, Samuel
Fulk, Harry
Fulk, John G.
Fulk, George C.
Fulk, William
Funk, A.D.
Funk, Hopkins R.
Funk, James
Funk, Milton E.
Funk, T.W.
Funk, William
Good, Jacob
Grabill, Charles
Grabill, Cornelius

Grabill, R.C.
Haisley. W.T.
Hall, Rasin
Harris, John, H.
Hollar, Samuel B.
Horn, Alrazi
Hulvey, Jonathan
Hulvey, Peter
Hupp, Charles T.
Jones, Evan
Jones, Israel
Keyes, Erasmus L.
Leacy, John
Lindamood, James
Lindamood, Sylvanus
Magruder, John H.
Mason, Henry
May, George
Messick, William
Miller, Isaac
Miller, John
Miller, William
Minnick, Levi
Minnick, William
Moore, George
Moore, John W.
Moore, Samuel
Morris, Alfred
Muller, Emanuel
Muller, George
Muller, S.F.
Neff, Erasmus
Neff, John H.
Neff, Michael
Newham, William P.
Pennybacker, B.R.
Pennybacker, D.D.
Pennybacker, Isaac
Pennybacker, John

Pennybacker, John S.
Phillips, John
Rader, C.S.
Rader, George
Rader, George C.
Rader, Jacob L.
Rader, Peter
Reedy, Isaac
Richey, Frank J.
Richey, Isaac
Richie, Isaac
Riddle, Joe N.
Ritchie, Solomon
Scott, J.T.
Shoup, Jacob G.
Shoup, John C.
Showalter, Abraham
Showalter, Joe
Showalter, Michael
Silvius, Uriah
Simmers, John
Sprinkle, William F.
Stickley, Dan
Stickley, Phineas
Swanson, William
Taylor, Edmund
Thomas, John
Trumbo, Benjamin
Turner, Jacob
Turner, Moses
Wean, Abram
Wean, E.J.
Wean, Jacob
Wean, Noah
West, John
Will, C.B.
Wood, George M.
Zirkle, David, P.
Zirkle, Henry

COMPANY C[3]
Officers

Myers, Samuel B., Captain
Myers, J.E., Captain
Bowers, Philip, First Lieut.
Murphy, George, First Lieut.
Rosenberger, R., Second Lieut.

Lantz, R.M. Second Lieut.
Allen, J.E. Second Lieut.
Clark, S.G., Third Lieut.
Miley, J.R., Third Lieut.

Enlisted Men

Allison, William
Artz, Peter
Baker, James
Bird, Hite
Bird, Samuel
Bishop, Charles
Bishop, Thomas
Bowers, Ezra
Bowers, Harvey
Bowers, Jacob
Bowers, Johnson
Bowman, Calvin
Bowman, Daniel
Bowman, L.B.
Bowman, Whiten
Bradford, William
Brenner, Casper
Bretts, Joseph
Burke, John
Burke, John T.
Carper, William
Cheek, Joseph
Chilcott, Jonathan
Clarke, E.
Clinedinst, A.B.
Clinedinst, Augustine
Clinedinst, D.C.
Clinedinst, Isaac
Clinedinst, William
Coffelt, Ananias
Coffelt, Joseph
Coffman, A.
Coffman, Addison
Coffman, B.
Coffman, E.
Conn, W.
Cook, H.
Crabill, J.
Day, James
Day, John
Day, Robert
Dellinger, Amos
Dellinger, Emmanuel

Dellinger, James
Dellinger, R.
Dirting, John
Dirting, P.J.
Dudley, William
Estep, Jack
Estep, Robert
Emswiller, Lemuel
Evans, A.J.
Evans, Samuel
Fadely, Eli
Fadely, Joseph
Fadely, William
Farrow, William
Fleming, Harvey
Fogle, Harvey
Font, Enoch
Foster, James T.
Fravel, F.M.
Fravel, William
Fry, Israel
Fry, James
Fry, Joseph
Fry, R.
Gaw, Robert
Granstaff, Lem
Grechnour, David
Griffith, John
Grimm, Franklin
Grove, William
Hallar, Robert
Hanson, Aquilla
Hanson, William
Helsley, Washington
Hollar, John
Hollar, Mahlon
Hollar, Reuben
Hollar, Samuel
Hollar, William
Holtzman, Beverly
Hottel, D.J.
Hottel, Isaac
Kagey, John

Kees, Alfred
Kerns, Isaac
Lantz, George
Larkins, William
Lewland, Lemuel
Lindamood, George
Litten, Ben
Litten, Eli
Long, Eli
Lorenzo, Fadely
Lutz, William
Magruder, John
Myers, John
Olinger, William
Pain, J.O.
Palmer, J.
Patton, George
Patton, John
Pullin, Andrew
Racey, Luke
Racey, Mat
Ran, Ansben
Ran, David
Ran, James
Ran, John
Reed, John
Riddlemoser, D.
Rinehart, G.C.
Rosenberger, C.
Ross, D.
Ross, S.
Ruby, David
Russell, M.
Russell, T.
Shadwell, H.
Sheets, Ananias
Sheets, Elias
Sheets, Isaac
Shorts, Frederick
Stoneburner, William
Strickler, Abe
Varner, John
Watson, John

COMPANY D[4]
Officers

Coyner, S.B., Captain
Jordan, Macon, Captain
Summers, George W., Lieut.
Lionberger, John H., First Lieut.

Reid, Peter C., First Lieut.
Brown, Booton, Second Lieut.
Bell, James H., Third Lieut.

Enlisted Men

Alger, Emmanuel
Alther, Andrew
Alther, Jacob
Alther, John
Bailey, Samuel
Baumgardner, David
Batman, B.F.
Beagles, H.F.
Beylar, George
Booten, Reuben
Bradley, W.F.
Brittain, James
Brooks, James
Brown, W.R.
Broaddus, C.L.
Brubaker, A.D.
Brubaker, F.F.
Burner, H.B.
Burner, Masson
Bywaters, A.J.
Campbell, Isaac
Campbell, J.N.
Carder, B.S.
Comer, Samuel
Compton, E.H.
Connelly, John
Connelly, Noah
Crider, Jacob
Davis, S.B.
Dashsman, Reuben
Dawson, Benjamin
Dofflemoyer, Daniel
Dofflemoyer, John
Dofflemoyer, Richard
Dovel, C.W.
Dovel, David
Dovel, George
Dovel, G.D.
Dovel, H.C.
Dovel, Joseph
Dovel, Noah
Dovel, P.S.
Dovel, William A.
Dulaney, W. Larkin
Dulaney, William
Durrough, James
Emmerson, Henry
Foltz, Hiram

Freeze, Wharton
Good, James M.
Gray, John H.
Hahn, J.
Ham, J.V.
Ham, Samuel
Hammer, William H.
Harrison, Jno. B.
Hiden, R.C.
Huffman, A.J.
Huffman, F.M.
Jordan, Hubert
Judd, George, W.
Judd, Lorenzo W.
Judd, Samuel N.
Keyser, J.A.
Keyser, John W.
Keyser, Joseph
Keyser, E. Thomas
Keyser, W.H.
Kibler, A.J.
Kibler, Albin,
Kibler, Simeon
Kibler, Willis,
Kite, Adam
Kite, David
Kite, Enoch
Kite, Jackson
Knicily, Joseph
Knight, William
Koontz, Jacob D.
Koontz, Newton
Lillard, S.T.
Long, Peter
Long, Reuben
Lucas, Henry
Lucas, Jefferson
Lucas, John
Lucas, Samuel
Lynch, John
Mayes, J.H.
Mays, F.L.
McCormick, George
McCormick, John
Meadows, T.S.
Menefee, H.
Menefee, S.L.
Menefee, W.B.

Miller, Hampton, H.
Miller, William Franklin
Milton, Joseph
Milton, William R.
Morris, I.
Morris, William H.
Ortz, Daniel
Painter, R.
Plum, John M.
Plumber, J.M.
Plump, John
Pound, J.J.
Printz, David J.
Printz, J.J.
Putnam, Robert
Reid, J.H.
Rhodes, Lafayette
Rickard, C.B.
Rickard, W.A.
Rodgers, Joseph
Rogers, J.P.
Rowe, William H.
Samuels, J.H.
Shenk, Abram (Abraham)
Shenk, F.M.
Shenk, H.C.
Shenk, Isaac
Shenk, James H.
Shenk, John
Shenk, Joseph
Shenk, Samuel
Shenk, T.F.
Short, John
Stover, John W.
Strickler, Daniel H.
Strickler, Henry
Strickler, John R.
Strickler, R.T.
Strickler, S.W.
Summers, George
Walter, B.F.
Walter, J.W.
Welfley (Welfby), W.F.
Wetherholt, Jonathan
Wilson, W.C.
Winsborough, John D.
Yates, Yancey

COMPANY E[5]
Officers

Buck, Thomas H., Captain   Willis, W.H., Second Lieut.
Simpson, Samuel, J., First Lieut. Buck, Walter, Third Lieut.

Enlisted Men

Adams, A.	Cook, Giles	Lacy, J.R.
Ash, J.H.	Cook, Scott	Little, W.D.
Bayly, R.B.	Cook, Wythe	McKay, A.A.
Beaby, I.L.	Doran, B.	Mitchell, Shipp
Beren, William	Eastham, Philip	Naid, George
Boone, J.W.	Foster, G.A.	Neville, J.D.
Bowling, W.A.	Foster, J.L.	Neville, P.G.
Brown, Edward	Garrison, M.L.	Oliver, J.W.
Brown, J.H.	Green, F.W.	Orndoff, O.
Brown, J.M.	Grubbs, Nathan	Parkins, A.D.
Brown, J.W.	Heater, Henry	Putman, J.K.P.
Buck, C.N.	Heater, John	Ray, T.M.
Buck, Edwin, G.	Helm, Robert	Richardson, C.M.
Buck, John N.	Henry, Charles	Richardson, Marcus
Buck, T.W.	Henry, Hugh	Robinson, William
Buck, W.A.	Henry, John	Roger, W.A.
Churchill, W.A.	Houser, W.F.N.	Royston, T.
Clapsaddle, Byrd	Irwin, Marcus	Spicer, B.B.
Clapsaddle, M.A.	Jackson, William	Steed, F.
Cline, H.C.	Jenkins, J.R.	Steed, W.T
Cline, W.R.	Johnson, John I.	Vaughan, George
Cloud, D.M.	Kendrick, J.W.	Wines, Burwell
Cloud, W.M.	Lacy, Henry	

COMPANY F[6]
Officers

Sheetz, George F., Captain   Baker, George H., Second Lieut.
Kuykendall, Isaac, Captain   Vandiver, Charles H., Second
McDonald, Angus W., First Lieut.   Lieut.

Enlisted Men

Allen, Elijah	Bonney, James	Clark, William F.
Allen, Hiram	Bower, Page	Cupp, Jesse
Alexander, Eugene	Bowers, Charles I.	Cunningham, George F
Arnold, John S.	Bowers, M.B.Y.	Cunningham, James H.
Baker, Henry	Cahil, William H.	Cunningham, James W.
Baker, Jacob A.	Cahill, Joseph	Davis, Charles
Baker, John W.	Cain, Anthony	Davis, Leslie
Baker, Levi	Carroll, Zedekiah	Davis, Reuben S.
Bane, James A.	Cayner, William	Davis, Samuel R.
Berry, Samuel	Chancy, Thomas	Dawson, Dory W.

Dignan, Patrick
Douphit John
Edwards, Robert
Engle, Samuel C.
Ervin, W.D.
Everitt, George W.
Fay, John B.
Fox, David
Gassman, Jacob
Gates, Charles
Gill, James
Goldsborough, Thomas
Grayson, William
Grim, M.V.
Harlan, Scott
Harman, Joseph
Harmison, M.G.
Harness, Adam C.
Harness, W.W.
Harrison, Isaac E.
Harrison, Thomas
Harrison, William B.
Healy, Maurice
Healy, Thomas
Heironimus, Jacob
Heitt, James
Heltzel, Samuel J.
High, Frederick
High, Samuel
Hollenback, Thomas
Houseworth, William
Hopewell, John
Hutton, J.S.
Inskeep, James
Inskeep, John W.
Inskeep, W.V.
Irvin, Elias L.
Johnson, George H.
Johnson, Isaac
Johnson, John
Johnson, Robert
Jones, David
Kackley, George
Kackley, Joseph
Kelley, J.T.
Kelley, Patrick
Kuykendall, J.W.

Lamar, William
Leise, George
Leise, James
Leise, John W.
Leps, John C.
Leps, William
Liggett, Calvin
Liller, Isaac
Lovett, Mortimer M.
Lyons, William
Marts, Michael
Maslin, James
Maslin, W.H.
Mathias, G.W.
McAloy, Warren
McBlain, Duncan
McCauley, B.F.
McCord, Thomas
McKee, Smith, F.
McInturff, __
Miller, H.C.
Millison, B.F.
Moore, Joseph
Myers, Samuel
Neal, Thomas
O'Brien, James
Offutt, Jonathan
Pancake, Silas
Paran, John
Parker, James T.
Parrill, J.A.
Parrill, James R.
Parrill, John C.
Parrill, William H.
Parsons, William L.
Pierce, J.T.
Pollock, James
Powers, Daniel
Price, Richard C.
Pugh, James
Pugh, John
Pugh, John W.
Rine, James H.
Rine, John J.
Rinehart, Chandler H.
Rollings, Sanford
Seymour, M.

Shaw, John
Sherrard, Robert
Shillenburg, Amos
Shoemaker, G.W.
Short, James
Shriver, Anthony
Shriver, Henry
Shriver, John
Sisk, C.H.
Skelton, W.M.
Smith, William
Smith, Isaac
Smoot, Charles W.
Stover, John
Taylor, James
Tayor, James H.
Taylor, John W.
Taylor, Rufus
Throckmarton, W.W.
Tilden, Robert J.
Tremon, Eurbrige
Ulum, John
Vance, James
Vandiver, Charles H.
Van Horn, John M.
Vanmeter, Charles W.
Vanmeter, R.B.
Van Meter, David G.
Van Meter, David P.
Van Meter, Edwin
Van Meter, Isaac
Van Meter, Milton
Vest, A.J.
Vest, Charles F.
Warden, Jacob
Warden, James
Warden, William
Welch, Lewis
Welch, Robert
Welton, Aaron
Welton, James
Williams, J.V.
Wood, James
Wright, M.F.
Zell, James A.
Zell, Robert

COMPANY G[7]
Officers

Mason, Dr. J.F., Captain

Davis, Sturgis, Lieut.

Thrasher, Thaddeus, Second
Lieut.

Smith, Jeff, Third Lieut.

Enlisted Men

Annan, Roger
Boone, Daniel
Bouic, J.P.
Brashears, T.P.
Brown, B. Bernard
Brown, Robert
Buck, James
Burns, William
Caldwell, Edward
Canter, John
Carlisle, Charles
Clemens, Ridgley
Contwell, Joseph
Crampton, B.P.
Cross, Lew
Crown, Frederick
Crown, John
Crown, Josh
Dormedy, John
Dorsey, Charles
Dorsey, Nick
Dunlop, John
Edwards, William
Emerson, Ridgley
Gatch, Thomas
Gilbert, Stevens
Gilmor, Harry
Gilmore, Howard
Gittings, Edward
Gover, William

Graham, Israel
Green, John
Grubb, Richard
Hannon, Henry
Higgins, Henry
Higgins, James
Hilleary, Clarence
Hilleary, Thomas
Hoax, Robert
Howell, Rodney
Hughes, Irving
Keller, Ab.
Kemp, William
King, Thompson
Knott, Frank
Lee, Edmund
Marlow, Robert
Marshall, Humphrey
Merriman, Richard
Miller, William
Minor, Fairfax
Money, Ephraim
Mooney, William
Motter, Jake
Norris, James
Orndorf, Jim
Orrison, Town
Osburn, Joseph
Owens, Charles
Paul, William

Peyton, Henry
Philpott, Blanchard
Rate, Charles
Rench, Charles
Ridge, Emerson
Ritenour, W.H.
Russell, Dr. Charles
Sakers, Sam
Shepperd, Abe
Shepperd, Thomas
Singleton, Thomas
Smith, Clapham
Staub, R.P.H.
Stoaks, Brad
Stocks, Thomas
Stone, William
Thomas, Charles
Thomas, James H.
Trapnell, Joseph
Wagner, Charles
Wakenight, William
Welsh, Warner
West, Eugene
West, J.P.
White, E.V.
Wilson, C.P.
Young, Dorie
Young, T.J.

COMPANY H[8]
Officers

Sharp, I.C., Captain

Sharp, Jacob, First Lieut.

Pennybacker, Durich, Second
Lieut.

Enlisted Men

Altafer, J.M
Bean, William
Black, Richard
Bowman, Edward
Bowman, Michael
Brock, Godfrey
Brock, William
Deppo, David

Deppo, Phil
Diddier, Hiram
Dinkle, Enoch
Ettinger, David
Finnegan, Richard
Fitzwaters, Isaac
Folk, John
Good, Jacob

Harlow, Samuel
Harner, George
Hesley, Milton
Hesley, William
Holtsinger, Andrew
Jordan, John

COMPANY I[9]
Officers

Shands, E.H., Captain
Lincoln, A.C., Captain
Roudabush, Noah, D., First Lieut.
Rader, Derrick, First Lieut.
Crawford, John, Second Lieut.

Rease,_____ Third Lieutenant.
Michael, Jacob, Third Lieut.

O'Brian, Moses, Third Lieut.
Hughes, John W., Third Lieut.

Enlisted Men

Archer, Peter
Armentrout, Abraham
Armentrout, David
Baldwin, James
Baxter, Frank
Bazle, Moses
Black, Samuel
Bowman, Benjamin
Bowman, Jacob
Bowman, Michael
Brown, Isaac
Bryan, Jeremiah
Bryan, Robert
Bull, Henry
Bush, Erasmus
Bush, Henry
Cook, John
Depoy, Henry
Depoy, Isaac
Depoy, Philip
Desser, John
Desser, Milton
Detrick, Harvey
Detrick, Jackson
Dinkle, Allen

Dinkle, Enos
Dinkle, John
Flarity, John
Flemming, H.F.
Flemming, J.H.
Flemming, John
Foster, Frank
Gaither, James
Garland, William
Gills, Daniel
Gills, William
Good, Jacob
Good, William
Grannels, Christopher
Gyer, John
Harrington, Henry
Harrison, David
Harrison, William
Hayes, John W.
Hess, Abraham
Hinton, John
Holland, Jerry
Homan, Washington
Homan, William
Hoover, Jacob

Hume, Benjamin
Joseph, John
Joseph, Moses
Joseph, Strother
Kearney, James H.
Kelly, David
Kerigan, Henry
Landis, George
Landis, Robert
Landis, Washington
Latham, James
Laymen, Philip
Laymen, Reuben
Lee, Jack
Lincoln, David
Loftes, Arch
Loftes, Ralph
Loker, Marion
Maupin, Horace
McDorman, John
McDorman, Samuel
McKey, Edward
Michael, R.T.
Morris, George
Morris, Henry

Morris, P.
Odewalt, John
Pennybacker, Joseph
Pirkey, E.
Pirkey, Henry
Planger, Jacob
Planger, Jacob, Jr.
Planger, John
Rader, John
Rader, Peter
Ray, David
Ray, Joseph
Reedy, George
Rhodes, Preston

Richards, James
Riley, Michael
Riley, Owen
Rinehart, John
Robinson, John
Robinson, John, Jr.
Robinson, Richard
Robinson, William
Roudabush, William R
Scott, George
Simpson, Thomas
Smith, Samuel
Terrill, William
Terrill, St. Clair

Thomas, Michael
Thomas, Samuel
Turner, James
Webster, George
Webster, Robert
Webster, William
West, D.
Whisman, Charles
Whisman, James
Whitmore, Frank
Whitmore, John
Winegard, John
Wood, George

COMPANY K[10]
Officers

Miller, William, First Captain
Koontz, H.R.T., Second Captain
Neff, J.G., Third Captain

Mohler, J.A., First Lieut.
Basye, Naason, Second Lieut.

Enlisted Men

Albright, John
Alger, John
Alger, Nathaniel
Andes, Dilmon J.
Baker, Milton O.
Barb, Amos S.
Barb, David
Barb, David A.
Barb, Elias
Barr, Joseph
Bayse, Jonas
Bird, P.M.S
Bird, William Wirt
Bolinger, Adam
Branner, Philip
Bridagum, Isaac
Bridges, Marian F.
Brumbaugh, Green S.
Cave, Benjamin F.
Cave, John H.
Cave, Noah
Clem, Ammon W.
Clem, William B.
Coile, Cain
Coile, Samuel
Cook, Cornelius
Dingledine, Adam

Drummond, Jacob
Drummond, William
Eckard, John
Elbon, Lorenzo D.
Estep, George
Estep, Jesse
Estep, Moses
Estep, William
Fadely, Daniel
Fansler, George W.
Fansler, Siram
Feller, Mahlon G.
Fitzmoyer, Lemuel
Fisher, Joel S.
Foltz, Joseph
Foltz, Nathaniel S.
Foltz, Samuel J.
Fry, Jacob
Frye, Reuben
Frye, William
Funkhouser, Christ. B.
Funkhouser, David
Funkhouser, Isaac
Funkhouser, Jacob H.
Funkhouser, John H.
Funkhouser, Peter
Funkhouser, Samuel H

Funkhouser, Simon
Funkhouser, William
Garber, Joseph, J.
Getz, John
Getz, Samuel D.
Good, Jacob
Good, John W.
Griffith, Mark
Hansbarger, J. Lemuel
Hanson, Samuel
Hanson, William
Harpine, Jonathan J.
Harpine, Silone
Haun, Joseph
Hepner, Dice
Hepner, Gideon
Hepner, Henry
Hepner, Jacob L.
Hepner, James
Hepner, John J.
Higgs, Frank L.
Higgs, Noah
Hollar, Robert S.
Hottel, David H.
Hottel, Nathaniel (Dock)
Hottinger, David (Dwarf)
Keller, Amos

Keller, Ananias
Kelley, Brian T.
Kibler, William
Kipps, Adam
Kipps, Jacob
Kipps, Lewis
Lambert, Joseph
Lichliter, A.J.
Lichliter, Cornelius B.
Lonas, J. Benton
Long, Benjamin F.
Matthews, Robert L.
McInturff, A.P.
McInturff, J.B.
McMullen, David
McWilliams, David
McWilliams, Reuben
Middleton, John
Mohler, Thomas J.
Mohler, William A.
Moomaw, David
Moomaw, George W.
Moomaw, Jesse
Moomaw, Samuel
Moore, William P.
Neff, J. Michael
Nesselrodt, A.J.
Nesselrodt, Job. S.
Orndorff, George W.
Orndorff, John H.

Orndorff, Philip
Overholser, Samuel P.
Peer, John W.
Peer, Joseph
Pence, Adam
Pence, Harrison
Pence, John M.
Pence, John W.
Pence, Micahel J.
Pence, Milton
Pence, Samuel
Pence, William A.
Pennywitt, Reuben
Peters, Amos
Prophet, Jacob
Rau, Samuel
Reedy, David S.
Reedy, John
Rickard, John
Rinker, Israel R.
Ritter, Joseph
Rude, William S.
Ryman, David
Ryman, Thomas J.
Schaeffer, George W.
Schaeffer, John L.
See, Craigen
See, John C.
Sheets, Will
Shutters, Christopher

Shutters, David
Showalter, John H.
Sibert, John M.
Smootz, Harvey
Snarr, John H.
Steinhart, John
Stickley, George
Stickley, Joseph
Straub, Frederick
Swartz, John
Tussing, Henry
Wakeman, John
Walker, Levi
Walters, Lemuel
Webb, Henry
Webb, Isaac
Webb, Jacob
Webb, Reuben
Will, John
Wunder, Henry S.
Zehring, George, W.
Zehring, Jacob
Zehring, John
Zehring, Samuel
Zehring, William
Zirkle, A.J.
Zirkle, J. Michael
Zirkle, Silone

MUSTER ROLL OF ELEVENTH VIRGINIA CAVALRY (LAUREL BRIGADE) ARMY OF NORTHERN VIRGINIA

COMPANY A[11]

Officers

Turner, A.J., Captain
Seibert, J.B., First Lieut.

Wilson, L.F., Second Lieut.

Enlisted Men

Betts, James
Britner, Thad
Butler, John

Callan, Neal
Crane, George
Cross, D.W.

Cross, J.A.
Cross, J.W.
Doran, Joseph

Fooks, J.D.
Harris, C.T.
Hedges, F.F.
Hodson, Louis
Jenkins, James
King, R.A.
Kitchen, Charles
Lillard, Hall
McNamar, Michael
Miller, Henry
Miller, Samuel

Mingle, John
Mowery, John
Norman, Matthew
Patterson, Frank
Patterson, James
Patterson, John
Pifer, George
Post, James
Ritter, Abe
Ritter, J.W.
Rockwell, G.W.

Royce, William
Runk, B.
Satterfield J.W.
Sayles, William T.
Smith, Frank
Sperry, William
Strode, Joseph
Swagard, Louis
Wilson, T.G.

COMPANY B[12]
Officers

Harness, William H., Captain
Alex, S.H., First Lieut.

Lobb, Charles, J, Second Lieut.
Wilson, James, Third Lieut.

Enlisted Men

Albin, James
Amick, Henry
Ashenfelter, David
Bean, Joseph
Beohm, T.S.
Berry, J.W.
Bovinger, George
Branson, William
Cartmell, M.B.
Cartmell, Thomas K.
Cleaver, George
Clem, James H.
Coffman, W.W.
Combs, Armstead
Cook, Abner
Crawford, L.W.
Crites, Daniel
Crites, William
Culdice, William
Cunningham, D.C.
Custard, St. Clair
Daugherty, James H.
Demond, Edward
Dyer, J.W.
Early, James O,.
Fishel, David
Fisher, J.P.C.
Fitzwater, Levi
Fitzwater, _____

Fon, George
Halter, John
Halterman, H.W.
Halterman, Jacob
Halterman, Michael
Hardy, John
Harper, William
Hawes, Jasper
Heiskell, Joe Dan
Hudson, Thomas
Hoffman, Christian
Hulver, Isaac
Hutton, Daniel M.
Judy, Enoch
Ketterman, Aaron
Ketterman, Abraham
Ketterman, Gabriel
Larrick, George B.
Lloyd, Robert
Lloyd William
Longacre, Benjamin
Longacre, C.J.
Lynch, John W.
Lyons, William
May, James M.
Mayhew, James
McDermott, Henry
McKeever, H.C.
McKeever, Isaac

McKeever, William
Miller, Ambrose
Mungold, Solomon
Neff, Mortimer W.
Newhouse, Thomas
Orndorff, Henry J.
Orndorff, Morgan
Pains, John
Painter, Absolom
Parsons, Adam
Pownell, David
Pratt, Job H.
Pratt, John
Reed, H.J.
Riffey, Harvey
Sager, Jacob
Saroil, John
Sherman, Noah
Sine, Bazil
Sine, Benjamin
Sine, Elijah
Snyder, Martin V.
Smith, Daniel
Smith, David
Smith, Joseph
Smith, Reuben
Sulser, John T.
Teetes, Levi
Thorpe, Benjamin F.

Van Meter, David   Webb, Thomas   Witzel, Jacob
Vameter, Isaac   Wilson, George
Violet, W.H.   Wilson, John

COMPANY C[13]
Officers

Pendleton, John R., Captain   Fauley, John, Second Lieut.
Mitchell, E.S., First Lieut.   Pendleton, Edwin, Third Lieut.

Enlisted Men

Aubry, Polk   Hess, Harvey   Showalter, B.F.
Bailey, Henry   Holsinger, John   Showalter, G.W.
Beam, Abraham   Holsinger, Phil   Snyder, D.C.
Beery, I.N.   Hulvy, George   Smith, Harrison
Bennett, Joshua   Jones, Thomas   Smith, Henry
Bragoiner, Hally   King, Wilson   Smith, Thomas
Bull, Henry   Lonthan, James L.   Somers, Reuben
Bush, Charles   Miaphes, Charles   Spencer, Edward
Bush, Samuel   Nane, Joseph   Sprinkel, Calvin
Clem, Ashford   Nazlerod, William   Taylor, Henry
Clem, Frank   O'Roark, Charles   Tennington, Harvey
Cline, Henry   Reed, Abraham   Thomas, Perry
Cook, Joseph   Reedy, Joseph   Vandiver, John
Durrow, Marion   Ritchie, Philip   Vanmeter, Isaac
Erman, James   Ritchie, Simon   Vanmeter, James
Eversole, Peter   Roadcap, Harvey   Walters, William
Famkin, John   Roadcap, Jacob   Wetzel, Simon
Faught, Joseph L.   Roudabush, William   Wilson, George R.
Feller, John :   Sanger, Levi   Witting, Harry
Fink, Noah   Shaner, G.W.   Zetty, Daniel
Gray, Richard   Shipe, Joseph

COMPANY D[14]
Officers

McDonald, E.H., Captain   Blue, John, Second Lieut.
Taylor, William, First Lieut.   Parsons, Isaac, Third Lieut.

Enlisted Men

Abbee, Frederick   Bowers, John W.   Carder, Charles
Abbee, Philip   Brady, Isaac T.   Carder, Frederick
Adams, John   Brill, Mathias   Carroll, Jed
Bane, Samuel   Brown, Frank   Carroll, John
Barnet, Frank   Brown, John   Casler, John O.
Bobo, J.W.   Brown, Richard   Chapman, Charles

Chressap, Robert,
Clary, Dick
Clary, Thad
Clayton, Charles
Conrad, Charles
Conrad, Holmes, Y.
Dailey, Benjamin
Dailey, John
Davie, James
Davie, John
Davis, Morris
Davis, Randolph
Duvall, George
Feshel, S.
Fridle, Samuel
Grove, J.
Haines, Jasper
Hanas, Stephen
Hartman, Ike
Holt, G.
Holt, George
Houser, Henry
Huddleson, Healey
Huddleson, Henry
Hunot, E.
Inskeep, J.V.
Kelley, John

Kidd, R.B.
Leese, Uriah
Light, Edward
Lovett, C.S.
McDonald, William N.
Moorehead, Robert
Moorehead, William
Murphy, Frank
Myers, Frank
Nixon, Lem
Nomstat, Conrad
Pancake, John S.
Pancake, Joseph A.
Pancake, S.
Parsons, James D.
Parsons, John D.
Parsons, William M.
Poland, Amos
Poland John W.
Pownell, Jasper
Ream, James
Riley, Charles
Robinson, Amos
Robinson, Joel
Rudolph, John
Rudolph, Simon
Ruse, John M.

Seibert, Charley
Senoff, Herman
Seward, Joseph
Seymour, Dan
Seymour, John N.
Shelley, James
Shingleton, Abe
Shingleton, Elisha
Sivell, John
Smith, James
Spurline, Luke
Starns, John
Stewart. John
Swartz, Edward
Taylor, D.K.
Taylor, Dudley
Taylor, Enos
Taylor, John
Taylor, Rufus
Uston, John
Washington, Edward
Watkins, Charles
Watkins, H.M.
White, Thomas
Wolfe, Isaac

COMPANY E[15]

Officers

Hess, Joseph, T., Captain
Hooff, J.L., Captain
McGuire, H.H., Captain
Brent, J.W., Lieut.

Hottel, G.W., Lieut.
Hockman, William, Lieut.
Spiker, G.W., Lieut.

Enlisted Men

Agnew, Oscar
Baker, Daniel
Baker, G.W.
Baker, Henry
Baker, Nicholas
Barrenger, Joseph
Beaver, J.E.
Beach, Jacob
Bell, R.F.
Bell, _____
Biers, Charles

Bly, Mason
Bly, Richard
Booth, C.S.
Booth, John F.
Borden, A.P.
Borden, D.M.
Borden, Joseph
Bowman, J.K.
Boyer, Bent
Boyer, J.A.
Brown, J.W.

Buck, Bruce
Bushong, Isaac
Chase, Daniel
Coffman, Walter
Collins, Carson
Cooper, William
Crabill, Benjamin
Crabill, D.G.
Crabill, Hal
Crabill, Jacob
Crabill, L.C.

Crabill, O.H.
DeHaven, Martin
Dewar, J.J.
Dickenson, James
Dodd, R.D.
Eberly, Jacob
Eberly, Isaac
Eberly, Joseph
Effenger, William
Fauver, Noah
Feeley, John
Feeley, Silas
Feeley, William H.
Funkhouser, Amos
Glaize, G.W.
Green James
Green, Zack
Grove, S.M.
Hammond, John
Hammond, Lawrence
Harrison, Howard
Hefline, James
Hess, L. Dow
Hinkins, G.A
Hinkins, J.H.
Hironemoss, Hutch
Hockman, J.W.
Hodges, John
Holler, George
Holler, John
Holler, John A.
Holmes, H.W.
Homes, James
Hoover, William
Hottel, William F.
Huffman, A.J.

Hyde, D.B.
James, Samuel
Kerns, Ephraim
Killmer, James
Lee, G.W.
Lee, Samuel
Luke, William
Lutholtz, Robert
Luttral, Archibald
Lynn, G.B.
Lynn, James
Maphis, George
McCloud, James
McGlincy, R.P.
Miller, J.F.
Miller, J.H.
Miller, William, first
Miller, William,
Mort, Jerry
Omps, James
Pangle, Abe
Pangle, Joseph
Pangle, William E.
Pingley, D.M.
Pogue, R.L.
Reedy, Abe
Rhyne, John
Ridenour, Alfred
Rudy, Isaac
Rutherford, J.A.
Rutherford, Tom, first
Rutherford, Tom,
Scroggins, J.E.
Sensenuey, E.D.
Shafer, Theodore
Shambaugh, Charles

Shambaugh, Cline
Sheets, Daniel
Shotts, Mark
Showalter, Tom
Sievers, G.W.
Smith, James
Snyder, Henry
Snyder, John
Sonner, J.H.
Sonner, J.W.
Stickley, Benjamin
Stickley, David E.
Stickley, D.E
Stickley, D.H.
Stickley, G.W.
Stickley, J.H.
Stickley, Josiah
Stickley, P.D.
Stickley, Walter
Stickley, William
Stover, David
Warner, Philip
Watson, Benjamin
Watson, Jacob
Watson, Samuel
Welch, James
Welch, Joseph
Welch, Samuel
Whitington, Gershen
Whitington, Joseph
Williams, J.J.
Windle, William
Winegood, John
Winegood, Joseph
Wright, Milton

COMPANY F[16]
Officers

McChesney, A.G., First Captain
Ware, A.J., Second Captain
McClintic, Henry, First Lieut.

Gatewood, A.C.L., Second Lieut.
Poage, H.M., Second Lieut.
Bonner, S.A., Second Lieut.

Enlisted Men

Acord, George
Ailstock, Robert
Anderson, Samuel

Banner, S.A.
Beard, E.L.
Beard, John G.

Beard, J.J.
Beard, Moffett
Beard, W.W.

Bradshaw, J.B.
Bratton, A.S.
Bratton, J.F.
Bratton, W.A.
Burger, David
Burnside, James
Callison, J.C.
Chandler, David
Chandler, Samuel
Cleek, D.G.
Cleek, George W.
Cochran, Clark
Cochran, G.B.
Criser, John S.
Criser, R.J.
Dean, William
Dickenson, J.S.
Douglass, Calvin
Douglass, B.
Dunlap, James R.
Eagle, Newton
Edmiston, Andrew
Edmiston, Matthew
Edmiston, Richard
Estes, William
Frazier, James A.
Fry, William
Gibson, Lewis
Gillespie, Joseph, G.
Ginger, George
Grose, Henry
Gwinn, J.K.P.
Gwinn, J.S.
Gwinn, William
Hamilton, Charles
Hamilton, J.A.
Hamilton, J.E.

Hickman, L.W.
Hodge, James
Jordan, James
Jordan, John
Jordan, William
Kennison, Davis
Kennison, J.L.
Keyser, D.W.C.
Keyser, James
Keyser, Hezekiah
King, A.C.
King, Spotswood
Landes, Joseph
Lockridge, David
Lockridge, Stephen
Maffett, George H.
Maffett, W.B.
Martin, W.A.
Mayse, Anderson
McCarty, John
McChesney, James Z.
McDonald, J.P.
McDonnald, G.W.
McElwee, B.D.
McElwee, D.B.
McElwee, Francis
McElwee, John
McNeil, A.G.
Moore, W.H.
Mustoe, David
Mustoe, James
Mustoe,Michael
O'Meara, James
Pauturff, James
Payne, J.E.
Payne, Lewis
Payne, W.H.

Payne, William G.
Porter, A.S.
Price, Henry
Revercomb, Archie
Revercomb, C.T.
Revercomb, George
Revercomb, John
Rosser, John
Shultz, John
Silvers, Joseph
Sittington, Alex. H.
Snead, Robert
Snead, William
Stewart, J.H.
Surber, M.P.
Swarts, Lewis
Swarts, Samuel
Swartz, John
Thomas, Charles
Thomas, David
Thomas, George
Thomas, Samuel
Thompson, Henry
Tinsley, James
Tinsley, W.H.
True, Thomas
Wallace, C.R.
Wave, G.
Wave, O.
Wilkinson, James
Wilfong, Jacob
Williams, E.B.
Williams, E.T.
Williams, Thomas
Windom, John
Wise, Jonathan
Woods, P.A.

COMPANY G[17]

Officers

Dangerfield, Foxhall A., Captain

Mayse, Joseph, First Lieut.

McClintic, Archibald M., Second Lieut.

Warwick, John A., Second Lieut.

Enlisted Men

Ailstock, C.F.
Ailstock, Jordan

Ailstock, Zorobabel
Anderson, William H.

Archie, Robert
Armstrong, Dr. J.M.

Armstrong, Peter
Bishop, George
Booth, _____
Brattan, James
Brattan, J. Mitchell
Brattan, William R.
Brodkin, Ami
Burger, David
Burger, Samuel C.
Burns, John
Burns, Presley F.
Cade, Balis
Cauley, Lee
Cleek, Eli
Cleek, James G.
Coffee, Henry
Cosby, Benjamin G.
Cosby, David
Cosby, John
Crizer, John
Crizer, Lewis
Crizer, Thomas J.
Crizer, W.H.
Curry, Andrew
Dean, William
Donnella, Fendall C.
Donavan, Stephen
Eagle, Newton
Ervin, James
Friel, James
Furr, _____
Gayheart, Joseph
Gendy, Robert
Gladwell, John W.
Glendy, Benjamin
Glendy, John
Glendy, Robert J.
Glendy, Thomas
Green, William
Hively, Thomas J.

Holcomb, Joseph
Hook, Elisha
Hoover, David
Hopkins, William H.
Husk, Thomas J.
Jackson, Peyton
Johnson, _____
Karnes, William H.
Keister, William R.
Kemp, _____
Kincaid, Joseph B.
King, Alexander
Lange, Henry C.
Lange, John
Langridge, Richard
Law, Aaron
Law, Benjamin
Law, James
Law, Stephen
Lewis, Jasper C.
Lockridge, Cooper
Lockridge, John
Lynch, W.L.
Mayse, Allan C.
Mayse, Charles F.
Mayse, George
Mayse, Thomas
McClintic, Adam,
McClintic, Andrew B.
McClintic, George T.
McClintic, James
McClintic, John S.
McClintic, Robert
McClintic, William S.
McDannald, D. Crockett
McDannald, William C.
McDannald, William R.
McMath, Samuel S.
Oliver, C.H.
Oliver, Joseph

Payne, Charles
Phillips, Thomas
Phillips, William
Price, Andrew G.
Reynolds, William H.
Richy, Joseph
Richy, William
Rogers, Stephen
Silvers, Joseph
Shumate, John K.
Simpson, George
Simpson, John
Simpson, William
Smith, Charles
Smith, James
Smith, Stuart
Taylor, Almond C.
Thomas, Charles
Thomas, Jacob
Thomas, Samuel
Thompson, Benjamin
Thompson, Charles
Thompson, George
Thompson, Mason
Thompson, William P.
Wallace, Andrew
Wallace, Christopher
Warwick, J.W., Jr.
Wilkinson, Robert S.
Williams, Anthony G.
Williams, Erasmus
Williams, Harvey
Williams, James
Williams, Lewis
Winthrow, Jack
Woodzell, B.F.
Woodzell, William
Young, George

COMPANY H[18]

Officers

Pierce, A.M., Captain   Braxton, _____, Second Lieut.
Sherrard, Joseph, First Lieut.

Enlisted Men

Ashwood, Joseph	Frye, B.F.	Orndorff, Lemuel
Bowman, John	Frye, James	Orndorff, M.
Cauplin, P.	Frye, Joseph P.	Orndorff, Phineas
Clark, James	Green, J.B.	Orndorff, Setz
Conner, James	Himelright, James	Shell, Samuel
Conner, Morgan	Himelright, Joseph M.	Smith, Sandy
Cooper, R.M.	Huff, John	Smith, William
Crosin, Randolph	Keiffer, James	Whetzel, James
Dinkel, Peter	Lichliter, Daniel	White, Ira
Eskridge, Heck	Linaburg, Martin	Wilson, Martin
Fauver, John	Marker, Amos E.	Wimer, Jack
Fauver, Samuel	Orndorff, Amos	Wireman, John
Frye, Al	Orndorff, Ananias	
Frye, A.N.	Orndorff, Joseph B.	

COMPANY I[19]
Officers

Ball, M.M., Captain	Moore, Alfred, Lieut.
Kirby, William H., Lieut.	Reid, William H., Lieut.

Enlisted Men

Alexander, B.	Dodd, Markus	Morter,_____
Alexander, D.	Donatini, L.G.	Nelson, James W.
Ball, Charles H.	Estes,_____	Nelson, Joseph
Ball, John H.	Everson, Doyle	Perry, Alex
Ball, John T.	Fairfax, John	Ratcliffe, C.W.
Ball, Lewin T.	Fenton, J.B.	Reid, E.C.
Ball, Summerfield	Ford, W.E.	Ritenour, David
Ball, William S.	Gheen, G.	Rutler, G.W.
Ball, William W.	Grigsby, P.C.	Saunders, Plunk
Bell, B.A.	Grigsby, T.M.	Smith, A.M.
Bell, G.H.	Harding, G.	Smith, F.M.
Billings, Edward	Harrison, George H.	Speaks, J.H.
Billings, William	Heath, J.B.	Stalcup, Joshua
Burke, T.T.	Hughes, D.	Summers,_____
Butler, W.B.	Hughes, John T.	Taylor, John S.
Carrigan, J.P.	Hughes, L.T.	Thompson, Joseph
Cashman, T.	Jeffries, Richard	Toole, John
Catlett, H.C.	Kirby, Asbury	Toole, Patrick
Cleveland, H.C.	Kirby, George F.	Utterback, William H.
Clump, John	McCartney,_____	Ward, Joseph
Cockrell, Seth	McClannahan, John	Williams, R.
Cooksey, J.W.	McClung,_____	Winn, John
Cooney, Patrick	McCorkle,_____	

COMPANY K[20]
Officers

Powell, William, Lieut.   Smith, Jack, Second Lieut.

Enlisted Men

Chappell, George   Murphy, J.T.   Smith, Jackson
Drish, Donk   Murphy, Moses B.   Stickles, Henry
Furr, Frazier   Powell, Lute   Stickles, Jno. M.
Furr, Harris   Powell, Watt   Thompson, William
Grimes, George   Pyles, William   Tomblin, James
Grimes, Joseph   Shafer, John T.   Wiley, James
Moore, James   Shell, Alfred   Willingham, George
Moore, Joseph C.   Smith, George

MUSTER ROLL OF TWELFTH VIRGINIA CAVALRY (LAUREL BRIGADE), ARMY OF NORTHERN VIRGINIA
Regimental Officers

Harman, Asher W., Colonel   Knott, John Locher, Major
Massie, Thomas E., Lieut. Col-
onel   Harman, Lewis, Captain

COMPANY A[21]
Officers

Isabel,_____, First Captain   Engle, Jacob, First Lieut.
Henderson, John, Second Cap-
tain   Engle, Samuel M., Second Lieut.
Glenn, James W., Third Captain   Owen, Charles, Third Lieut.
Morrow, W.H., Fourth Captain

Enlisted Men

Ashby, G.H.   Blue, John   Burns, Isaac
Ashby, John   Blue, Joseph G.   Butt, J.W.
Barrett, Charles   Bolus, Thomas   Cameron, William H.
Barringer, Frank   Boyer, George   Cincindiver, George
Belt, Adam S.   Briscoe, William   Cincindiver, James
Billmyer, William   Brown, Joe   Cincindiver, John
Blackford, Corbin   Brown, Thomas   Cincindiver, Samuel
Blake, George V.   Burner, C. Eldridge   Cockrill, Thomas

Colbert, John
Coleman, John
Coyle, I.M.
Coyle, Jerome, B.
Coyle, Joseph H.
Cramer, Robert
Dailey, John
Dailey, Richard
Dillow, Joe
Dixon, George
Dooley, Lewis
Doran, James
Doran, J.W.
Doran, Matthew
Dorsey, Patrick
Driscol, Daniel
Engle, Benjamin
Engle, Brent
Engle, Henry
Engle, William
Foreman, Charles
Foreman, Perry
Fraley, David
Fritts, John
Gainor, Patrick
Garrison, Lewis
Geisling, Harrison
Gheisling, James
Glassford, Alexander
Grove, Henry
Harrold, Elihu
Hawthorn, J.J.
Hess, J. Frank
Hicks, John
Hiser, John
Homer, Sandy
Homer, Thomas
Homer, William
Hosier, James
Hughes, Thomas

Jones, George
Jones, James
Jones, John
Kane, Maurice
Keller, John
Kerfott, P.
Kimmell, Isaac
Kimmell, John
Lance, James
Langdon, James A.
Lattimer, T.
Lewis, George M.
Lyons, Jeff
McCann, Patrick
McGarry, James W.
McGlone, Edward
McSherry, William
McWinkle, J.
Manuel, Columbus
Manuel, Jasper
Manuel, John
Manuel, Lucien
Manuel, Thornton
Mercer, Fenton
Miller, James
Moore, Albert
Moore, A.L.
Moore, Vincent
Morgan, Samuel
Nelson, Isaac
Niceley, A.D.
Noland, Charles
O'Bannon, Alfred
O'Bannon, Hiram
O'Connell, Patrick
Osborn, James
Painter, Jacob
Painter, James
Painter, Lewis
Pearl, Burt

Piper, James
Piper, William
Ramey, Isaac
Ramey, Michael
Reed, Benjamin
Roberts, Samuel
Roberts, William
Rockenbaugh, John W.
Sager, John
Seldon, Carey
Sencindiver, G.W.
Shepherd, William
Shipway, Thomas
Skinner, William
Small, A.S.
Souders, F.B.
Spates Charles
Staley, Parin
Staub, Jesse
Staub, Lewis
Taylor, John
Thompson, Charles
Thomspon, Josiah
Trist, John
Vaughn, S.
Wageley, William
Way, Harrison A.
Webster, Dallas
Webster, Thomas D.
Whittington, Daniel
Whittington, James C.
Whittington, James N.
Whittington, John N.
Wiltshire, Charles, B.
Wiltshire, James G.
Wright, Joseph T.
Wright, W.H.
Yoll, Stephen
Zombro, George

COMPANY B[22]
Officers

Baylor, R.W., Captain
Rouss, Milton, First Lieut.
Roland, George, Second Lieut.

Washington, B.C., Second Lieut.
Baylor, George, Third Lieut.

Enlisted Men

Abril, Robert P.
Aisquith, E.M.
Aisquith, William
Alexander, Charles
Alexander, Herbert
Allen, William
Anderson, Isaac
Averill, William
Baker, William H.
Baney, Thaddeus
Barringer, James
Baylor, Richard C.
Baylor, Robert W., Jr.
Beall, H.,D.
Bell, Daniel
Berry, Charles
Boley, Frank
Bonham, Edward
Butler, J.D.
Callahan, Ferdinand
Cameron, William H.
Castleman, Robert
Chew, John
Clapsaddle, William
Colbert, Joseph
Coleman, John
Conklyn, C.C.
Conklyn, J.H.
Conrad, J.M.
Conrad, Morris
Cooke, B.W.
Cookus, Robert
Copeland, Philip D.
Coyle, James W.
Craighill, Robert
Crane, Charles L.
Crane, James C.
Crane, Joseph
Creaton, George
Dovenberger, Daniel
Easterday, John S.
Easterday, Joseph H.
Eastham, Jackson
Eddins, H.C.
English, W.D.
Faughnder, Daniel
Faughnder, Fenton
Frazier, W.C.
Fry, Jesse P.

Fry, Joseph D.
Furley, John
Gallaher, Edward
Gallaher, James N.
Gallaher, J.H.
Gallaher, J.S.
Garrison, Thomas
Gibson, William H.,
Gordon, Abraham
Grantham, John S.
Hardesty, Charles R.
Harvey, William
Hatcher, William R.
Hendeson, Charles E.
Henderson, Robert
Heskitt, William
Hesser, C.F.
Hilbert, George
Hilbert, John E.
Hoffmaster, John W.
Howell, John M.
Hunter, H.C.
Hutchinson, Julian
Huyett, R.D
Isler, C.H.
Johnson, Charles G.
Jordan, M.F.
Kanode, B.W.
Lackland, E.M.
Lewis, B.F.
Lewis, David
Lewis, Elisha
Lewis, F.J.
Lewis, John L.
Locke, William F.
McCluer, John
McDonough, James
McKown, Warner
Manning, Addison D.
Manning, Charles J.
Manning, F.J.
Manning, George U.
Manning, William P,.
Mason, William S.
Moore, Monrose
Mumaw, W.H.
Myers, Thomas
Neill, Samuel B.
Nicely, Charles

Noland, Samuel C.
Partlow, E.L.
Randall, James
Ranson, B.B.
Ranson, Thomas D.
Redman, Thomas B.
Rickamore, George C.
Ridgeway, Josiah
Rouss, Charles B.
Rowland, J.H.
Rucker, S.
Ryman, F.
Sadler, L.L.
Selden, W.C.
Shewbridge, J.H.
Smith, John W.
Starry, Tustin
Strider, Isaac H.
Tearney, George
Tearney, Leonidas
Terrill, John U.
Terrill, Philip
Thomson, William S.
Timberlake, George
Timberlake, Harry
Timberlake, James H.
Timberlake, Joseph E.
Timberlake, Richard
Timberlake, Stephen
Timberlake, S.W.
Timberlake, T.W.
Trussell, C.W.
Trussell, E.C.
Trussell, J.T.
Trussell, Moses E.
Wade, Algernon S.
Walker, George
Walker, John
Washington, George
Washington, James C.
Watkins, John
West, A.J.
Whittington, Benjamin
Whittington, James
Willis, Albert
Willis, Frank
Willis, W. Beale
Wilson, William L.
Wiltshire, J.C.

Wingard, George   Wysong, R.L.   Zombro, John D.
Wolfe, John W.   Yates, John O.   Zombro, Thomas B.
Workman, John   Young, Mason E.
Wright, Samuel   Zombro, James W.

COMPANY C[23]
Officers

Ford, John H., Captain   Wood, Joseph R., Second Lieut.
Myers, W.H., First Lieut.   Sydnor, Richard, Third Lieut.

Enlisted Men

Adams, John D.   Fenwick, William   Miller, Robert
Ashwood, Eli   Flowers, Frank   Patterson, Henry
Ashwood, Thomas   Fry, Jesse   Patterson, Newton
Baker, Henry   Fry, Marshall   Perry, Joseph
Baker, John   Fugerson, Charles   Piper, Calvin
Baker, William   Fugett, George   Piper, William
Baylis, Milton   Ginn, C.H.   Pitcher, William
Beemer, John   Glaze, Henry   Pitman, Archie
Bell, Henry   Grove, Josiah   Pitman, John
Bell, John   Harris, Sulton   Pitman, Joseph
Bell, Joseph   Heitt, J.T.   Pitzer, Alexander
Bennett, Peter   Heironomus, R.S.D.   Pitzer, Charles
Bowers, Frank   Herbert, William   Reed, W.E.
Brown, James   Hilliard, George   Rudolph, Joseph
Brown, Joseph   Hilliard, Jacob   Rudolph, N.
Brumback, Dallas   Hunter, George   Roderick, Thomas
Brumback, Jacob   Huntsberry, Henry   Russell, J.W.
Brumback, Joseph   Huntsberry, Jacob   Shank, Henry C.
Carter, Charles   Jackson, T.J.   Sharley, John
Carter, Joseph   Jenkins, John   Shepherd, I.N.
Chenowith, George   Jones, Charles   Shroad, David
Colsten, John T.   Kaufman, G.   Shroad, George
Copenhaver, Morgan   Keefer, Frederick   Shrout, Lewis
Crisman, Jacob   Kramer, William   Shull, Briscoe
Daugherty, William   Leopard, William   Snapp, Sydner
Davis, Edgar   Lupton, John   Sperry, W.S.
Diffendiver, Benjamin   Loge, Jacob   Stricker, Robert
Dugans,_____   Marker, J.M.   Stump, Calvin
Dugans,_____   Marshall, Edward   Sydnor, Cyrus
Eddy, Theodore   McDonald, James   Sydnor, Fauntleroy
Eddy, Thomas M.   McDonald, Joseph   Tanquary, Henry
Everhart, Jackson   McDonald, Marshall   White, John
Everhart, Newton   McDonald, Samuel   Wisecarver, A.
Everhart, Thomas   Meade, James   Wright, Joseph
Fenwick, Ignatius   Miller, Dudley   Yeakley, Martin
                                                Yole, J.P.

COMPANY D[24]
Officers

Kearney, H.W., Captain   James, J.W., Second Lieut.
Engle, George, First Lieut.   Lucas, Benjamin, Third Lieut.

Enlisted Men

Adams, W.A.	Fincham, H.	Keys, James
Allen, James	Flanagan, William	Keys, J. Richard
Allen, John	Fraley, Dave	Kilmer, Harry
Andrews, Daniel	Fraley, James	Kirby, T.L.
Andrews, John	Frazier, James	Kisner, Joseph
Athey, James	Furrey, John	Knott, Charles, H.
Backus, H.C.	Furrey, Martin	Knott, George S.
Badger, John	Gall, George	Knott, Samuel M.
Bane, Garrett	Gay, James	Lambert, Charles
Banks, Washington	Goodwin, Charles	Leopold, Andrew
Barnhart, George	Hagley, George H.	Lewis, David
Berlin, Charles	Haines, Charles	Lewis, John
Beyer, Gus	Halpin, Robert	Licklider, Frank
Bowers, George W.	Hanby, William	Licklider, John
Brantner, George	Hartman, George	Licklider, Joseph S.
Brubaker, Isaac	Hastings, Daniel	Loudon, John
Burley, P.	Hayslett, John	McBee, William
Caton, George W.	Hayslett, William	McCleary, J.W.
Chambers, I.M.	Heckroach, William	McGarry, James W.
Chambers, M.	Hendricks, Daniel W.	Mackin, Patrick
Chambers, T.T.	Hendricks, J.M.	Melvin, James
Claw, A.J.	Hendricks, Tobias	Melvin, William
Clymer, Dan	Henkle, D. Grove	Merritt, Henry
Clymer, Frank	Henry, William	Minghinni, Joseph
Coffinbarger, J.W.	Herr, E.G.W.	Moler, D. Griff
Colbert, Richard	Hess, Charles	Moler, George
Conrad, Alexander	Hicks, J.W.	Moler, H. Clay
Conrad, Nathaniel	Higgins, Andrew	Moler, Jacob
Cook, George	Higgins, Owen	Moler, Newton
Cook, James	Hipsley, Thomas P.	Moler, Raleigh
Currie, Charles	Hoffman, David	Moler, Rollin
Day, Samuel	Hoffman, George	Moler, Sanders
Deck, E.C.	Hoffman, John	Moler, William J.
Deck, Fred	Holmes, David C.	Moore, Bart
Dickson, J.C.	Hough, Mason	Moore, George
Dodson, Thomas	House, Samuel	Moore, Hedley
Doran, W.	Hudson, Charles	Morgan, Frank
Elliott, Charles	Johnson, E.C.	Morningstar, Charles
Engle, Benjamin	Johnson, George	Nichols, Lewis
Engle, H.C.	Johnson, William	Ogden, John J.
Eskridge, Thomas	Kephart, Jacob	Osbourn, A.L.
Farnsworth, John B.	Kephart, W.H.H.	Osbourn, George W.

Osbourn, James B.
Osbourn, Robert.L.
Patten, James
Polly, Samuel
Prather, Charles
Prather, Denton
Pretzman, Wallace
Reed, Samuel
Reinhart, A. Phillip
Reinhart, William
Ritter, James
Roberts, James
Roberts, Robert
Roe, George
Ronemous, George

Rowdan, John
Rutherford, Thomas
Shewbridge, John H.
Shirley, James
Show, Collin
Simpson, John T.
Slavin, John
Smith, George
Smith, William
Snyder, James
Snyder, John
Staley, William
Strider, Howard
Swimley, H. Harrison
Swimley, J. Samuel

Walker, T.L.
Ware, Richard
Watson, Bart
Watson, Eph
Watson, G.W.
Watson, William
Welch, Michael
Whittington, James
Wilson, John
Wintermoyer, William
Wright, James
Yates, John R.
Zombro, Isaac

COMPANY E[25]
Officers

Marshall, James, Captain
McKay, J.C., First Lieut.

Marshall, Thomas, Second Lieut.
Marshall, James, Second Lieut.

Enlisted Men

Amiss, J.B.
Bauserman, W.H.
Berryman, George
Berryman, Thomas
Berryman W.A.
Biedler, Jacob
Bolen, A.R.
Bowman, Allen
Bowman, John
Bowman, W.H.
Boyd, M.A.
Brannan, A.J.
Brewer, J.W.
Brown, J.W.
Bushong, Calvin
Bushong, Edward Mark
Bushong, James
Bushong, Mark
Castillo, John
Conrad, W.B.
Crabill, Silas
Cullers, L.H.
Delinger, John
Derflinger, James
Forsythe, William

Fox, Sidney
French, James H.
Garrett, R.M.
Green, E.A.
Hall, David
Hall, Elijah
Hall, Jeff
Hall, Wesley
Hockman, Henry
Hottle, Nathaniel
Hyde, Peter S.
Jenkins, Gabriel
Johnson, Joseph
Keiser, Edwin
Kelley, Patrick
Kern, Hy
Knight, George
Lake, A.
Lambert, William
Legg, Bushrod
Legg, J.B.
Lichliter, Wayman
Maddox, C.J.
Maddox, J.N.,
Maddox, J.W.

Maddox, R.B.
Maddox, T.S.
Maddox, W.B.
Majers, Hy, Coleman
Marshall, Alfred
Marshall, Charles
Marshall, James
Marshall, Thomas
McDonald, George
McInturff, James
McKens, H.
Miller, David
Mills, Charles
Mills, John
Mills, Robert
Painter, W.H.
Pence, Lemuel
Pickrell, George
Pickrell, Hy. C.
Riley, R.V.
Rouzee, Benjamin
Rucker, Samuel
Ryman, George
Ryman, Isaac
Sealcock, George

Sealves, George   Smith, John   Williams, William
Shipe, Jacob   Smoot, Philip   Wright, A.M.
Silmond, Richard   Strickler, Abram   Wright, Silas
Smith, A.M.   Strickler, Martin
Smith, Ch.   Strother, John A.

COMPANY F[26]
Officers

Gilmor, Harry, Captain   Hurst, Maury, Second Lieut.
Clarke, James, Captain
Welsh, Warner, First Lieut.

Enlisted Men

Cook, John H.   Hansburger, Samuel   Richardson, W.H.

The company was not strong numerically, but was composed of splendid fighting men, and it is unfortunate no record of its brilliant achievements on detached service and with the brigade has been obtainable, and that only a partial roll of officers and men seems to have been preserved.

COMPANY G[27]
Officers

Willis, A.M., Captain   Eastham, John , Third Lieut.
Swindler, A.C., First Lieut.   Brownell, W.F., Third Lieut.
Anderson, W.F., Second Lieut.

Enlisted Men (partial listing)

Anderson, H.B.   Fogg, Joseph   Schwartz, John
Baggarly, Charles   Grigsby, Elijah   Schwartz, Thomas
Byers,_____   Hackley, James   Sindle, Samuel J.
Carter, F. Pendleton Howard, H.R.   Turner, Jordan
Dearing, James A.   Jenkins, Mat   Turner, Thomas
Dodson, Lloyd   Kirby, Thomas   Van Horn, Samuel
Dodson, Stephen   Partlow, Leonard   Weakley, James K.
Dodson, William   Pierce, Brock   Wood, R.J.
Fincham, Fidler   Priest, Mason
Finchams, Jack   Rosson, John

COMPANY H[28]
Officers

Sipe, Emanuel, Captain

Randolph, E.C., First Lieut.

Arehart, Casper H., Second Lieut.

Kratzer, Joseph, Second Lieut.

Horn, O.P., Third Lieut.

Simpson, John R., Third Lieut.

Keller, J.W., Fourth Lieut.

Enlisted Men

Adams, George W.
Alford, Robert
Altoffer, J.M.
Altoffer, John
Altoffer, Joseph
Altoffer, Martin
Altoffer, William
Arehart, Nason
Arehart, W. Harvey
Arehart, W.H.
Ary, John A.
Baker, Isaac
Baker, Jacob
Baker, Samuel
Bare, David
Bare, John S.
Bateman, Elijah
Bouman, Berryman T.
Bouman, Casper
Bouman, David H.
Bouman, Ephraim
Bouman, John S.
Bouman, J.W.
Bouman, Socrates
Bowman, Alpheus, M.
Bowman, Franklin M.
Bowman, Paul C.
Bowman, Solon M.
Bowman, S.S.
Brannaman, Milkiah
Bright, John
Brooks, Hess
Brooks, John
Brown, John M.
Brunk, Abraham
Carpenter, W.J.
Clatterbuck William
Cool, Littington
Crann, John S.

Crann, Samuel
Danner, David
Dinkle, Calvin
Dovel, Lucious
Dundore, David
Dundore, Samuel
Ettinger, William
Fately, Sylvanus
Fifer, Jerry
Fitch, Buck
Frankum, John
Frankum, Walker
Garber, Daniel
Glovier, J.H.
Glovier, Madison
Gowl, Daniel
Gowl, Peter
Gowl, William
Grandstaff, Branson
Groves, William H.
Hawkins, Jacob
Hawkins, W.H.
Hidecker, William
Hile, Samuel
Hinegardner, Jacob
Holsinger, Abraham
Holsinger, John D.
Holsinger, Martin
Holsinger, Peter, P.
Holsinger, Samuel
Holsinger, Silas J.
Huffman, John W.
Huffman, Joseph H.
Jennings, Dallas
Jimison, John W.
Jones, Adam
Keller, Phillip
Lacky, Robert
Lairy, John

Loker, Thomas
Long, Cooney
Long, Samuel
Marshall, Thomas
Maston, John
May, Joseph F.
McLaughlin, Joseph
Miller, Jacob
Moore, John H.
Moyers, Jacob
Nyres, E.P.
Naras, Patrick
Neff, Washington L.
Oaks, Dick
Orebaugh, William H.
Painter, Allen
Painter, Robert
Painter, Romannus
Painter, Uriah
Parry, Thomas
Phillips, John
Phillips, Nathaniel
Pitt, Samuel
Plecker, William
Rice, Bram. M.
Rice, Joseph
Rinker, Erasmus
Ritchie, Dallas
Ritchie, George
Ritchie, Joseph
Ritchie, Polk
Roller, Emanuel
Roller, Henry
Roller, Peter
Ryman, Samuel A.
Saufley, Joseph
Saufley, William
Sherman, D.W.
Showalter, Samuel

Slusser, Samuel
Slusser, William
Smith, Allen
Smith, David
Smith, Noah
Spader, John

Stover, Jacob
Strickler, B.F.
Sylvins, Moses
Treavy, J.C.
Trobough, John
White, Milton

Whitesell, Jacob
Wilberger, David
Will, Nason
Will, William A.
Wine, John
Wine, William

COMPANY I[29]

Officers

O'Ferrall, Charles T., Captain
Harman, Lewis, Captain

Eastham, Granville, First Lieut.
Rust, John R., Second Lieut.

Enlisted Men

Ash, Buckner
Ash, George A.
Ashby, John W.
Ashby, Lewis
Ashby, Russell
Baker, Jonas
Biggs, Elias
Black, Benjamin F.
Black, Henry A.
Breedlove, Samuel
Brown, John T.
Burk, Thomas
Chapman, J.A.
Cooley, Peter F.
Cooley, Samuel C.
Cooley, Smith
Coomes, Joseph R.
Costello, Edward
Coverstone, Lewis
Crawley,_____
Cunningham, John F.
Davis, A.C.
Eichelberger, D.S.
Flynn, James A.
Furgeson, Abner
Green, Casper, W.
Grubbs, James
Harrison, William H.
Haskins, Daniel
Haskins, William A.

Heiflebower, Edward
Holmes, William F.
Johnson, Thomas
Kem, Henry R.
Lake, Enoch A.
Lake, John H.
Long, Isaac
Massie, Edward G.
McKay, John W.
McKay, Joseph
Mitchell, I. Ship
Muman, William
Oliver, Alfred
Oliver, John B.
Page, Thomas D.
Palmer, Robert
Payne, Edward S.
Petty, George N.
Petty, Thomas W.
Powers, John W.
Putnam, W.R.F.
Reid, George W.
Reid, John R.
Reiley, J.M.
Reiley, J.W.
Rice, Benjamin F.
Ridgeway, Joseph
Ridgeway, Newton
Robinson, James T.
Ruffner, Benjamin F.

Ruley, William A.
Russell,_____
Rust, Bushrod
Santmyers, D.M.
Seibert, George W.
Sherrard, William
Stokes, Newton
Stout, George
Strother, George W.
Strother, James W.
Strother, John I.
Strother, John W.
Strother, Lewis
Strother, R.F.
Strother, William
Tally, John
Templeman, James
Thornhill, Philetus
Tolbert, Charles W.
Turner, James C.
Vermillian, James
Wade, Horace, M.
Warwicks, John
White, James W.
Woodward, Thomas E.
Yuille, A.B.
Yuille, A.C.
Yuille, Thomas

MUSTER ROLL OF THIRTY-FIFTH VIRGINIA CAVALRY (WHITE'S BATTALION) LAUREL BRIGADE, ARMY OF NORTHERN VIRGINIA

Regimental Officers

White, Elijah, V., Colonel   Myers, F.M., Major
Ferneyhough, George N., Major

COMPANY A[30]
Officers

Myers, F.M., Captain   Marlow, R.C., Second Lieut.
Barrett, William F., First Lieut. Conrad, B.F, Third Lieut.

Enlisted Men

Anderson, Colmore	Dove, Joseph	Jacobs, George W.
Bales, Charles A.	Drish, Edwin	Jenkins, J.J.
Ballenger, Benjamin F.	Edwards, William	Jenkins, Samuel
Barker, Rufus C.	Ellmore, George	Jones, Edward F.
Barrett, C. Boyd	Ellmore, John D.	Kabrich, Peter J.
Bennett, Edward L.	Everhart, George F.	Kane, Doc
Bicksler, John F.	Fletcher, James H.	Keighn, Samuel
Brown,_____	Fletcher, John T.	Kephart, Jasper C.
Brown, William	Fletcher, John W.	Kephart, John
Bussard, Lycurgus	Foley, Fenton	Kidwell, James E.
Buzzard, O.M.	Freeman, James	Kilgore, Mortimer
Carper, Philip W.	Galloway, Charles	Kyle, William P.
Chadwell, John R.	Galloway, Charles F.	Lee, David J.
Cockerill, A.J.	Galloway, William	Lee, Edgar A.
Coe, Aurelius	Garrett, Albert T.	Lee, George
Conner, Joseph, E.	Goard, John	Lee, James E.
Conrad, Jonathan T.	Grubb, H.	Lee, John F.
Cook, Alfred, M.	Grubb, T.	Lee, William W.
Craig, George W.	Hancock, James W.	Leslie, Benjamin F.
Crumbaker, Samuel W.	Harding, Albert	Lewis, John
Curry, William F.	Harding, Richard	Lewis, Thomas R.
Cuizen, William T.	Harper, James W.	Luckett, William H.
Darr, James W.	Hayes, Brook	Lyon, William L.
Debutts, John	Herndon, Joseph	Marlow, John H.
Donohoe, Legrand	Hibbs, Henry C.	McCauley, John F.
Douglas, Edward	Horseman, William H.	McDonough, W.W.
Douglas, James R.	Householder, William O.	McFarland, Henry C.
Douglas, John	Howard, John	McFarland, Richard
Douglas, Ross	Hummer, Braden	McFarland, William A.,
Douglas, Samuel E.	Hummer, Henry O.	Miller, George
Douglas, Theodore	Hutchenson, John R.	Minor, Fairfax C.
Dove, John	Hutchinson, George C.	Mobberly, John W.

Mock, G.
Moore, Henry R.
Moreland, William, H.H.
Muse, John W.
Myers, Charles P.
Myers, Thomas J.
O'Neal, James W.
O'Niel, Edward
Orrison, John W.
Oxley, E.R.
Palmer, Mortimer, M.
Pettingall, D.C.
Pickett, Enoch F.
Polland, James E.
Presgraves, Philip
Presgraves, Samuel T.
Price, Joseph
Prince, Daniel L.
Richards, Lewis

Riley, James
Robertson, Jacob R.
Ryan, Henry C.
Ryan, James M.
Ryan, William
Saffer, B.F.
Sampsell, Henry G.
Selman, Henry
Sheeves, W.M.J.
Shugars, C.H.
Simpson, Henry
Simpson, John F.
Sinclair, John H.
Sloper, John T.
Smith, James B.N.
Snoots, William
Spates, T.G.
Stephenson, John
Survick, George W.

Tavenner, Edward
Tavenner, E.H.
Tipper, Thomas C.
Titus, William
Tribby, James W.
Tribby, John T.
Van Devanter, T.H.
Walker, Charles C.
Walker, John
Walker, William T.
Wenner, C.C.
Whaley, Charles A.
Whaley, C.M.C.
Whaley, J.W.
White, John W.
Wooten, D.
Wycoff, A.C.

COMPANY B[31]
Officers

Christwell, G.W., Captain
Crown, J.R., First Lieut.

Dorsey, Nicholas, Second Lieut.
White, S.C., Third Lieut.

Enlisted Men

Allen,_____
Alridge, Robert
Beall, Thomas
Bezant, William T.
Boswell, William
Brady, Edward
Brisnan, John
Butler, Charles E.
Butler, George
Cantwell, Michael
Carlyle, David
Carlyle, William
Cecil,_____
Christwell, Edward
Christwell, William
Coberth, David
Craft, John
Crown, Frederick
Crown, John O.
Dade, Lee
Dade, Robert T.

Darne, William
Davis, James
Davison, John
Durham, James
Eader, Charles
Eader, Lewis
Elgin, John O.
Fitch, William
Fitzsimmons, Nicholas
Gallager,_____
Green, Charles
Gordon,_____
Grahame, William
Harding, Abraham
Harewood, Thomas
Hays, Brook
Hays, R.P.
Heffner, Stephen
Henderson, G.
Herbert, William
Jones, Benjamin

Key, Daniel
Lamar, Ab.
Lowry, James
Magaha, Joseph
Martin, Pinckney
Maxwell, John
McCormick,_____
Morris, George
Morris, John
Needhammer, Lewis
O'Boyle Charles
O'Boyle, James
Oden, William
Orme, Henry
Orme, Lindley
Peter, J.P.C.
Peters, Thomas
Phillips, Crome
Price, Elias
Pyles, Frank
Pyles, Thomas

Scholl, C.E.
School, John
Sellman, Alonzo
Sellman, H.O.
Shehan, William
Smith, Charles
Smith, Rice
Stallings, Richmond
Stewart, Henry
Stone, William

Tabler, John
Taylor, Martin
Thomas, Byron
Thomas, Edwin
Thomas, Frank
Thomas, Jacob
Thomas, L.
Trundle, Joseph
Van Bussum,_____
Veirs, Boling

Veirs, Elijah
Veirs, William S.
Vinson, Joseph
Welsh, Edward
White, J.C.
White, S.C.
White, Thomas
White, William
Williams, Frank
Yingling, Zadoe

COMPANY C[32]
Officers

Grubb, Richard, B., Captain
Dowdell, William Flavius, Second
Captain

Grubb, Samuel E. First Lieut.
White, Thomas W., Second
Lieut.

Enlisted Men

Armstrong, William H.
Beans, Aaron T.
Beans, Elwood, H.
Beans, William Flavius
Beans, William H.
Best, E.J.
Birkby, Collins T.
Boling, John
Boling, William D.
Burress, Thomas
Campbell, E.T.
Canada, Thomas
Carlisle, John H.
Chamblin, George
Chamblin, John M.
Chamblin, Richard
Clendening, John J.
Clendening, William T.
Compton, Burrell
Compton, J. Booten
Copeland, Dr. James E
Copeland, James R.
Copeland, Silas
Davis, Edgar
Davis, William H.
Davisson, John William
DeButts, Welby
Dorrell, James A.

Douglas, John
Elgin, Thomas G.
Elmore, George
Elmore, John H.
Fogg, Elias W.
Follin, Ira
Follin, J.N.
Follin, Richard
Foster, James M.
Fouche, Sydney
Fritts, James
Fritts, William
Gooding, J. Edward
Gooding, William D.
Graham, James M.
Grubb, Rev. James W.
Grubb, John Caden
Grubb, Joseph M.
Grubb, William Hilt
Hammerly, John W.
Hart, Joseph S.
Henderson, Charles
Hood, James
Hood, Smith
Hough, James W.
Hough, Thomas E.
Houser, John H.
Howell, Benton D.

Jenkins, Norval
Jenkins, Reuben
Jett, William
Jones, William R.
Keith, E.J.
Keith, William
Keyes, Landon H.
Kilgour, Franklin
Kilgour, J. Mortimer
Lay, Craven C.
Marion, Gabriel
Matthews, Rodney
McDaniel, James W.
Milburn, John
Moffet, Thomas J.
Moran, Thomas J.
Morrison, James
Morrison, Richard
Murphy, J.F.
Murphy, J. Franklin
Neer, N. Frank
Orrison, George
Pierson, John S.
Potts, E. Fletcher
Potts, William C.
Price, Charles D.
Price, Joseph
Purcell, Frank

Roach, Philip   Thompson, Magnus, S.   Turner, William
Roberts, John D.   Thompson, Malcolm   Van Pelt, N. Brown
Scanlin, Patrick   Thomason, William H   White, John J.
Sexton, John W.   Tollen, Richard   White, Josiah Robert
Simpson, Eben   Torreyson, Thomas N.   White, Robert Hunter
Simpson, Thomas P.   Touche, Sidney   Wilson,_____
Tavenner, Jonah   Tribett, William H.   Wilson, William
Taylor, B.C.   Triplett, Manley   Wood, Gip S.
Taylor, Maitland   Triplett, W.H.
Thompson, John Early   Turner, Creed

COMPANY D[33]

Officers

Trayhern,_____, First Captain   Spangler,_____, First Lieut.
Anderson,_____, Second Cap-
tain   Baker, Samuel, Second Lieut.

No roster of enlisted men available.

COMPANY E[34]

Officers

Grabill, John, Captain   Grubbs, A.C., Second Lieut.
Strickler, H.M., First Lieut.

Enlisted Men

Brumback, Isaac N.   Hockman, Philip A.   Rogers,_____
Burnett, George   McInturf, Marcus

COMPANY F[35]

Officers

French, Marcellus, Captain   Watts,_____, First Lieut.
Ferneyhough,_____, Captain   James, Charles A., First Lieut.

Enlisted Men

Broy,_____   Rhodes,_____   Sinclair, Charles
Grogan,_____

MUSTER ROLL OF CHEW'S BATTERY (LAUREL BRIGADE) ARMY OF NORTHERN VIRGINIA[36]

Officers

Chew, R. Preston, Captain   Carter, John W., Third Lieut.
Thomson, James W., First Lieut. Yancey, E.L., Fourth Lieut.
Williams, James H., Second
Lieut.

Enlisted Men

Ainsworth, T.	Dash, George	Hattle, H.H.
Allen, James	Davis, George	Helsley,_____
Ambler, John	Davis, Henry	Henkel, Al
Anderson, George	Davis, Thomas	Henry, J.W.
Anderson, William	Dawson, George E.	Hetzall,_____
Asberry, Frank	Deahl, Henry	Hicklin, George W.
Atkinson, R.C.	Deck, J.	Higgs, John
Baker, Samuel	Deck, Morgan	Hill, William
Baker, S.	Deck, William	Holliday, B.T.
Bird, Derrick	Dennis, Alfred I.	Homan, Hiram C.
Blair, James	Dingledine, Jacob	Homrick, James
Bliss, A.	Edmunds, Joseph A.	Hoofmaster, George
Bliss, Thomas	Everly, Amos F.	Hoshour, Robert
Boston,_____	Everly, George	Huff, George
Bowley, E. Devereaux	Everly, Samuel	Huff, H.
Boyd, Philip W	Farris, Moses	Johnson, T.D.
Brady, George	Few, Samuel	Jolliffe, John
Brady, Louis	Fiser, Jacob	Jones, Thomas
Britner, Gregory	Fisher, Isaac	Kagey, Benjamin
Brook, J.A.	Fitzsimmons, Matthew	Kagey, John
Brooks, E.C.	Fravel, Henry	Kagey, Joseph
Brown, Bailey	Fravel, J.W.	Kapeharte,_____
Brown, Charles	Fravel, John H.	Kendall, Carthage
Brownough, J.W.	Fravel, Kyte	Kerr, Upsher
Buck, Willie	Frazier, William	Keyes, Newton
Bull, Americus	Fry, Jesse	Knisely, G.
Burgess, A. Bealle	Fultz, Joe	Knisely, H.
Butts, Samuel	Fultz, Reuben	Kolhenhousen, Luther
Callahan, George	Furry, Robert	Lakin, Charles
Carpenter, Charles	Furry, Van	Landon,_____
Carr, J.B.	Furry, William	Lewis, John
Chew, John	Gillock, John	Lindsay, John
Cline, Samuel	Golladay, Perry	Long, Benjamin
Conrad, Charles F.	Good, Anthony	Longerbeam, Abe
Conrad, Frank E.	Green John	Longerbeam, Charley
Cooper, George	Haas, Isaac	Longerbeam, George
Crawford,_____	Hammer, Junius B.	Longerbeam, John
Dabney, Basil G.	Hare, John	Loveday, John

Lyman, William R.
Lyon, John D.
McGuire, William P.,
McVicar, Charles W.
McWilliams, George
Magruder, William
Markell, Samuel
Marstella, William
Matheny, Randolph
Miller, A.
Miller, Cal
Miller, F. Thomas
Miller, Stephen
Miller, William
Morrill, Louis D.
Mosher, Frank
Myer, P.H.
Neese, George M.
Nelson, D.
Nicely, George
Nicely, H.
Nisewander, Abe
Nisewander, George
Noland, C.C.
Noland, L.
Oakes, R.
O'Roark, J.
O'Roark, J.C.
Page, John B.
Painter, George
Phillips, George
Phillips, Reuben
Pierce, John

Pifer, Jacob
Powell, P.
Powell, Raleigh
Procter, John
Procter, Noah
Purl,_____
Ramey, W.H.
Reed, Edward
Richard, George W.
Riely, Frank
Rinker, Fenton
Rivercomb, H.
Rivercomb, W.
Roberts, John
Roberts, Stephen
Rodeffer, John
Rodeffer, Mark
Rodeffer, Samuel
Rodeffer, Theodore
Roderick , Philip
Ruffin, W.N.
Shaffer, Amos
Shaffer, Ferd
Shaffer, J.
Shaffer, William
Sheetz, John
Shell, George
Souder, A.J.
Stickley, Laban
Stribbling, Frank
Stuart, George
Stuart, John
Suddith, Edward

Supinger, C.B.
Supinger, Lemuel B.
Taylor, J.W.
Teawalt, William
Thompson, Pem, B.
Thompson, William
Thornton, J.R.
Thornton, R.A.
Thuma, Chap.
Venable, James
Vorhees, George
Ware, Nimrod
Weymer, John
Wharton, Isaiah
Wheeler, Mack
Whitaker, F.B.
White,_____
Wickes, William
Williams, Andy
Williams, James H.
Williams, John
Williams, John J.
Williams, Samuel
Williams, T. Clayton
Williamson, Levi
Wiltshire, James G.
Wooten, John R.
Wright, James
Wright, S.
Wunder, J.C.
Wunder, Reuben
Zea, Martin
Zirkle, A.P.

FOOTNOTES FOR APPENDIX

1. *Virginia Confederate Roster*, Vol. 9, pp. 126-133; Ramey, Emily. and Gott, John K., *The Years of Anguish, Fauquier County, Virginia, 1861-1865.* pp. xxii-xxvi; McDonald, *Laurel Brigade*, pp. 382-388.
2. McDonald, *Laurel Brigade*, pp. 388-392.
3. *Ibid.*, pp. 392-396.
4. *Virginia Confederate Roster*, Vol. 9, pp. 159-165.
5. McDonald, *Laurel Brigade*, pp. 396-398.
6. *Ibid.*, pp. 399-405.
7. *Ibid.*, pp. 405-408.
8. *Ibid.*, pp. 408-410.
9. *Ibid.*, pp. 410-413.
10. *Virginia Confederate Roster*, Vol. 9, pp. 211-215.
11. McDonald. *Laurel Brigade*, pp. 414-419.
12. *Ibid.*, pp. 420-421.
13. *Ibid.*, pp. 421-424.
14. *Ibid.*, pp. 425-427.
15. *Ibid.*, pp. 427-430.
16. *Ibid.*, pp. 430-434.
17. *Ibid.*, pp. 435-438.
18. *Ibid.*, pp. 439-443.
19. *Ibid.*, pp. 444-446.
20. *Ibid.*, pp. 446-448.
21. *Ibid.*, pp. 448-449.
22. *Ibid.*, pp. 450-454.
23. *Ibid.*, pp. 454-458.
24. *Ibid.*, pp. 459-462.
25. *Ibid.*, pp. 462-467.
26. *Ibid.*, pp. 467-469.
27. *Ibid.*, pp. 469-470.
28. *Ibid.*, pp. 470-471.
29. *Ibid.*, pp. 472-476.
30. *Ibid.*, pp. 476-479.
31. *Ibid.*, pp. 480-485.
32. *Ibid.*, pp. 485-488.
33. *Ibid.*, pp. 488-493.
34. *Ibid.*, p. 494.
35. *Ibid.*, p. 494.
36. *Ibid.*, pp. 494-495.
37. *Virginia Confederate Roster*, Vol. 18, pp. 164-171; McDonald, *Laurel Brigade*, pp. 496-499.

BIBLIOGRAPHY
Manuscript Material

Turner Ashby Papers. Chicago Historical Society. Chicago, Ill.
Turner Ashby Papers. National Archives. Washington, D.C.
Turner Ashby Papers. Virginia Historical Society. Richmond, Va.
Alexander Robinson Boteler Papers. Duke University, Durham, N.C.
Samuel D. Buck Papers. Duke University. Durham, N.C.
Holmes Conrad Papers. Virginia Historical Society. Richmond, Va.
Mrs. Ralph Dorsey Papers. Berryville, Va.
Fauquier County Records. Warrenton, Va.
Laura Virginia Hale Papers. Front Royal, Va.
Jedediah Hotchkiss Papers. Library of Congress, Washington, D.C.
Jefferson County Records, Charles Town, W. Va.
Thomas T. Munford Papers. Duke University. Durham, N.C.
William N. Pendleton Papers. Southern Historical Collection. University of North Carolina. Chapel Hill, N.C.
Green W. Penn Papers, 1764-1894. Duke University. Durham, N.C.
Thomas Lee Settle Papers. Duke University. Durham, N.C.
Virginia Confederate Rosters, Virginia State Library, Richmond, Va.

Personal Reminiscences and Unit Histories

Avirett, James B. *The Memoirs of Turner Ashby and His Compeers.* Baltimore, Md.: Selby and Dulany. 1867.
Baylor, George. *Bull Run To Bull Run: or Four Years in the Army of Northern Virginia.* B.F. Johnson Publishing Company. 1900.
Casler, John O. *Four Years in the Stonewall Brigade.* 2nd. Ed. Marietta, Ga. Continental Book Company. 1951.
Cockrell, Monroe F. ed. *Gunner with Stonewall: Reminiscences of William Thomas Poague.* Jackson, Tenn. McCowat-Mercer Press. 1957.
Cooke, John Esten. *Surry of Eagles Nest: or The Memoirs of a Staff Officer Serving in Virginia.* New York. 1866.

_____. *Wearing of the Gray.* New York. 1867.

Douglas, Henry Kyd. *I Rode with Stonewall.* Chapel Hill, N.C. The University of North Carolina Press. 1940.

Eby, Cecil D., Jr., *A Virginia Yankee in the Civil War: The Diaries of David Hunter Strother.* Chapel Hill, N.C. University of North Carolina Press. 1961.

Gilmor, Harry. *Four Years in the Saddle.* New York, N.Y. Harper & Brothers. 1866.

Johnson, R.V. and Buel, C.C., eds. *Battles and Leaders of the Civil War.* 4 Vols. New York, N.Y. The Century Company. 1884-1888.

McDonald, Archie. ed. *Make Me a Map of the Valley: the Civil War Journal of Stonewall Jackson's Topographer.* Dallas, Tex. Southern Methodist University Press. 1973.

McDonald, Cornelia. *A Diary with Reminiscences of the War and Refugee Life in the Shenandoah Valley, 1861-1865.* Nashville, Tenn. Cullom & Ghertner. 1934.

McDonald, William N. *A History of the Laurel Brigade: Originally the Ashby Cavalry of the Army of Northern Virginia and Chew's Battery.* Baltimore, Md. Sun Job Printing Office. 1907.

Neese, George M. *Three Years in the Confederate Horse Artillery.* New York, N.Y. Neale Publishing Company. 1911.

Opie, John N. *A Rebel Cavalryman with Lee, Stuart, and Jackson.* Chicago, Ill. W.B. Conkey Company. 1899.

Robertson, James I., Jr. *The Stonewall Brigade.* Baton Rouge, La. Louisiana State University Press. 1963.

Taylor, Richard. *Destruction and Reconstruction: Personal Experiences of the Late War.* New York, N.Y. D. Appleton and Company. 1879

Thomson, O.R. Howard and Rauch, William H., *History of the "Bucktails" Kane Rifle Regiment of the Pennsylvania Reserve Corps.* Philadelphia, Pa. Electric Printing Co. 1906.

Biographical Works

Ashby, Thomas A. *Life of Turner Ashby.* New York, N.Y Neale Publishing Company. 1914.

Bean, William G. *Stonewall's Man: Sandie Pendleton.* Chapel Hill, N.C. University of North Carolina Press. 1959.

Bushong, Millard K. *Old Jube: a Biography of General Jubal A. Early.* 2nd Printing. Boyce, Va. Carr Publishing Company. 1961.

Cooke, John Esten. *Stonewall Jackson: a Military Biography.* New York, N.Y. D. Appleton and Company. 1876.

Cunningham, Frank. *Knight of the Confederacy: General Turner Ashby.* San Antonio, Tex. The Naylor Company. 1960.

Dabney, R.L. *Life and Campaigns of Lieutenant General Thomas J. Jackson (Stonewall).* New York, N.Y. Blelock & Company. 1865.

Dufour, Charles L. *Gentle Tiger: the Gallant Life of Roberdeau Wheat.* Baton Rouge, La. Louisiana State University Press. 1957.

Hamlin, Percy G. *Old Bald Head.* Strasburg, Va. Shenandoah Publishing House. 1940.

Freeman, Douglas S. *R.E. Lee: a Biography.* 4 Vols. the Pulitzer Prize Edition. New York, N.Y. Charles Scribner's Sons. 1947.

Henderson, G.F.R. *Stonewall Jackson and the American Civil War.* Authorized American Edition. New York, N.Y. Grosset & Dunlap. n.d.

Reese, Lee Fleming. *The Ashby Book: Descendants of Captain Thomas Ashby of Virginia.* Vol. I Bicentennial Edition. San Diego, Calif. Western Press. 1976.

Sigaud, Louis A. *Belle Boyd: Confederate Spy.* Richmond, Va. The Dietz Press. 1944.

Stutler, Boyd B. *Captain John Brown and Harper's Ferry.* Charleston, W. Va. 1926.

Thomas, Clarence. *General Turner Ashby: the Centaur of the South.* Winchester, Va. The Eddy Press Corp. 1907.

Vandiver, Frank E. *Mighty Stonewall.* New York, N.Y. McGraw-Hill Book Company. 1957.

Villard, Oswald G. *John Brown, 1800-1859, a Biography Fifty Years After.* New York, N.Y. Alfred A. Knopf. 1943.

Periodicals

Baltimore Weekly American, 1859. Baltimore, Md.

Baltimore Weekly Sun, 1859-1860. Baltimore, Md.

Confederate Veteran. 40 Vols. Nashville, Tenn. 1893-1932.

Independent Democrat, 1859. Charles Town, W. Va.

Rockingham Register and Virginia Advertiser. Vol. 40, No. 28 (June 20, 1862), Harrisonburg, Va.

Southern Historical Society Papers. 1876-1959. 52 Vols. Richmond, Va.

Spirit of Jefferson, 1929. Charles Town, W. Va.

The Century Illustrated Monthly Magazine, Aug., 1885. Vol.
XXX, No. 4

The Shepherdstown Register. 1886. Shepherdstown, W. Va.

Virginia Free Press. 1859. Charles Town, W. Va.

West Virginia History; a Quarterly Magazine. Vol. XXVII, No. 2
(Jan. 1966). Charleston, W. Va. State Department of Archives
and History.

General Studies

Allan, William. *History of the Campaign of General T. J. (Stonewall) Jackson in the Shenandoah Valley of Virginia.* Dayton,
Ohio. Press of the Morningside Bookshop. 1974.

Ambler, Charles H. *West Virginia the Mountain State.* New York,
N.Y. 1940.

Ashby, Thomas A. *The Valley Campaigns.* New York, N.Y. 1914.

Bean, William G. *The Liberty Hall Volunteers: Stonewall's College Boys.* Charlottesville, Va. The University Press of Virginia. 1964.

Boatner, Mark M., III. *The Civil War Dictionary.* 6th Printing. New
York, N.Y. David McKay Company. 1969.

Brannon, Selden W. ed. *Historic Hampshire, a Symposium of
Hampshire County and Its People, Past and Present.* Parsons, W. Va. McClain Printing Company. 1976.

Bushong, Millard K. *Historic Jefferson County.* Boyce, Va. Carr
Publishing Company. 1972.

Cartmell, T.K. *Shenandoah Valley Pioneers & Their Descendants: a History of Frederick County, Virginia.* Berryville,
Va. Chesapeake Book Company. 1963.

Couper, William. *History of the Shenandoah Valley.* 3 vols. New
York, N.Y. Lewis Historical Publishing Company. 1952.

Daniel, Lizzie Cary. *Confederate Scrap-Book.* Richmond, Va. J.L.
Hill Printing Company. 1893.

Davis, Julia. *The Shenandoah.* Rivers of America Series. New
York, N.Y. Farrar & Rinehart. 1945.

Evans, Clement A. ed. *Confederate Military History.* 12 vols. At-
lanta, Ga. 1899.

Evans, M. Louise. *An Old Timer in Warrenton and Fauquier
County, Virginia.* Warrenton, Va. Virginia Publishing. 1955.

Fauquier County Bicentennial Committee. *Fauquier County, Virginia, 1759-1959.* Warrenton, Va. Virginia Publishing. 1959.

Freeman, Douglas S. *Lee's Lieutenants.* 3 Vols. New York, N.Y.
Charles Scribner's Sons. 1943.

Hale, Laura Virginia. *Four Valiant Years in the Lower Shenandoah Valley, 1861-1865.* Strasburg, Va. Shenandoah Publishing House. 1968.

Hungerford, Edward. *The Story of the Baltimore and Ohio Railroad. 1827-1927.* 2 Vols. New York, N.Y. G. P. Putnam's Sons. 1928.

Johnson, Allen & Malone, Dumas. eds. *Dictionary of American Biography.* 25 Vols. New York, N.Y. 1928-1936.

Johnston, Mary. *The Long Roll.* New York, N.Y. Houghton Mifflin Company. 1911.

Livermore, Thomas L. *Numbers and Losses in the Civil War in America, 1861-1865.* Bloomington, Ind. Indiana University Press. 1957.

Maxwell, Hu and Swisher, H.L. *History of Hampshire County, West Virginia from Its Earliest Settlement to the Present.* Reprint. Parsons, W. Va. McClain Printing Company. 1972.

Miller, Francis T. *The Photographic History of the Civil War.* 10 Vols. New York, N.Y. The Review of Reviews Company. 1912.

Morton, Frederic. *The Story of Winchester in Virginia.* Strasburg, Va. Shenandoah Publishing House. 1925.

Pollard, Edward A. *Lee and His Lieutenants, Comprising the Early Life, Public Services, and Campaigns of General Robert E. Lee and His Companions in Arms with a Record of Their Campaigns and Heroic Deeds.* New York, N.Y. E. B. Treat & Company. 1867.

Ramey, Emily G. and Gott, John K. *The Years of Anguish, Fauquier County, Virginia, 1861-1865.* Warrenton, Va. The Fauquier Democrat. 1965.

Register of Former Cadets, Virginia Military Institute. Centennial Edition. Roanoke, Va. Roanoke Printing Company. 1939.

Steele, Matthew F. *American Campaigns.* 2 Vols. Washington, D.C. Combat Forces Press. 1951.

Summers, Festus P. *The Baltimore and Ohio in the Civil War.* New York, N.Y. G. P. Putnam's Sons. 1939.

Tanner, Robert G. *Stonewall in the Valley: Thomas J. "Stonewall" Jackson's Shenandoah Valley Campaign, Spring, 1862.* Garden City, N.Y. Doubleday & Company. 1976.

The Advanced Engineer Manual. 5th Ed. Harrisburg, Pa. The Military Service Publishing Company. 1938.

The South in the Building of the Nation. 13 Vols. Richmond, Va. The Southern Publication Society. 1909.

U.S. War Department. *The War of the Rebellion: a Compilation of the Official Records of the Union and Confederate Armies.* 70 vols. in 128 books. Washington, D.C. 1880-1901.

Wayland, John W. *Stonewall Jackson's Way.* Staunton, Va. The McClure Company. 1940.

——————————. *Twenty-Five Chapters on the Shenandoah Valley.* Strasburg, Va. The Shenandoah Publishing House. 1957.

Wharton, H.M. *War Songs and Poems of the Southern Confederacy, 1861-1865.* 1904.

INDEX

255